PRAISE FOR MIC[

In this wonderfully quirky music- and art-focused book, Welch concentrates on his New Orleans—the New Orleans that he and his friends know. There is plenty of information on many aspects of artsy New Orleans: Mardi Gras festivities, literary New Orleans, art galleries, burlesque clubs, theater, comedy clubs, thrift stores and costume shops, record stores, as well as a discussion of the Mardi Gras Indians, profiles of local musicians, and even a chapter on family fun.

—*Chicago Tribune*

I've been friends with Michael Patrick Welch for a number of years, and in New Orleans he seems to have really found his place. On my first visit from New York, before the flood, he took me on an epic bike ride tour of the city. We saw everything from grand mansions to beautiful bombed-out neighborhoods, and no matter where we went that day, Michael knew someone. Michael obviously loves New Orleans very much, and on my visits there he has shown me so much that I never expected, and would have not seen otherwise.

—Jonathan Ames, creator of HBO's *Bored to Death* and author of *The Extra Man* and *The Double Life Is Twice as Good*

Michael Patrick Welch is a true community light.

—Chuck D, Public Enemy

Your boyfriend is very, very talented.

—Ray Davies of The Kinks to Michael Patrick Welch's girlfriend, Jazz Fest 2003

To John, 9/25/14
Love
Annette ♡

THIRD EDITION

NEW ORLEANS
THE UNDERGROUND GUIDE

MICHAEL PATRICK WELCH

with Brian Boyles

PHOTOGRAPHS BY ZACK SMITH AND JONATHAN TRAVIESA

 LOUISIANA STATE UNIVERSITY PRESS   BATON ROUGE

Published by Louisiana State University Press
Copyright © 2014 by Louisiana State University Press
First and second editions published by the University of New Orleans Press,
2009 and 2011
All rights reserved
Manufactured in the United States of America
First printing

Designer: Barbara Neely Bourgoyne
Typefaces: DubTone and Helvetica Neue, display; Ingeborg, text
Printer and binder: Maple Press

Maps are by Morgana King.

Library of Congress Cataloging-in-Publication Data

Welch, Michael Patrick, 1974–
  New Orleans : the underground guide / Michael Patrick Welch with Brian
Boyles ; Photographs by Zack Smith and Jonathan Traviesa. — Third Edition.
     pages cm
  Includes index.
  ISBN 978-0-8071-5606-3 (pbk. : alk. paper) — ISBN 978-0-8071-5607-0 (pdf)
— ISBN 978-0-8071-5608-7 (epub) — ISBN 978-0-8071-5609-4 (mobi) 1. New
Orleans (La.) —Guidebooks. 2. New Orleans (La.) —Description and travel. I.
Boyles, Brian, 1977– II. Smith, Zack, 1975– III. Traviesa, Jonathan. IV. Title.
  F379.N53W44 2014
  917.63'3504—dc23
                           2013033661

ACKNOWLEDGMENTS

We would first like to acknowledge that any attempt to comprehensively document every one of New Orleans' music and art communities would be impossible. Further editions of this book will fill in any embarrassing holes we may have left this third time around.

We would like to thank Benjamin Simmons and Katrina Arnold for two of the cover photographs and Morgana King for the neighborhood maps.

Most photographs for this edition were taken by Zack Smith and Jonathan Traviesa. Other photo contributors were Katrina Arnold, Rachel Breunlin, Mark Caesar, Paul Cheenne, Geoff Douville, Alleyn Evans, Sierra Hudson, Katja Liebing, Gary LoVerde, Louis Maistros, Benjamin Simmons, Scott Stuntz, Matt Uhlman, Taslim Van Hattum, Robin Walker, and Kim Welsh.

We also want to thank those we interviewed and those who gave recommendations, favorites, or otherwise contributed to the text: Mark Caesar, Geoff Douville, Otis Fennell, Jonathan Ferrara, Brian Greiner, DJ RQAway, Juicy Jackson, Catherine Lasperches, Walt McClements, Leo McGovern, Alex McMurray, Justin Peake, Katey Red, Matt Russell, Veronica Russell, Jason Songe, Nick Thomas, Andrew Vaught, Paul Webb, and Mike IX Williams.

Special thanks to Alison Fensterstock, Dirty Coast, Creighton Durrant, and also Edward Jackson, Katie Hunter-Lowery, *Gambit Weekly, OffBeat,* and *Antigravity* magazine.

NEW ORLEANS
THE UNDERGROUND GUIDE

WELCOME TO NEW ORLEANS

It's Not What You Think!

We wrote this third official edition of *New Orleans: The Underground Guide* to counter the incomplete image of New Orleans that you have in your head. It's not your fault. New Orleans is marketed, largely from within, as its old self. New Orleans does still sound like brass bands, Mardi Gras Indians, and trad jazz. But New Orleans' old-school image has been a marketing template the tourist industry is loath to relinquish. New Orleans is marketed as if the French Quarter is still bursting with culture, when really it has turned into a beautiful shopping mall where almost none of the city's important modern-day music is made, or even played (Bourbon Street in particular is more than happy to accommodate your outdated notions of the city). New Orleans' past should be glorified, its amazing traditions kept alive, but not if it means the world ends up thinking New Orleans' most important artistic days are behind us! There are things happening here, now, that have the power to change the way the world views music and art—again, as New Orleans always has.

We continue making these music-focused guidebooks partly to show that new-millennium New Orleans sounds pretty damned different, and that our artistic communities are still as unique and vibrant, and conjure up as many important new creations as ever. We made *New Orleans: The Underground Guide* for tourists who don't want New Orleans marketed to them. You want natural adventures! Though all guidebooks purport to be street-level accounts of where the locals hang out—well, our writers and photographers have lived in New Orleans for many years, participating wholeheartedly in its music, art, journalism, and publishing scenes, and when we scribbled down hundreds of places where we regularly go hang out for the music and art, few of our awesome, historic, truly popular, New Orleans culture–defining choices could be found in almost any other guidebook.

As you see, something needed to be done.

And we figured that the best thing we could do would be to act as friends of yours who live here, who want you to meet our wild, artistic local friends and to truly understand how much fun we have, and why we love living here. And that reason, mainly, is music. Even our extensive food section features, almost exclusively, eating spots that also host live music.

As for how to read our guidebook, we hoped that *New Orleans: The Underground Guide* would be, even for a local, a somewhat enjoyable read from the first page to the last. Within the listings we pause for short informative essays and interviews—called "N.O. Moments"—about the New Orleans places and people we like best. Rapper **Katey Red** suggests where to go and where not to go to hear bounce rap in New Orleans, while **Mike IX Williams** of **EyeHateGod** lets you know where to go in New Orleans to throw the goat. The book's crown jewel is its music sections, wherein we describe over one hundred of New Orleans' best modern, nontraditional bands, solo artists, rappers, and DJs— musicians who sound like New Orleans, without playing old New Orleans music.

We've practiced this same ideology with all our choices here, hoping to prove, to you, that New Orleans is not what you think.

—Michael Patrick Welch

SEVEN AWESOME NEIGHBORHOODS

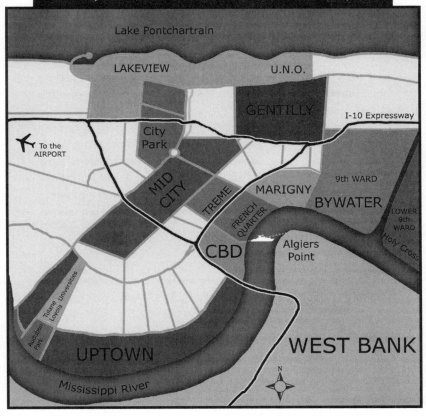

As a visitor, you will understand and enjoy New Orleans more if you think in terms of neighborhoods. Locals always rep their wards and blocks as distinctly flavored places with different accents and styles. Many of New Orleans' neighborhoods were creamed by floodwaters, hoods that tourists rarely visited. Rebuilding is still incomplete in many areas—just as a trip to our city is incomplete if one doesn't stray beyond the French Quarter.

This book admittedly overlooks many New Orleans neighborhoods that were wiped out and are slowly rebuilding. We opt instead to help you explore the surviving heart of the city, which is also the most easily traversable. It should be noted, though, that New Orleans' farthest reaches and suburbs and still-struggling areas all possess their own charms—the still-thriving Vietnamese community in flood-ravaged New Orleans East (see "More Foods" section) is one great example. Not incidentally, the burbs often feature some of the best locals'-favorite restaurants, from seafood on the Lakefront to Italian in Kenner. But for our purposes, we'll skip the outlying parishes for the most part and stick to the basics—downtown (Marigny/Bywater) and its most immediate walkable, bikable, public transport–accessible environs.

Also, when we refer to "neighborhoods," we rarely mean the French Quarter. The Quarter is technically a neighborhood, too (which is why the city fines bars and restaurants that host unregulated live music. Can you believe that?), but nowadays the Quarter is mostly a picturesque mall that caters/panders to tourists. It has its cool little secrets and stalwart holdouts, as well as historical curiosities (that Laundromat on Rampart was once **Cosimo Matassa**'s legendary recording studio), but we're here to make sure you spend time exploring New Orleans' real neighborhoods, enjoying good conversation and adventures with the many friendly, interesting, artistic locals you won't meet on Bourbon Street (unless they're bussing your table, or giving you a lap dance).

We will address these seven hoods as they are connected, one to the next, starting in the east and moving downriver, west: 1) **Bywater**, 2) **Faubourg Marigny**, 3) **The French Quarter**, 4) **Central Business District (CBD)**, 5) **Uptown**. Then north of the Quarter there's 6) **Mid-City** and 7) **Faubourg Tremé**.

BYWATER

**Boundaries: Florida Ave., Mississippi River, Industrial Canal
and levee, Press St. railroad tracks**

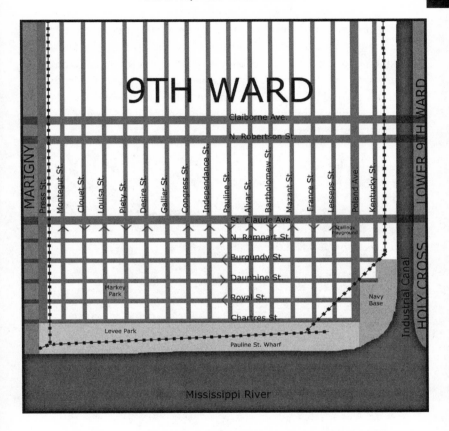

In this guide, we will harp on Bywater (and its sister neighborhood, Marigny) the way other guidebooks focus on the French Quarter. Bywater's art and music scenes are hip, but rarely pretentious. Many locals claim that long ago, real estate agents coined the term "Bywater" (meaning it's by both the river and the Industrial Canal) to disassociate the area from the rest of the Ninth Ward. But especially since the neighborhood survived Katrina, the rents for Bywater's many classic, hundred-year-old shotgun houses have gone up and up and up. Developers talk of a giant cruise terminal (possibly Disney) in the hood, and new luxury loft spaces pop up monthly. Brooklyn- and Portland-style eateries and boutiques nibble at Bywater's unique core. Still, the neighborhood's dense community of artists and musicians have deep roots here, and it will be a while before they're forced out.

For now the neighborhood is pleasantly mixed: a house flipper's dream stands freshly painted between dilapidated beauties that more-or-less poor residents ain't giving up any time soon (thank god), partly because they're right down the street from the world's greatest bars. If you came to New Orleans for truly unique art and fun, and if you came to follow strange new friends on adventures often involving bikes and beer and pot and music, then Bywater. Bywater.

Zack Smith

FAUBOURG MARIGNY

(FAW-borg MER-ih-nee)

Boundaries: St. Claude Ave., Mississippi River, Franklin Ave., Esplanade Ave.

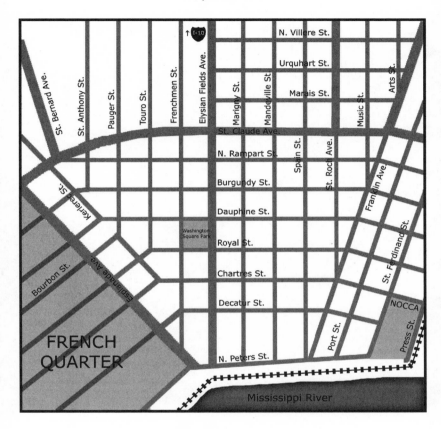

The Faubourg Marigny is cleaner, more expensive, and more charmingly crammed together than Bywater, but everyone from all over the city comes to hear and play music on Frenchmen Street and its surrounding neighborhood venues, including those around the corner on St. Claude. The Marigny is half-entertainment district (the mellow Bourbon Street), and half-residential streets lined with nineteenth-century Creole cottages in pastel pinks, yellows, and blues. The residents have money (lots of

good-looking gay folks in the Marigny), but they aren't generally snobs. Don't be lulled, though, by the smell of high rents;
muggers are drawn to that smell too. Keep your wits about you,
remain on your bike, look around, stay alert, and move with
friends whenever possible.

THE FRENCH QUARTER

Boundaries: Pretty much a big lopsided square, bordered by Rampart St., Decatur St., Esplanade Ave., and Canal St.

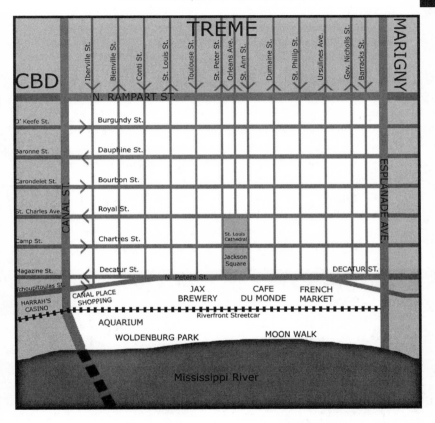

Part national landmark, part American party zone, the French Quarter remains a functioning mixed-use residential/commercial neighborhood. It's also a giant open-air mall of bars, antique shopping, street performers, more bars, bad art, strip clubs, daiquiri stands, and, in its margins, old-timey New Orleans music. Even if the Quarter isn't overrated, it's definitely overexposed, considering so many tourists spend their whole vacations there, neglecting all other New Orleans exploration. It's a fun section of town, but the only locals you'll likely meet are your waiter or bartender (who'll give you the inside info if you ask and tip them correctly). Even many of the strippers come from out of town for our local holidays.

Make no mistake: the blocks between Canal and Esplanade are utterly beautiful, and perfect for endless wandering and stumbling. Every other block or so, you'll discover a place like the Chart Room (300 Chartres St.), which allows for amazing people-watching, and often charges just $2.50 for a stiff drink. **Jackson Square** hosts tarot readers, "psychics," questionable artists hawking their wares, and gold-painted statue people, all to the tune of good brass bands (many of the city's best traditional players hone their chops in the Square, passing the hat) and bad folk music. There's also the old **French Market** on lower Decatur (near the river just off Esplanade), which features a giant selection of cheesy New Orleans souvenirs, and more cool cheap sunglasses than you've ever seen, two pairs for $7!

But if the weather's nice, after a full day of drinking and shopping, gravitate down to the **Mississippi River** and its romantic **Moon Walk,** named for former New Orleans mayor **Moon Landrieu** (a good place to smoke pot, if you're vigilant for bike

You never know what to expect, even in the morning, at the Abbey bar on Decatur in the French Quarter.

Zack Smith

cops). We also suggest taking the **Algiers ferry** (free for pedestrians and bikes!) located at the foot of Canal Street, across the Mississippi to interesting and quaint Algiers Point on the West Bank (ferry leaves New Orleans every thirty minutes, on the :15 and :45, from 6 a.m. to midnight). **William Burroughs** lived for many years in Algiers at 509 Wagner Street, and was once visited there by Jack Kerouac, as documented in *On the Road*.

Despite whatever hype, you will and should spend a day or two wandering unself-consciously around the French Quarter, drinking before sunset out of your go-cup until you're tipping every street performer. Just promise us you won't party there the whole time.

CENTRAL BUSINESS DISTRICT (CBD)

Boundaries: S. Claiborne Ave., Mississippi River, Canal St., Lee Circle

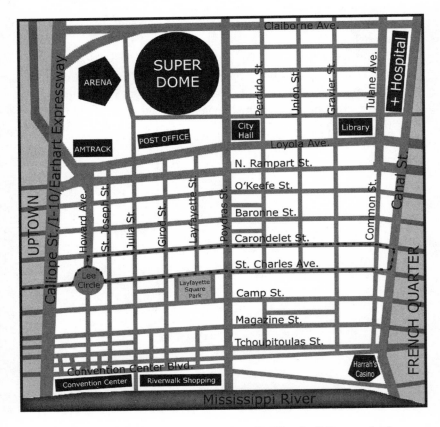

The CBD hosts all of New Orleans' tall office buildings, which would make any outsider think it's our "downtown." In local parlance, it's actually the midway point between Uptown (Garden District) and downtown (everything below Canal Street). In recent years the booming sports entertainment zone around the Superdome and New Orleans Arena has created new buzz in the area. The CBD boasts some decent New Orleans restaurants, though many are open only for weekday lunch, catering to the working stiffs.

The **Julia Street Arts District** is continually open and nice to stroll down, though there's more cutting-edge, street-level art downtown on St. Claude. In the end, you'll probably get all you need of the CBD on your streetcar tour, rolling between the giant old New Orleans office buildings on your way to better vistas.

The portion of the CBD nearest the river is called the **Warehouse District**, though many of the area's old nineteenth-century warehouses were converted into condominiums. Redeveloped around the time of the 1984 World's Fair, the Warehouse District is also home to the **Contemporary Arts Center** (CAC) (900 Camp St.) and the **Ogden Museum of Southern Art** (925 Camp St.), as well as the venerable **Howlin' Wolf** (907 S. Peters St.) rock club and (in the Wolf's old space) the Republic (828 S. Peters St.). The condos and the Convention Center have served impetus for added nighttime fun options in the Warehouse District, in the form of music clubs and upscale restaurants, including **Cochon** (930 Tchoupitoulas St.) and **RioMar** (800 S. Peters St.). If you're in town for a convention, a drink or lunch is recommended in this part of the CBD, but nightlife bubbles better in other quarters.

UPTOWN

Boundaries: Carrollton Ave., Mississippi River, Carrollton at
the river bend, Lee Circle

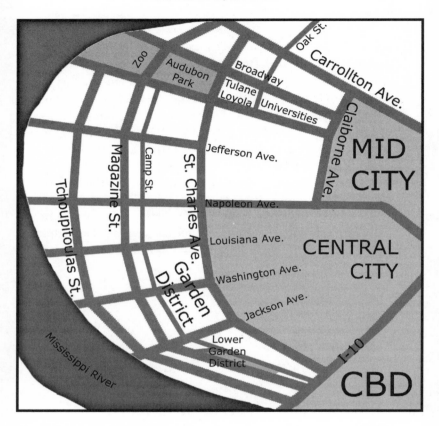

The designation "Uptown" is mostly an umbrella term to describe
the neighborhoods and areas of New Orleans that are west of
"above" Canal Street. Uptown is seen (perhaps wrongly) as one
of the more stable parts of the city in terms of population and
crime, but it's good to see the area as several distinct neighborhoods, split by St. Charles Avenue.

If you're riding the streetcar, you enter Uptown once you cross
beneath the interstate at Calliope. The first stretch of St. Charles
features many eateries and fast food joints, and we recommend

it if you're viewing Carnival parades. Get off around Jackson Avenue to explore the Lower Garden District (LGD), a funkier, slightly unkempt neighborhood that features the dog-and-bum friendly **Coliseum Square Park** (intersection of Coliseum and Euterpe Streets), plus numerous cool dive restaurants and bars. In the late '90s, *Utne Reader* dubbed the LGD America's hippest neighborhood. You may judge for yourself. On the other side of Magazine Street from the Garden District is the **Irish Channel** and its community center–bar–restaurant **Parasol's** (2533 Constance St.). The Irish Channel, along with the Lower Garden District, has seen somewhat of a resurgence since the St. Thomas housing projects were shut down in the early 2000s. It's also known as the "Sliver on the River" since Katrina, due to its being actually above sea level and one of the least ravaged parts of town.

The Uptown neighborhood of Central City lies across St. Charles from the LGD and remains one of the nation's most dangerous places. Most of the projects that birthed legends of New Orleans hip hop are gone, but indigenous culture is still thick, if uncommercial and more difficult to pierce. Central City is home to Mardi Gras Indian celebrations, important jazz landmarks, and, particularly in the fall, frequent second-line parades, and locals can hip you to the best times to check these out. Moving upriver from Central City past Louisiana Avenue, you'll encounter the diverse Uptown that includes Freret Street. Along St. Charles, a lovely New Orleans moment can be had on the veranda of the **Columns Hotel** (3811 St. Charles Ave.), just downtown of Napoleon. Across St. Charles above Napoleon is the Upper Garden District, and it's the "uptown" you'd expect, with grand mansions of the well-manicured and old-moneyed, plus more than enough eating and shopping along Magazine Street.

After passing Tulane and Loyola Universities, the streetcar turns at the Riverbend into the Carrollton section of Uptown, home of college-kid-friendly restaurants and bars, as well as the popular Oak Street. We recommend **Lebanon's Cafe** (1500 Carrollton Ave.) for Middle Eastern food and **Boucherie** (8115 Jeannette St.) for fancy-but-not-too-pricey local and southern cuisine.

MID-CITY

Boundaries: The Canal streetcar line (starts at the riverfront in the French Quarter at Esplanade) turns onto Canal Street and heads through the Central Business District, before continuing into the heart of Mid-City.

Mid-City sits midway between the Mississippi River and Lake Pontchartrain—making it a prime area for flooding, were it not for Esplanade Ridge, one of the longest, highest shelves in the city (which didn't really save it from the floods of '05). This mixed-income, visually stunning neighborhood was damaged badly by Katrina but has managed to come back strong. The Fair Grounds horse-racing track hosts every **Jazz Fest**. The **New Orleans Museum of Modern Art** (NOMA) is still representing in vast and wondrous **City Park**. Mid-City also hosts many mini-

A safety-minded tuba player goes in for a drink at Pal's bar in Mid-City.

hoods you can and should explore, including Bayou St. John and Bayou Road. Gawk at the big houses, which are as gargantuan as in Uptown but colorful and unpretentious. During the day, Mid-City is mostly safe and beautiful; still, it's easy at night to wander somewhere you might not want to be.

FAUBOURG TREMÉ

(FAW-borg Trem-May)

Boundaries: Claiborne Ave., Rampart St., Esplanade Ave., Canal St.

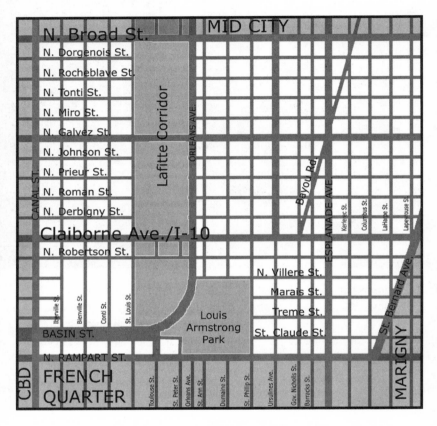

The relatively small but culturally invaluable Tremé neighborhood is famous for being the first area in America where black people could buy and sell land, even as the country was still enmeshed in slavery. After a run on HBO and an influx of gentrification, the neighborhood remains a beautiful, unruly place where you'll always find something interesting on the streets and in the doorways. Its many corner bars, churches, and funeral homes were the breeding ground for centuries of musicians to hone their horns and drums. In many ways, the Tremé's unique energy—which has endured surprisingly well since the storm—is

the biggest reason why New Orleans will always be "a chocolate city," as former mayor Ray Nagin called it.

Along with a lot of great shotgun houses and corner stores (some of the best food in the city comes not from Galatoire's, but from various corner stores), Tremé is home to several homegrown museums dedicated to celebrating African Americans' cultural, historical, and artistic achievements. The **Backstreet Museum** (1116 Henriette Delille St.) and the **New Orleans African American Museum** (1418 Governor Nicholls St.) make for good, idiosyncratic stops.

Tremé is also where the biggest, most beautiful second-line jazz funerals occur. Regular churchgoers will be welcomed at traditional, very musical, New Orleans–style services at the country's oldest black Catholic church, **St. Augustine** (1210 Governor Nicholls St., 504-525-5934).

Zack Smith

Music, food, and drinking in the streets are the main attractions in New Orleans. The French Quarter definitely does not have the market cornered on music, with a huge percentage of its offerings consisting of cover bands and drunken karaoke joints—although it is home to the excellent **Preservation Hall** and **One Eyed Jacks**. In any case, great clubs thrive in every neighborhood.

ALLWAYS LOUNGE

Marigny, 2240 St. Claude Ave.,
504-218-5778; theallwayslounge.com

The longtime home of Cowpokes, a gay bar with a rootin'-tootin' theme, this space was taken over by a punk-rock and theater-friendly, sex-positive contingent. The back room serves as the community Marigny Theatre, hosting all manner of local, alternative performances. It's also just a friendly bar, always offering something wild and daring and fun.

BACCHANAL

Bywater, 600 Poland Ave.,
504-948-9111; bacchanalwine.com

Hosts live jazz and serves up excellent creative foods in a verdant outdoor courtyard.

BANKS STREET BAR

Mid-City, 4401 Banks St.,
504-486-0258;
banksstreetbarandgrill.com

Before this Mid-City neighborhood even had power after Katrina, Banks Street Bar was serving beer by candle-light. (You can see photos of the flood damage on the bar's website.) Lots of local bands play—from R&B to electro to reggae to metal—and there's rarely a cover. It's small enough that the bands run their own PA, but the club often hosts multiple shows per day—a rarity even in New Orleans. Be warned that, in New Orleans, rock shows can often be very poorly attended, so if you go to Banks Street, bring a friend to talk to just in case. They've also got free red beans and rice on Mondays and free oysters on Thursdays. Not much else is around in that area (as of this writing) except a few pioneer neighbors living on sadly torn streets in beautiful sagging buildings, but Banks Street is a great spot to see where and how people in New Orleans actually live.

BJ'S LOUNGE

Bywater, 4301 Burgundy St.,
504-945-9256

Charles Bukowski would have loved sitting in BJ's listening to the great jukebox with a host of colorful alcoholic musician types. On Thanksgiving and other holidays, BJ's hosts live music and potluck dinners with smoked duck and crawfish mac-n-cheese, among dozens of other neighborhood dishes. Monday nights feature live downtown R&B music by **King James and the Special Men.** No credit cards.

CHICKIE WAH WAH

Mid-City, 2828 Canal St., 504-304-4714; chickiewahwah.com

Named for the song recorded by **Huey "Piano" Smith and the Clowns** in 1958 for the French Quarter–based **Ace** label, this Mid-City joint books a cheerful grab bag of homegrown acts, from **Evan Christopher**'s trad jazz to **Jumpin' Johnny Sansone**'s barroom blues, and hosts late late-night gigs during Jazz Fest. They have a small bar-food menu, including a sloppy Cuban sandwich, for soaking up booze. Plus, it may be the closest bar featuring live music in proximity to Orleans Parish Prison.

CHRIS OWENS CLUB

French Quarter, 500 Bourbon St., 504-523-6400; chrisowensclub.net

Bourbon Street may be the most American of alleys in our fair city, so surprises are few and nipple-based. Chris Owens remains a fixture from another era, a performer and club owner who's graced this stage from the 1960s and appears (eerily unchanged) on weekends as a time capsule/one-woman floor show of sequins and pizzazz. If you're on Bourbon, check in and don't be surprised to find bounce music and furious dancers. Saturdays also feature a very local Latin night in a room perfect for dreams of a Puerto Rico on Mars.

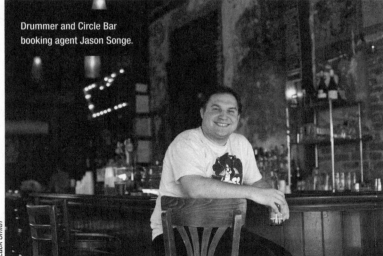

N.O. MOMENT

UPTOWN MUSIC, PART 1

Drummer and Circle Bar booking agent Jason Songe.

Zack Smith

JASON SONGE AND THE CIRCLE BAR

CBD, 1032 St. Charles Ave. at Lee Circle, 504-588-2616; circlebarnola.com

Under the watchful eye of General Robert E. Lee, this teeny-tiny living room-esque venue that holds maybe seventy-five concertgoers hosts shows almost every night. The jukebox—courtesy of original owner **Kelly Keller**, a legendary underground-rock personality who passed away in 2004—boasts one of the finest collections of punk, garage, and Louisiana R&B and soul as ever there was. Since 2007, Jason Songe has booked bands at the Circle Bar. Here is a short list of his favorites:

BANTAM FOXES (bantamfoxes.com). Brothers **Sam** and **Collin McCabe** present fierce rock with screeching guitar and heavy bass.

CARBON POPPIES (carbonpoppies.bandcamp.com). Twee rock with vocal harmonies and shaker/tambourine, the Poppies are a little bit edgy, and will get you sweaty.

CARDINAL SONS (cardinalsons.com). Three brothers combine to create pop rock structure with organ solos. Spoon guitar, and Ben Folds Five everything else.

GLISH (glish.bandcamp.com). New Orleans shoegaze/reverb/dreampop with sweet female vocals.

HABITAT (habitatband.bandcamp.com/releases). Instrumental experimental noise rock—think Lightning Bolt and Vampire Weekend's miscarriage.

THE KID CARSONS (thekidcarsons.com). Country band of brothers and sister featuring deep pedal steel plus a lot of nuance and space. They tour quite a bit and have played with Shovels & Rope, and comedian Steve Martin's bluegrass group the Steep Canyon Rangers.

NATIVE AMERICA (nativeamericamusic.wordpress.com). Plentiful hooks of which the Beach Boys and Beatles would approve.

SUNRISE: SUNSET. Wizened vets of the metal scene, including **Zack Smith** (**Rotary Downs**) on drums, and **Tom Beeman** shredding on guitar.

SWEET CRUDE. Percussion-heavy seven-piece indie rock band with French Cajun flavor and meticulously arranged tunes.

YELEPHANTS (yelephants.bandcamp.com). Tropical psych garage rock.

WHERE TO GET NAKED

As hot as New Orleans is, there are not nearly enough swimming pools. Unless you hit a hotel, then the funky, nice, clothing-optional pool and hot tub area of the **Country Club** (Bywater, 634 Louisa St., 504-945-0742; thecountryclubnew orleans.com) is one of your only options. The club's crowd is majority gay, with more of a mix of neighborhood people and service industry folks at night. The restaurant—which also serves a poolside menu—features surprisingly fancy snacks like seared mahi mahi with chutney and cilantro spaetzle alongside standard country-club fare (club sandwiches, chef's salad). Ten dollars will get you in for a visit, while $299 will get you a year's membership. Ask about discounts for service-industry slaves, which are significant.

Intermittently there is also the "DIY strip club" experience at **Big Dick's House of Big Boobs,** which purports to feature "Gender-bending bouncers, auto-fellating performance artists, dozens of glorious glory holes, and the longest C-section scars in the city GUARANTEED!" Guests are encouraged to "bring an act, take off all your clothes, or just watch teenage runaways perform feats of lewd, crude entertainment in a sexual jamboree that would make R. Kelly blush." Genital Portraits, Cuntfessional Booth, Free Sex Advice, and Tarot and Nipple Readings are available, plus special fun hosts and DJs. BDHoBB usually goes down at the **Mudlark Public Theatre** or else **AllWays Lounge**. Don't forget to bring singles!

DRAGON'S DEN

See page 34.

ELLIS MARSALIS CENTER FOR MUSIC

Upper Ninth Ward,
1901 Bartholomew St., 504-940-3400,
ellismarsaliscenter.org

The centerpiece of the **Musicians' Village**, this 17,000-square-foot facility serves as a performance, education, and community venue. The center includes a 170-seat performance hall, recording studios and teaching facilities for individual and group instruction, and a gathering place for the community. From music to dance, theater to film, the goal of the center is to harness the exceptional talents of the residents and students in the surrounding Musicians' Village.

HOWLIN' WOLF

CBD/Warehouse District,
907 South Peters St., 504-529-5844;
thehowlinwolf.com

The Wolf is a hard place to pin down. Once a major contender in the city, its status has been significantly shrunk over the years by the **House of Blues**, which, with Clear Channel money behind it, can outbid any truly local club. The Wolf is just one sprawling room, with nowhere to go but outside for any kind of break. But the sound is pristine, and the dude who owns it—who also manages the **Rebirth Brass Band**—has been championing the local scene forever. This may not be where you wander over looking for a random good time, but if they book a brass or local hip-hop show, you know it will sound perfect.

KERMIT'S MOTHER-IN-LAW LOUNGE

Tremé, 1500 N. Claiborne Ave.

Ernie K-Doe had a hit in the '60s with the track "Mother-in-Law," and though that was his career high point nationally, locally he became a beloved icon for his flamboyant presence in the bars and as a DJ on WWOZ and WTUL radio. "Emperor of the Universe" **Ernie K-Doe** passed away in 2001, and the bar was run by his wife Antoinette until she died on Mardi Gras Day 2009. It's since been purchased by trumpeter **Kermit Ruffins**, who had a Fat Tuesday party there in 2013 but hasn't opened it again on a regular basis. The bar's outside walls are covered with artist **Daniel Fusilier**'s explosively colorful mural depicting K-Doe, his widow Antoinette, and their favorite local music personalities.

LE BON TEMPS ROULÉ

Uptown, 4801 Magazine St.,
504-895-8117;
myspace.com/4801magazine

Le Bon Temps is a ramshackle old honky-tonk with a couple of pool tables, a great, greasy kitchen, and local music almost every night with no cover. The booking is generally just good-time rock 'n' roll, free oysters on Friday, and a regular free weekly gig (Thursdays, at press time) from the **Soul Rebels Brass Band** that's been shaking the walls there since forever.

BRIAN GREINER
OF THE
HI-HO LOUNGE AND MAISON

508 Frenchmen St., 504-371-5543; maisonfrenchmen.com
2239 St. Claude St., 504-945-4446, hiholounge.net

Since opening in 2010, **Maison** has moved to the head of the pack among larger venues on Frenchmen. Rarely charging a cover for shows on its window stage and upstairs DJ lounge, Maison books national hip-hop acts on its main stage and serves decent food all night. In 2013, Maison proprietors **Brian Greiner** and Jeff B took over the **Hi-Ho Lounge,** a club on St. Claude Avenue known for edgier downtown acts and cheaper drinks. We asked the manager of these two strikingly different clubs, Brian Greiner, to recommend a few of his favorite local acts:

The **BRASS-A-HOLICS** (brass-a-holics.com). These guys are the next great brass band to come out of New Orleans. While a lot of the other brass bands in the city settle for traditional songs that everyone knows and everyone plays, the Brass-A-Holics set is different every time you see them. They seamlessly mix traditionals with originals, '80s covers, current pop hits, and rare party anthems no one else does.

EARPHUNK (earphunk.com). If hard funk grooves with a dash of rock and electronic mixed in is your thing, then you will love Earphunk. Following in the path **Galactic** forged a generation before, the members of Earphunk are making a name for themselves with their diverse sets. They have performed full-set tributes to acts like Daft Punk, Zapp, and Roger, and have acted as backing band for Nola hip-hop legend **Mannie Fresh**. Their own sets are littered with these influences.

THE ESSENTIALS. The Essentials are an 11-piece '60s soul cover band that plays all the Motown hits and other gems from that era exactly how they were written and meant to be played. The Essentials features three male and three female singers, go-go dancers, and sometimes even has burlesque performances during their set.

LIVE MUSIC CLUBS

MID-CITY LANES ROCK 'N' BOWL

Mid-City, 3000 S. Carrollton Ave.,
504-861-1700; rockandbowl.com

Rock 'n' Bowl has been a city institution for decades, and is a favorite
for New Orleans natives who want to
two-step and jitterbug on the dance
floor to bands like the late, legendary
Snooks Eaglin and his big red guitar,
who played here almost monthly until
his death in 2009. It's usually the spot
that zydeco and Cajun acts play when
in town. It's likely you'll see owner **John
Blancher**—in the turquoise '50s-style
bowling shirt that's the club uniform—
dance on the bar or take over the mic
from whatever band's onstage.

NEW ORLEANS HEALING CENTER

Marigny, 2372 St. Claude Ave.,
504-940-1130;
neworleanshealingcenter.org

With a stated mission of providing services and programs promoting physical, nutritional, emotional, intellectual,
environmental, and spiritual well-being,
the 55,000-square-foot Healing Center
also hosts entertainment, with drinks,
at the Café Istanbul Performance Theater. The Crossroads Arts Bazaar and
the Art Gallery both feature the work of
local artists and artisans. Other options
inside this center include the Island of
Salvation Botanica, Fatoush Coffee and
Juice Bar, the Movement Room Dance
Studio, Wild Lotus Yoga, Worldwide
Concepts Travel Agency, a co-op grocery store and bank, and more.

ONE EYED JACKS

French Quarter, 615 Toulouse St.,
504-569-8361; oneeyedjacks.net

Downtown's premier independent
rock club has a delicate balance of
punk and swank, with ornate flocked
red wallpaper that evokes equal parts
Storyville and '70s porn. (They've also

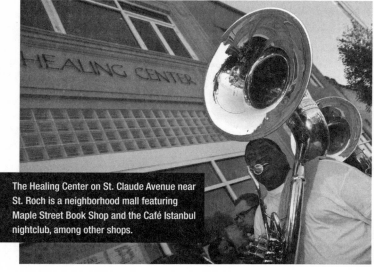

The Healing Center on St. Claude Avenue near
St. Roch is a neighborhood mall featuring
Maple Street Book Shop and the Café Istanbul
nightclub, among other shops.

Zack Smith

got an excellent collection of velvet nudie paintings.) The building started life as a theater, which means the gently raked floor of the showroom guarantees generally awesome sightlines from anywhere in the 400-capacity space. The calendar usually includes equal parts big-name indie-rock and shows from big local players in the bohemian scene. Thursday night is a screamingly popular '80s DJ night, and Mondays usually feature low-key free early shows in the front bar.

N.O. MOMENT

UPTOWN MUSIC, PART 2

Ambitious young booking agent Nick Thomas of the Republic nightclub in the CBD.

Zack Smith

NICK THOMAS OF THE REPUBLIC

828 S Peters St., 504-528-8282; republicnola.com

Then 23-year-old Nick Thomas got his feet wet booking bands at the **Republic**, starting in 2006. Early booking-career milestones included **TV on the Radio, Gogol Bordello**, and **Pretty Lights.** He founded the hugely popular **Throwback** concert and dance party series (described below). These days Thomas says, "There are a ton of EDM [electronic dance music] promoters who are willing to work in partnership, and not as many in rock or indie, so our roster hasn't been as full of indie and rock as it used to, which is unfortunate." Republic often hosts a younger crowd in the college demographic, but it is also a club known for growing local talent, especially in the DJ and electronic music scene. Thomas was the first to nurture **Force Feed Radio**'s big visual and sound spectacle. Here are several other New Orleans acts Thomas suggests you check out:

G-EASY (g-eazy.com). "A live rapper, hip-hop artist. Right now he's touring with a live drummer and backing tracks, but sometimes plays with a whole live band. We gave him a ton of opportunities to play in front of big crowds and he came hard with great material and great performances. The crowd got bigger and bigger every time and by the time he went out of town he was selling out thousand-seat venues almost everywhere."

ROYAL TEETH (royalteethmusic.com). "A full band that is just now kind of blowing up nationally and cutting their teeth with some big stuff. We've booked them so many times over the years, and watched them growing their fan base, polishing their live show. I loved it at first but it was a little raw, but these guys now put together amazing live shows that are just seamless. They're doing big stuff."

BIG ROCK CANDY MOUNTAIN (bigrockcandymountain.net). "Neither of these next two bands are necessarily doing big things on a national scale, but they always kill it at the Republic, and they're both doing something different. BRCM is hard rock meets pop, with the synths like LCD Soundsystem mixed with the heavier guitars."

GLASGOW. "Glasgow is rock with a more theatrical style, almost like a musical."

DAMION YANSEY (damionyancy.net). "Original DJ for our throwback night, we were able to build his name until he kind of outgrew New Orleans, and now he's in Miami. He had that raw talent with song selection, really complicated changeovers. DJ G who took over Damian's spot is also killin' it."

THROWBACK SERIES (weekly event at the Republic). "Nearing the ten-year mark, the weekly Friday night themed dance party Throwback pays homage to '80s and '90s indie music and pop culture. Each night starts off with a different indie rock or hip-hop band before a DJ delves into '80s and '90s music, plus modern stuff like MIA and LCD Soundsystem. Popular with the college crowd, Throwback has the feel of a house party party, with cheap drinks and tons of free '80s and '90s video games. Solve the Rubik's Cube on the bar and get a free drink. Throwback averages over 800 people in the door."

PRESERVATION HALL

*French Quarter, 726 St. Peter St.
between Bourbon and Royal,
504-522-2841; preservationhall.com*

For only $10–$15, listen to real traditional jazz with an impeccable pedigree in a sparse but still charming environment with limited distractions (no booze, no smoking). From 8 p.m. to midnight the band plays several 30-minute sets, and your ticket is valid all night. But there's far more to the Hall than just trad jazz: under the stewardship of **Ben Jaffe**, son of Hall founders **Allan and Sandra Jaffe** (way back in 1961), Pres Hall has been steadfastly keeping it fresh and exciting, collaborating with the likes of **My Morning Jacket, Lenny Kravitz,** and rapper **Mos Def**. Look for a series of album releases featuring the band's talented heavyweights doing their own thing.

SATURN BAR

*Bywater, 3067 St. Claude Ave.,
504-949-7532; saturnbar.com*

Saturn Bar (whose awesome old-school neon sign appeared in the movie *Ray* through the miracle of CGI) is a bona fide New Orleans legend. Its irascible original owner, **O'Neil Broyard**, legendarily disliked making change, talking to customers, and running a bar in general. He filled the club to bursting with a collection of priceless New Orleans art, keepsakes and garbage. Broyard passed away in 2006, and the bar is now run by his nephew **Eric Broyard** and his niece **Bailee Broyard**, who cleaned up the cat pee smell and most of the garbage. It now hosts any type of music

from avant-garde jazz to metal to DJs. Their iconic calendars, T-shirts, and day planners are the hippest souvenirs you could hope for. Saturn is also across the street from **Mr. Quintron's Spellcaster Lodge**.

SIBERIA

*Marigny, 2227 St. Claude Ave.,
504-265-8855; siberianola.com*

A small, empty black rock club with a pool table and a tight PA. Heavy on the heavy: garage rock, punk, metal, and all else wild from around the world. Kick-ass Slavic food in the back (see "Restaurants").

SIDNEY'S SALOON

*Tremé, 1200 St. Bernard Ave.,
504-947-2379*

North Claiborne and St. Bernard Avenues, which run perpendicular to each other in Tremé, were once the heart of New Orleans' black commercial district. St. Bernard in particular was a major neon strip, full of bars and music spots. In the '60s, the construction of the I-10 overpass, which runs over Claiborne like a gloomy, noisy canopy, cast a pall over the hood. St. Bernard still is home to a host of neighborhood bars that cater mostly to an older African American crowd; Sidney's, recently purchased by horn player **Kermit Ruffins,** stands at the center of the strip. There's often live music, occasionally Kermit himself—and when he's not playing, he might be cooking up a pot of red beans with turkey necks. Also, **Preservation Hall** banjo player **Carl LeBlanc** can often be heard across the street at the **Perfect Fit**.

SPEAKEASIES

THE PEARL

Bywater

This house/speakeasy, the **Pearl**, by the river on Desire, is a huge, haunted-seeming Mardi Gras den *cum* junk shop full of Carnival paraphernalia and every other odd or end you could imagine. At concert parties hosted by **MC Trachiotomy** that last well into the next day, the Pearl hosts all types of crazy neighborhood bands and DJs—plus gourmet tacos, oysters, and other culinary delights. Pearl parties are rarely if ever advertised, and we can't give you the address. If y're in Bywater, maybe ask around.

Cousin Itt sips a leisurely drink at a speakeasy, the Pearl.

Jonathan Traviesa

FRENCHMEN STREET

The current music capital of New Orleans

Couples dance on the sidewalk out front of Three Muses restaurant on Frenchmen Street.

Zack Smith

Similar to Austin's famous 6th Street, **Frenchmen Street** is back-to-back clubs and funky, relatively inexpensive restaurants. Frenchmen is to be enjoyed as a whole, as a casual stumble door to door. Just go down and wander and you'll find what you want. But if'n you are interested, here are five favorite spots:

BLUE NILE

532 Frenchmen St., 504-948-2583; bluenilelive.com

This very eclectic club with two nice stages and sound systems (separate door costs) hosts everything from live hip-hop MCs and DJs to dancehall nights hosted by **DJ T Roy**, lots of traditional New Orleans music (from **Kermit Ruffins** to various **Nevilles**), a marginal amount of indie rock, a few fashion shows, and even the Open Ear experimental jazz series. Their programming varies so wildly, it's advisable to make sure you know who's playing before you pay the cover.

Drummer Simon Lott convinces the audience to lie on the ground at dba on Frenchmen Street.

dba

*Marigny, 618 Frenchmen St.,
504-942-3731, dbaneworleans.com*

dba often books two shows a night at 6 and 10 p.m.; a roster of New Orleans music—jazz vocals to rowdy funk to straight-ahead rattling blues. This is also where **Stevie Wonder** chose to pop in after Jazz Fest, and countless others. If you've visited dba more than a few years ago, the sound and the stage space have been much improved.

DRAGON'S DEN

*Marigny, 435 Esplanade Ave.,
504-949-1750;
myspace.com/dragonsdennola*

Up the precarious, twisty red stairwell you'll find a dim, red-lit room anchored on one end by the bar and on the other by a wrought-iron balcony overlooking the grassy Esplanade Avenue neutral ground and the mouth of the lower Decatur strip. After the flood, the Den (once a Thai restaurant with music upstairs) was sold to a crew led by local **DJ Proppa Bear**. Proppa installed turntables both upstairs and downstairs, where a second stage was also added. A host of electronic music parties such as **Bass Church** feature hip-hop, jungle, reggaeton, and the like, with a smattering of rock 'n' roll bands.

Those who enter this dark hallway will feel the bass from one of Dragon's Den's nightly electro, dubstep, and dancehall parties.

SNUG HARBOR

Marigny, 626 Frenchmen St., 504-949-0696; snugjazz.com

Though more adventurous spirits may find some of the jazz shows here a bit staid, Snug is nonetheless considered the city's premier spot for big-name local and international jazz acts, with sets nightly at 8 and 10 p.m. Jazz patriarch and educator **Ellis Marsalis** plays here monthly with his quartet. The building's other half is given over to a casual-upscale supper club focusing on steaks, burgers, and Gulf seafood. Tip: the often-pricey upstairs show is usually broadcast on a closed-circuit TV you can watch at the downstairs bar.

YUKI IZAKAYA

Marigny, 525 Frenchmen St., 504-943-1122

Hesitant to write much about this comfy upscale-ish Japanese place on Frenchmen, since it hasn't been here long. But for the sake of their menu of late-night fried dumplings, yakitori, and sake (modeled after the after-work spots Tokyo businessmen booze it up in), plus DJs and unusual live music—Yuki is a great place to catch cellist **Helen Gillet**'s French chanson combo, **Wazozo,** or semi-goth band **Morella & the Wheels of If**.

ST. ROCH TAVERN

Marigny, 1200 St. Roch Ave.,
504-945-0194

A 100 percent authentic, no-hype dive bar where you will feel charmingly unsafe while meeting some fucked-up locals and hearing music from under-the-radar local bands, ranging in styles from harmonica blues to metal. God and the cops willing, **DJ Rusty Lazer** spins bounce music every Saturday night. The city made the bar disallow animals, meaning it's no longer a dog bar, and the St. Roch's weekly "chicken drop" gambling event has been discontinued. But there's still cheap bar food, and sometimes blood on the floor.

First they came for our fliers . . .
Zack Smith

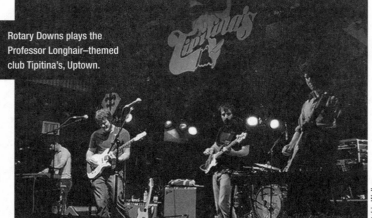

Rotary Downs plays the Professor Longhair–themed club Tipitina's, Uptown.

Soundman and studio engineer Andrew "Goat" Gilchrist meets real-life goat Chauncey Gardner outside of Vaughan's bar in Bywater.

VAUGHAN'S LOUNGE

Bywater, 4229 Dauphine St.,
504-947-5562

This dilapidated-looking saloon deep in the Bywater is without a doubt one of the city's best bars. Serious touring musicians from **Will Oldham** to the **Rolling Stones** have come down to see and hear proud viper and Louis Armstrong facsimile **Kermit Ruffins and His Barbecue Swingers** (or some fill-in brass band or other) get Vaughan's dancing, which Ruffins did on Thursday nights for nearly two decades. Vaughan's is generous with free grub given any halfway good excuse, and in the bar's shadows, there are plenty of smokey treats to be shared.

ZEITGEIST MULTI-DISCIPLINARY ARTS CENTER

Uptown, 1618 Oretha Castle Haley
Blvd., 504-352-1150; zeitgeistinc.net

More like a community center than a real theater, Zeitgeist is the premier venue in which to consume alternative film, dance, theater, and avant-garde music. Often, it's the only venue to catch the more outré film festival favorites on a big screen with the added benefit of knowing you're supporting truly marginal, bohemian culture. They host everything from the annual touring Sex Workers Art Show to a human rights film festival.

CITY GOVERNMENT'S WAR ON LIVE MUSIC

Until recently, New Orleans telephone poles were decorated with hundreds of colorful handbills keeping us abreast of concerts and reminding us that we lived in the world's music capital. In the summer of 2011, though, Mayor Mitch Landrieu's administration decided to crack down on fliers. Landrieu created the Office of Cultural Economy and immediately began enforcing many previously ignored music regulations, which helped to kill off nightclubs like jazz staple **Donna's** brass band club in the Quarter. The city made the **Circle Bar**—which harbored "illegal" music since 1999—cease live entertainment for months while it acquired the correct permits, then went after **Bacchanal,** a popular outdoor jazz spot. One night during peak business hours, Bacchanal was invaded by the NOPD's Quality of Life officers, the Fire Department, and the Department of Health. Shit got so intense that **Mimi's in the Marigny** (which had hosted "illegal" music seven nights a week since Katrina) voluntarily halted its bands and DJs.

Playing defense, the local music community started the **Music and Culture Coalition of New Orleans (MACCNO)** in 2012. New Orleans trumpet player **Kermit Ruffins** (of Tremé fame) began hosting Wednesday MACCNO meetings at his Tremé speakeasy club with representatives from the Jackson Square Task Force, the Sound Ordinance Task Force, the Visitors' Bureau, NOLA Business Alliance, and the Department of Economic Development. Since MACCNO's formation, the city has chilled out a little, though it hasn't stopped busting nightclubs. **Siberia,** which opened in 2011 among a cluster of other clubs (the **AllWays Lounge,** the **Hi-Ho Lounge,** and **Kajun's** karaoke club), was targeted by the permit police and voluntarily put a halt to shows in 2012. By playing nice, and with MACCNO's help, Siberia became the first in a series of venues allowed to continue hosting live music on a temporary basis while working with the city to acquire proper permits. Currently, the venue has made it through two out of three steps in the process toward attaining a conditional use permit. While in purgatory, Siberia's music must end at 2 a.m. and drinks cannot leave the premises in go-cups.

In March 2013, a harsh verdict was handed down to the ancient **St. Roch Tavern,** which was fined $10,000. Now music must end on Fridays and Saturdays by 1:30 a.m. and at 11:30 p.m. for the rest of the week—and DJs aren't allowed to perform at all on weekday nights. A new restriction on live animals will keep most of the dog-owning fauxbeaux away, while also ending the Tavern's popular weekly "chicken drop" gambling event.

"It was such a slap in the face," says **DJ Rusty Lazer,** who hosts St. Roch's bounce night. "I lived in Austin, and New Orleans' new campaign just reminds me of 'Keep Austin Weird.' That campaign was the moment Austin started to become unrecognizable."

Modern New Orleans music cannot be summed up with the words "jazz" or "funk" or "blues," or any genre tag. Well, there's rap, but. Many New Orleans musicians create a true sense of the city without sounding like old, traditional New Orleans music. Mardi Gras is just as big an influence on many of these bands— any rock band desiring to sound "heavy" should study New Orleans high school marching units. The city's seasonal banjo-strumming, accordion-tooting **fauxbeaux** bands even manage to sometimes subvert genres (other times they just mimic Tom Waits). Even the city's abstract/experimental/noise music scene is genuinely entertaining and fun in a way that can definitely be attributed to living where we do. The true heart of New Orleans music is not jazz, funk, or blues, but rather, originality! Here is an overview of New Orleans music in the 2000s:

THERESA ANDERSSON

theresaandersson.com

Andersson came to prominence as a talented fiddle player and singer who, with the help of other songwriters, hybridized various forms of American "roots music" into something almost her own. With the release of *Hummingbird Go!* and then *Street Parade,* Andersson began following her own unique muse, a muse who wanted her to use loop pedals and other modern instruments to create something truly unique, and very beautiful. It doesn't hurt that she's one of the best violinists in a state full of fiddle players, and that her voice is as strong as any American Idol contestant. Her current one-woman-band is standing-ovation worthy.

AU RAS AU RAS

myspace.com/tessbrunet

Tess Brunet, former drummer for **Deadboy and the Elephantmen** and **the Generationals**, creates a sensual, singing-focused panorama of electronics and guitars.

BABES

babesuniverse.net

Wild one-man-band **Rhodes**'s new band plays OC-style psych punk.

BIG HISTORY

Dual female singers lead this fresh-faced, wildly popular electro-pop-rock group. Backed by a mountain of laptops and synths, **Amanda Wuerstlin** soars on violin.

ANXIOUS SOUND PRODUCTIONS AND NOISE GUITARIST ROB CAMBRE

Guitarist Rob Cambre runs New Orleans' avant-garde music scene.

Jonathan Traviesa

Since 1997, guitarist **Rob Cambre's Anxious Sound Productions** has been the first name in adventurous modern music booking, with shows usually pairing international cult musicians with some hot New Orleans cats—including Cambre, who fits himself into almost every show he books. Luckily his "Sonic Youth meets Japanese-noise freeform guitar work" is often worth it. Cambre's sets run the gamut from solo improvised electric guitar to more structured acoustic pieces to off-the-cuff groups with drummers, bassists, saxophonists, dancers, and poets. His intermittent **Dry Bones Trio** with **Endre Landsnes** (drums) and **Bill Hunsinger** (bass) plays ferocious, high-energy music touching on aspects of free jazz and rock, while the **Death Posture** features Borbetomagus guitarist **Donald Miller** and butoh dancer **Vanessa Skantze**. The traditional rock band he sets aflame—and the group in which he really shines—is "garage gospel" purveyors **R. Scully's Rough 7**.

Cambre hosts shows once or twice a month. There are also a few Anxious Sound events you can mark on your calendars. On January 30 each year, Cambre hosts the Anxious Sound Holiday HO-Down at the **Hi-Ho Lounge**: a blowout of adventurous improvisers from New Orleans, Baton Rouge, and Mississippi, usually including the likes of **James Singleton** (bass), **Helen Gillet** (cello), **Bruce Golden** (perc/electronics), **Donald Miller** (guitar), and of course Cambre himself. More recently, Cambre also concocted the **Sound Circus** concert series (a more high level production supported in part by an **Arts Council** grant) at the **Big Top** arts center, featuring an international roster of improvisers that has included **Han Bennink, Ken Vandermark, Ab Baars**, and many, many others. In 2009, Cambre also helped bring about the first New Orleans installment of the **No Idea Festival**, curated by Austin-based percussionist **Chris Cogburn** and featuring musicians from Baltimore (**Bonnie Jones**), Mexico City (**Mario de Vega**), and Zurich (**Jason Kahn**). In short, if you enjoy difficult and/or complicated listening, look for the Anxious Sound label on the product.

Note—if you enjoy strange, experimental sounds, also check out purveyors of freaky jazz and software experiments like drummer **Justin Peake**, keyboardist **Brian Coogan**, trombonist **Jeff Albert**, or sax man **Dan Oestreicher**, just to name a few scatterjazz players in the New Orleans strange music conspiracy. Albert curates frequent improvisational jams (at the time of publication) under the umbrella of the **Open Ears Music Series**.

BIG ROCK CANDY MOUNTAIN

bigrockcandymountain.net

Rock with fuzzy guitars, analog keyboards, ultra-sweet harmonies, distorted bass-lines, and techno drum beats. Fun and loud.

BIPOLAROID

Bipolaroid's garage rock drips down the walls. Over the course of many years and many lineups, **Ben Glover**'s musical vision has evolved into something truly psychedelic, bent and beautiful. The band's most recent incarnation features garage-rock icon **King Louie** on drums.

BIRTHSTONE

Psych punk.

THE BLACKBELT BAND

sickroomrecords.com/Releases/SRR053.htm

Having played in various combinations for the last fourteen years, the members of Blackbelt have developed a signature style utilizing acoustic, electric, and electronic instrumentation to create a mix of experimental rock, blues, post-punk, reggae, and movie soundtrack.

BLIND TEXAS MARLIN

myspace.com/blindtexasmarlin

A feral cat–style songwriter/screamer/guitarist who has come a long way toward perfecting the "badass while almost falling apart" aesthetic.

RAY BONG

bongoloids.com

Actually from Lafitte, Louisiana, Ray is as close to a Hunter Thompson-esque character as anyone you'll ever meet (even in New Orleans): a drug-freak psychedelic-noise musician who, because he's also a wealthy independent engineer who put four kids through college, has attained guru status. Ray can be seen at rare solo shows pounding away like a caveman on totally unrecognizable analog gear (the Tri-Wave Generator, the Coron, the Superstar 3000 toy guitar).

THE BRASS-A-HOLICS

brass-a-holics.com

This multiracial brass band combines New Orleans brass and Washington D.C. go-go music, plus disparate influences from Miles Davis and Nirvana to Wham! and Kanye West. Trombonist **Winston Turner** is a former member of St. Augustine High School's **Marching 100**, plus the **Pinstripes** and **Soul Rebels** brass bands.

BRASSFT PUNK

Adventurous musician and sometime **Preservation Hall** soundman **Earl the Mad Wikkid** leads a tight, big brass band covering the songs of techno act **Daft Punk**.

CHEF MENTEUR

chefmenteur.org

A live space-rock band named after a famous New Orleans highway, Chef Menteur's (which means "chief liar") drone-oriented "songs" are built around murky loops and samples, and a tight rhythm section. More recently they've ditched the electronics and turned up the volume.

CLOCKWORK ELVIS

myspace.com/clockworkelvis

This Elvis cover band has an extensive personal narrative vision that connects the story of *A Clockwork Orange* to **Elvis Presley**. It's not immediately apparent in the performance—straight-ahead Elvis songs played honestly and with love (but not jumpsuits)—but you can ask lead singer **Elvis DeLarge** if you want the whole hypothesis. Actually, we suggest it. The band often plays shows with local burlesque troupe the **Billion Dollar Baby Dolls**, led by DeLarge's wife, **Reverend Spooky LeStrange**.

BANDS

N.O. MOMENT

COMMUNITY RECORDS AND THE HEY! CAFÉ

Get your coffee from Hey! Café, Uptown, and your New Orleans post-punk recordings from Community Records.

Zack Smith

communityrecords.org

This DIY record label collective started in 2008 by **Daniel Ray** and **Greg Rodrigue** distributes free downloads directly from their website. Community Records has released over 35 records on vinyl, CD, and cassette, and 65 records in digital formats. They regularly host all-ages DIY shows for New Orleans artists and touring acts.

For the last five-plus years, Daniel and Greg have hosted an annual music festival called **Block Party** at the **Big Top** arts and education center. Each year the festival showcases twenty bands, mostly Community Records artists. The label has also converted a diesel engine tour van to run on waste vegetable oil so that their artists can tour without heavy reliance on fossil fuels. While in town—or once you're back in your town—check out Community Records' bands live:

ALL PEOPLE. Four-piece punk/dub reggae/experimental New Orleans group. Daniel and Greg both perform with this band. For fans of: Fugazi and Lee Scratch Perry.

CADDYWHOMPUS (caddywhompusband.com). Two-piece noise/pop/experimental New Orleans group. Guitarist **Joel Gifford** is off the charts—he makes finger tapping absolutely acceptable. Tours regularly, amazing live shows. For fans of: Lightning Bolt and Animal Collective.

DONOVAN WOLFINGTON. Five-piece punk/rock/emo group from New Orleans. Youthful energy meets a southern vibe with reflective thoughtful lyrics. For fans of: Joyce Manor and Pavement.

HEAT DUST. Three-piece grunge/punk from New Orleans. Washed-over fuzzy tones and heavy guitar. For fans of: loud music and skateboarding.

WHOM DO YOU WORK FOR? (whomdoyouworkfor.com). Electronic/experimental/rock/noise/pop electronic music, named for an Ornette Coleman recording.

THE CONSORTIUM OF GENIUS

consortiumofgenius.com

Part band, part multimedia weirdness, the C.O.G. is a gaggle of costumed mad scientists who carry on the tradition of New Orleans' famous TV host **Morgus the Magnificent** in musical form while, according to them, trying to take over the world. With songs like "Lab Coat" and "Science Fight," they definitely have a shtick, and the rock shows are highly theatrical. Sometimes C.O.G. shows feature original films, which include their fifth member, a cartoon robot.

COUNTRY FRIED

countryfried.net

The best New Orleans has to offer in the way of twang, Country Fried is technically impressive, with virtuosic strings and perfect vocal harmonies in the old-fashioned acoustic country string band tradition. Some of the city's soul and R&B influences have also snuck in, and Country Fried's live covers of southern rock and contemporary alt-country acts like **The Band, Lucinda Williams, Gram Parsons,** and **Little Feat** add some fire to the mix.

COYOTES

Alt-country, Americana milieu. The band began life in Los Angeles before settling in the New Orleans indie rock scene. Citing the Flying Burrito Brothers as inspiration, the Coyotes describe their sound as "cosmic Americana."

DASH RIP ROCK

dashriprock.net

The 25-year-old world's greatest bar band—hits include "Locked inside a Liquor Store with You" and "(Let's Go) Smoke Some Pot"—is also edgy enough to release albums through **Jello Biafra**'s label, **Alternative Tentacles**.

Marcus Davis's Drumcart provides big-ass beats for wild walking parades, and creates spontaneous dance parties of its own wherever it goes.

DEBAUCHE

debauchemusic.com

Russian-born **Yegor Romanstov**, backed by his "Russian Mafia Band," croons and bellows rocking drunken versions of Russian folk songs, some more than a century old, written by prisoners and gangsters, hooligans, orphans, and gypsies. One crowd favorite tells of lesbians who marry in jail then escape, only to be killed.

PHIL deGRUY

guitarp.com

deGruy only comes out into the light if he doesn't see the shadow of his "guitarp" on April Fool's Day. The "guitarp" being the guitar deGruy invented, wherein a tiny audible 11-string harp built into the guitar body is played simultaneously or in syncopation with the other six strings. His constant dry but subversive sense of humor and otherworldly playing was described by former Zappa and David Lee Roth axman Steve Vai as "John Coltrane meets Mel Brooks at a party for Salvador Dali."

deGruy also shares the stage with fellow hilarious guitar wizards **Jimmy Robinson** and **Cranston Clemments** in the band **Twangorama**.

DIE RÖTZZ

dierotzz.tripod.com

A loud punk rock power trio who make fun musical mess. Die Rötzz does double time as **Guitar Lightnin' Lee**'s **Thunder Band**, which means they, improbably, hang out with Fats Domino sometimes, and play blues like a broken steamroller.

MIKE DILLON

myspace.com/mikedillonpercussion

This tricky percussionist and vibes man has played in jam-band-friendly musical experiments including **Les Claypool's Frog Brigade** and his own **Mike Dillon's Go-Go Jungle**. In New Orleans, he's often seen in combination with **Galactic**'s **Stanton Moore**, jazz/funk drummer **Johnny Vidacovich**, and bass weirdo **James Singleton**. A big favorite of the **Bonnaroo** crowd.

NEW ORLEANS HEAVY SOUNDS, PART 1

with Mike IX Williams of EyeHateGod

Metal godfather and published poet Mike IX Williams.

Gary LoVerde

Mike IX Williams has fronted slow punk-metal band **Eye-HateGod** for twenty-five years. Williams also published the excellent dark and hilarious poetry book, *Cancer as a Social Activity* (Southern Nihilism Front). Mike and his band are incredible, and so we interviewed him about EyeHateGod, its place in the pantheon of New Orleans metal, plus other heavy bands you may want to peep while in town.

Tell me the story of EyeHateGod.

We started in 1988. Now there's different members. The cool thing at the time was thrash metal, Slayer was cool. Even I had a thrash band in New Orleans. We heard the Melvins and we were also into Black Flag, side 2 of *My War,* and obviously we were into Black Sabbath and St. Vitus and stuff like that. We weren't even 100 percent serious at the beginning; it was just something to piss off people who would play these shows, and just have fun and watch people's reaction when we'd just do feedback for fifteen minutes, and throw in three riffs as slow as we possibly could.

So you didn't have a lot of company on the scene then?

Not in New Orleans. Before EyeHateGod, **Soilent Green** was around. But they were more influenced by Napalm Death and they kind of started playing slower later on—I'm not sure if that's our influence but. There was **Hawgjaw**. And we were all friends so it wasn't like anyone was stealing from each other. **Graveyard Rodeo** was a local band that had similar influences. EyeHateGod was like taking the Melvins even further, more filthy and dirty and with the bluesy southern feeling to it also. There were bands in other cities, Cavity in Fla., BuzzO*ven was kind of starting up in North Carolina or Richmond. There was a band in Boston called Grief. And there was Neurosis of course, who were still a hardcore band at the time but were starting to play slower. We were hated for a long time; people just didn't get it. We had a few fans who understood that it was just supposed to be heavy—in 1986 to 1988 as we were forming, people thought the faster you play the heavier you are, but that's obviously not true.

And now New Orleans is a metal capital of America!

Yeah, people have moved here from other states, man, even other countries, to be part of the scene here. Though a lot of people left after Katrina, a lot of people came down after Katrina. That was a great time for music actually, right after Katrina, with bands starting back up, and new bands forming. The greatest thing is around 1998 and 1999 when we did take a sort of hiatus because of personal problems and record label trouble—during that hiatus we noticed bands were popping up in England, and Japan even—a Japanese band called Green Machine—Iron Monkey in England, bands all over the world that were starting to kind of sound like this same exact kind of sound. That's when we noticed it was something bigger than us.

Tell me about your affiliation with Housecore Records.

I used to play with **Phil Anselmo** in **Arson Anthem**, where we had Hank III on drums, that since kind of fizzled out. Then Outlaw Order was a side project of EyeHateGod but

BANDS

that kind of fizzled out too—though we have been trying to keep it on the burner. Now we have **The Guilt of . . .** which is a noise band with me and **Ryan McKern.** We have a 12-inch out with Merzbow. The new record is coming out on New Orleans label **Last Hurrah,** this guy **Chad Hensely.** I also started a band with **Scott Kelley** from Neurosis, we did a three-week tour with no record, no press, no interviews, just got in a car and went out and we all did solo sets where I came out and did a reading, then Scott did his mildly dark acoustic stuff, and Bruce does experimental saxophone, and then we have this guy **Sanford Parker** with some drum machine stuff and just loud noise—then at the end we come out and do three songs together that we wrote. That band is called **Corrections House.** A new 7-inch should be out as we speak.

NEW ORLEANS HEAVY SOUNDS, PART 2

with Matt Russell and Paul Webb

Guitarist and music store owner Paul Webb and club owner/"singer" Matt Russell know the New Orleans metal scene intimately.

Zack Smith

Believe it or not, heavy metal rock could be considered a type of New Orleans roots music. Though not invented here, New Orleans metal has a distinctly slow, low, slithery sound, with a lineage stretching as far back as bounce rap's. Since the late '80s, New Orleans has offered up legends from **Soilent Green** and **EyeHateGod** to more recent successes like the slow, grinding **DOWN**, led by Louisiana natives guitarist **Pepper Keenan (Corrosion of Conformity)** and singer **Phil Anselmo (Pantera)**. Anselmo's **Housecore** record label (thehousecorerecords.com) not only releases albums by his own side-bands like **Arson Anthem,** but also works to preserve on vinyl Louisiana metal legends like **Crowbar,** and newer acts like sludge-metal band **Haarp** and heavy, spooky **Ponykiller.**

The websites **noladiy.org** and **nolaunderground.wordpress.com** will help you learn where you can "throw the goat" while in town. But personally, when I want me metal, I inquire with either **Paul Webb** or **Matt Russell.** Webb, owner of **Webb's Bywater Music,** plays guitar in mostly instrumental tech-metal combos such as **Mountain of Wizard** and **Spickle.** Matt Russell has for the last decade booked heavy bands at local bars, most recently through his Marigny club, **Siberia.** Matt currently "sings" while Paul plays guitar in the hardcore punk band **Classhole**, with **Gary Mader** from EyeHateGod and **Grant Tom** from Haarp. "The New Orleans metal scene is like Mexican food," says Webb. "There are just a few people in many different combinations." Knowing those combinations intimately, Webb and Russell suggest the following heavy New Orleans bands:

THE BASTARD SONS OF MARVIN HIRSH. Primitive, old-school teen punk led by the son of the bassist from Die Rotz and Guitar Lightning. The songs are about bombing McDonald's, and Abercrombie Zombies. Pretty funny.

BUCK BILOXI AND THE FUCKS. Fronted by cab driver **Joe Pestilence**, they sound like the Spits but stupider. They have stuff out on **Goner Records**' side label **Orgone Toilet**, and also local label **Pelican Pow Wow Records**.

CHRIST PUNCHER. Bywater dudes, like '90s, post-punk but more heavy. Like Helmet and Unsane but more technically driven.

CROWBAR. Twenty years and still heavy, these New Orleans doom-core legends were inspired by the down-tuned sludge of the Melvins and the over-the-top aggression of Carnivore. Crowbar's currently releasing new material and reissuing old records on the Housecore label.

DEMONIC DESTRUCTION. Spanish guys, transplants living in Kenner, Louisiana, playing death metal. Their Myspace page claims inspiration from Slayer, Morbid Angel, Possessed, Deicide and Monstrosity, adding, "The band's lyrics are highly based on satanism and tyranny."

DISCIPLES OF THRASH. A thrash metal cover band doing '80s and early '90s stuff like Metallica, Slayer, Testament, Megadeth, Sepultura, Kreator, Death Angel. The singer's really into it.

DONKEY PUNCHER. Nola sludge, hardcore thrash. They have a song called "Don't Drop Your Baby in the Crawfish Boil." Ridiculous.

EXCARNATE. Black metal with members of **High Priest,** Haarp**, Cancer Patient,** and **Missing Monuments.**

FAT STUPID UGLY PEOPLE. Power violence. **Hollis,** the lead singer, is kinda the mascot of the scene. He might wear a coconut bra, or you never know what's gonna happen with Hollis.

GOATWHORE (goatwhore.net). Black metal with Sammy from **Acid Bath/ Crowbar**, Ben from **Soilent Green**.

PONY KILLER. Almost goth-y, psychedelic rock band rolls with Phil Anselmo's Housecore records and has toured with DOWN and Arson Anthem, but Ponykiller is heavy in its own way.

DUMMY DUMPSTER

myspace.com/dummydumpster

This punkish, noisy, unpredictable anything-goes project started in Chalmette, Louisiana, in 2001. The microphone is mounted in the singer's decorated homemade shoulderpads, allowing him to rip around the room and petrify the crowd as he sings.

EARPHUNK

earphunk.com

This funk band mixes in electronic elements à la Galactic. They've served as backing band for Nola hip-hop legend **Mannie Fresh**.

STEVE ECK

myspace.com/steveeck

A dark singer-songwriter and guitarist, Eck bends compositions that could be played straight into beautiful and wholly unique shapes, then backs them with amazing New Orleans players from all over the musical spectrum. You won't party and dance to this music, but it kicks the ass of most New Orleans party music.

EMPRESS HOTEL

myspace.com/empresshotel

In this band named for one of New Orleans' skeezer lodging facilities, brothers **Ryan and Eric Rogers** (guitar/drums) and **Julie Williams** (keys) back

Little Maker singer **Micah McKee** playing '70s-esque folk music with touches of funk and punk. Stream-of-consciousness lyrics and dynamic vocal melodies.

N.O. MOMENT

TIP THE PERFORMERS!

Zack Smith

New Orleans is a haven for people who can do things well—but usually just one thing, to the point where they're otherwise unemployable, despite their musical talent. Music is many New Orleanians' sole source of income. So, this may seem over-obvious—and good for you if it does!—but some people don't realize: TIP EVERY PERFORMER that you enjoy! Not the weepy old terrible folk singer whose too-loud amplifiers pollute the air around Jackson Square, but that silver-painted ghost mime lady you took a picture of, you DAMN WELL better tip her. If you take a photo of a performer and don't tip them, plan on spraining your ankle or losing your car within forty-eight hours. No cover charge at the bar on Frenchmen? TIP. Only there for a drink? TIP. You wouldn't pull that in a strip club, don't pull it on Frenchmen Street.

THE ESSENTIALS

This 11-piece '60s soul cover band plays Motown hits and other gems from that era. Singer/songwriter **Micah McKee** of **Little Maker** leads this unit featuring six singers, go-go dancers, and sometimes burlesque.

FELIX

myspace.com/felixnola

Wild, messy, blues-punk band with a secret-weapon organ player who coats the guitar-and-drums in beautiful, creepy textures. (See **Blind Texas Marlin**.)

Adventurous cellist Helen Gillet.
Robin Walker

GAL HOLIDAY AND THE HONKY TONK REVIEW

galholiday.com

Undeniably retro, and undeniably pretty, Gal Holiday presents high-quality recreations of old country music.

GENERATIONALS

generationals.com

A strikingly pleasant version of a well-worn indie style: guitars shimmer behind passionate dual vocals swamped in reverb. Like a third generation **R.E.M.,** or a more hearty **Galaxy 500**.

HELEN GILLET

You've never witnessed a cellist rock this hard. Dynamic and experimental but unpretentious and fun, Gillet plays jazz and medieval music, sings French *chansons* and "musettes" in her band **Wazozo**, uses loop stations in her wild solo act, and helps reconstruct the abstract orchestra pieces of bass wiz **James Singleton**—to name just a few of her many successes. If you came to New Orleans for music, Helen is a must-see.

GLASGOW

Stalwarts of the New Orleans scene, brothers **Sam and Jack Craft** use eclectic instrumentation like electric violin and cello, creating rock akin to **ELO**, **Queen**, and **David Bowie**, all filtered through a **Zappa**-esque absurdism.

Live drum-and-bass electro funk group, Gravity A.

Zack Smith

GOLD AND THE RUSH

In low gear, the band strums bluegrass-tinged country Americana. Its high gear is reminiscent of Black Keys but with backup singers and a nice fiddle.

GOV'T MAJIK

myspace.com/govtmajik

By fusing free-form jazz and mind-melting atmospheric elements, this 10-piece afrobeat band aims for the psychedelic majesty of **Fela Kuti**, while whipping up a world-groove dance frenzy.

GRAVITY A

gravitya.com

Self-described as "funktronica," this jam band quartet combines New Orleans funk, drum 'n' bass breaks, and trippy trance.

DAVE GREGG

Primarily a street performer, Gregg plays New Orleans standards and other jazz and funk with one hand strumming a guitar around front, the other hand picking another guitar behind his back, while his bare feet play the bass. Turn your back and you'd never know.

GUITAR LIGHTNIN' LEE AND HIS THUNDER BAND

guitarlightninlee.com

Born and raised in the Lower Ninth Ward (and lifelong friends with **Fats Domino**'s son **Antoine Jr.**), Lightnin' studied blues guitar with masters like **Jimmy Reed** and **"Boogie" Bill Webb**, and has palled around with every major artist to come through New Orleans. His scrappy band of white punk rockers also make up the very loud band **Die Rotzz**. Together, they make sloppy, fuzzy, unhinged blues that will make you spill your drink and slap your mama.

A HANGING

myspace.com/ahanging

Grindcore-esque metal band with a hot chick singer. Their own Myspace description, in caps: "WILDCAT STUCK IN GARBAGE DISPOSAL."

HAPPY TALK BAND

myspace.com/thehappytalkband

Happy Talk is mostly frontman **Luke Allen**, whose bittersweet songwriting captures the bohemian, downtown New Orleans life where bartenders, strippers, junkies, artists, musicians, and other similar sorts live, drink, and

die. Allen, a guitarist, plays in several combinations, from a raw, electric alt-country/punk combo to a gentle ensemble with cello and pedal steel. His economy of words will break your heart.

HAWG JAW

myspace.com/hawgjaw

Hardcore music for people who don't think hardcore is interesting enough, Hawg Jaw was formed in 1996. The vocals are more expressive than in most metal, and the heavy music is twisted and brutal (see pages 48–50).

JAMES HAYES

A less ostentatious take on the Dinosaur Jr. aesthetic of big melodic fuzz. When not in town playing at **The Saint** or **Circle Bar,** songwriter Hayes regularly drives down and tours Central and South America.

THE HELP

reverbnation.com/thehelpfrom neworleans

Barbara Menendez fronted New Orleans new wave/punk band **The Cold** in the early 1980s. Three decades later, her band The Help cites (English) Beat, Blondie, X, and the Buzzcocks among its influences.

CLIFF HINES

cliffhines.com

A young jazz guitar graduate of the **New Orleans Center for the Creative Arts (NOCCA)** out to make a name for himself, Hines tours his ass off with his own adventurous jazz-esque bands,

Benjamin Simmons

or as sideman for percussion wildman **Mike Dillon**. You may even catch him leading a group at Frenchmen's "mainstream" jazz spot, **Snug Harbor**.

THE HONORABLE SOUTH

thehonorablesouth.com

Combining rock, soul, folk, hip-hop, funk, and a little more rock, Honorable South are more **Janelle Monae** than **Etta James**. Singer **Charm Taylor** and guitarist **Matthew Rosenbeck** bring along secret-weapon guitarist **Danny Kartel**, whose production credits include **Soulja Slim**, **Mystikal,** and **Juvenile**'s "Slow Motion." Good for dancing, good for the soul.

THE HOT CLUB OF NEW ORLEANS

hotclubofneworleans.com

The Hot Club perform the swing era music of **Duke Ellington,** plus **Django Reinhardt** and **Stephan Grappelli** among others, yet avoid sounding like

a museum piece by infusing the music with their own modern sensibilities. In keeping with the classic format of this music, Hot Club lacks a drummer—but will still make you dance.

HURRAY FOR THE RIFF RAFF

hurrayfortheriffraff.com

The best example of Bywater trainhopper music. Cat Power-esque singer/banjo player **Alynda Lee** actually did learn music by participating in trainhopping culture. As a result, Hurray for the Riff Raff uses acoustic instruments to spin 6/8 waltzes and modern country ballads about life's perils.

KING LOUIE

myspace.com/kinglouieandhisrock nroll

Harahan, Louisiana's most famous rock 'n'roller—as well known for his unpredictable behavior as his music—has played in a laundry list of revered local garage bands, most recently **Missing**

JAMES SINGLETON'S JAZZ

Animal bassist and modern-day jazz man James Singleton plays all styles.

Katja Liebing

The most amazing stand-up bassist you've ever heard or seen, the mop-haired, eternally youthful fifty-something **James Singleton** has played with everyone from **Ellis Marsalis** to **Clarence "Gatemouth" Brown** to legendary pianist **James Booker.** But unlike some of New Orleans' best-known musicians, Singleton is also original, daring, and multifaceted. "My overarching project is that I want my music to reflect two centuries," says Singleton, whose **James Singleton Orchestra** purports to perform jazz from 1913 to 2013.

Singleton is perhaps most famous for the progressive jazz outfit **Astral Project** (astralproject.com), which he's helped power since 1978 with saxophonist **Tony Dagradi**, guitarist **Steve Masakowski**, and drummer **Johnny Vidacovich.** Vidacovich and Singleton also share the band **DVS** with percussionist **Mike Dillon**—who plays in **Illuminasti** with Singleton and avant-garde trumpeter **Skerrik.** Singleton's **Bluebelly** is ostensibly an acoustic piano trio with every instrument run through laptops; drummer **Justin Peake** handles loops and effects. The **James Singleton Quartet** finds multi-instrumentalists using punk rock textures and swing rhythms smashed together in the jazz club with acoustic piano. If the money's right, Singleton can even put together his wild concert hall String Quartet.

"Part of my experience is always that someone has seen me doing my freaky shit," says Singeleton "Then they come up to me and say, 'Weren't you the guy we just saw at **Spotted Cat?**'" In the **Orleans 6,** Singleton plays traditional New Orleans jazz beside **Ben Polcer.**

Singleton doesn't like to tour, so you can almost always catch him in New Orleans. If not, he suggests you attend the weekly **Open Ears Music Series** (openearsmusic.org) on Tuesday nights upstairs at the Blue Nile (532 Frenchmen St.). Trombonist **Jeff Albert** curates this concert series featuring interesting and experimental music, often improvised and touching on jazz. Shows run fairly strictly between 10 p.m. and 12 a.m. The artists are paid via your donations. Then each fall the Open Ears series celebrates its anniversary with a festival of adventurous jazz-ish music.

Monuments. Louie shifts between power pop, Thin Lizzy-isms, and a one-man-band where he plays double bass and guitar simultaneously. His tight circle of friends dance their asses off at even his smallest shows, so he's always a safe bet if'n you need some fun.

LITTLE FREDDIE KING

littlefreddieking.com

Little Freddie King is the genuine article—a real-deal bluesman with a hardscrabble bio, a guttural, menacing mumble and a ferocious gutbucket guitar. King, who was shot twice on two different occasions by the same wife (and stayed married to her), released a record on **Fat Possum** a few years ago, and more recently put out the excellent *Messin' around the House* record of **R. L. Burnside**–style remixes.

A LIVING SOUNDTRACK

myspace.com/alivingsoundtrack

Electronics-driven instrumental indie rock act that mixes cinematic, experimental sound with a video projector for live performances.

THE LOCAL SKANK

myspace.com/thelocalskank

Talented all-girl ska band (with a dude drummer). Check out their delicious series of pin-up calendars.

LOST BAYOU RAMBLERS

lostbayouramblers.com

Based in Lafayette, the Michot brothers are here often enough and kick enough ass to qualify as New Orleans music.

Want some post-punk with your Cajun music? LBR songs are marked by long drones from **Andre Michot**'s accordion that collapse back into furious two-stepping underneath the rousing tenor of frontman **Louis Michot**. The effect is the rare iconoclasm that displays mastery over the very original it dissembles, a music for the humid trippiness of the South Louisiana landscape. The Ramblers contributed tracks to *Beasts of the Southern Wild,* and their live shows will get you screaming and flexing your guns.

MARS

myspace.com/marsdoom

Since 2006, Mars has made slow, simple stoner doom metal for the end times.

TOM McDERMOTT

mcdermottmusic.com

McDermott, a crafty and gifted pianist whose main idioms are traditional jazz and Brazilian choro, is most often seen around town with clarinetist **Evan Christopher,** messing with people's expectations of classic genres. His original work has a strong sense of humor and experimentation that smarty-pants jazz fans—including uptight moldy-fig traditionalists—will nonetheless totally enjoy.

KELCY MAE

kelcymae.com

Poetic roots music about the American South with acoustic instrumentation that'll surely appeal to the Canadian North.

ALEX McMURRAY

"They say if you can make it in New York, you can make it anywhere," Alex McMurray told us in a 2011 interview. "What I say about New Orleans is, if you can't make it here, don't leave." An invaluable force on the downtown scene, McMurray offers his adopted city an essential musical voice, a prolific performance schedule, and, each May, he offers up his own backyard.

Whether performing solo or as a member of the **Tin Men** trio, playing excellent guitar for any number of sympatico souls, or as the leader of the **Valparaiso Men's Chorus**, McMurray bundles an everyman's laments and furies with a keen eye for the landscape. Superficial ears might mention Tom Waits, but waiting for the train to pass at Press Street is the more consistent fodder for his songwriting and singing, delivered with a biting sense of humor. Odds are he'll be on stage somewhere while you're in town, but count yourself especially lucky if his Valparaiso Men's Chorus convenes its twenty-odd drunken howlers for a night of sea shanties.

By now, you've probably heard of **Chazfest** (see "Other Festivals"), the one-day, McMurray-led alternative to Jazz Fest hosted at his Truck Farm on St. Claude Avenue. Just know that a drunken afternoon among musician friends led to the creation of that glorious, drunken afternoon of music, and that the man in the middle is arguably the city's best contemporary songwriter. If you want to see what making it in New Orleans on New Orleans' terms looks like, catch Alex McMurray.

BANDS

MEADOW FLOW

myspace.com/meadowflow

Psychedelic, dreamy, rain-soaked lullabies; light summer jams molding pretty noise into pop.

METRONOME THE CITY

metronomethecity.com

This instrumental band of New Orleans natives has played together since high school. With guitar, bass, drum kit, keys, and effects, they somehow sound like a DJ seamlessly mixing together dub reggae, metal, and **Thrill Jockey**–style indie rock.

MICROSHARDS

myspace.com/themicroshards

Usually a ferocious, bass-wielding/tape-manipulating one-man-band, Microshards has recently enlisted a drummer and keyboardist to enhance his over-distorted rock instrumentals. On other occasions, the band has instead gotten trashed, disrobed, and just thrown their instruments around the room in a way that's somehow honestly artful and engaging.

MIKRONAUT

This solo artist and DJ drinks a lot of cough syrup and makes extremely listenable, drugged-out, minimalist, dub-influenced electronica on various Casios and a four-track cassette recorder. When performing, Mikro runs said four-track into effects pedals and creates live remixes like the old dub masters. Mikronaut, however, is a snowbird, and can mostly only be seen during New Orleans' winters.

MORELLA & THE WHEELS OF IF

myspace.com/morellaandthewheelsofif

This haunting and romantic co-ed cabaret dispenses free Lucid Absinthe from the stage, and sometimes also offers a peek at Vincent van Gogh's lost ear. Projections show original films, video, and photography created by musical siblings **Aeryk Laws** (pianist/composer/singer/guitarist) and **Laura Laws** (writer/singer), and their singing and writing partner **Anastacia Ternasky**. As much an "act" as a "band," Morella has performed at the **DramaRama** theater fest and the annual **Fringe** multimedia fest (see "Theater and Dance").

M.O.T.O.

myspace.com/moto

Masters of the Obvious: Hooky garage rock with song titles like "2-4-6-8 Rock 'n' Roll," "Gonna Get Drunk Tonight," and "Flipping You Off with Every Finger of My Hand." The phrase "so dumb they're brilliant" can be found in several M.O.T.O. reviews. Unfortunately for New Orleans, M.O.T.O.'s usually on tour.

MR. GO

mrgoband.com

A mostly laid back party grunge band with a '60s fetish and a penchant for studio experimentation.

MUTEMATH

mutemath.com

Though MuteMath somehow became literal arena rockers without ever participating in the local music scene (how does that happen?), these closet-Christian emo rockers are one of New Orleans' most successful rock bands.

NARCISSY

narcissy.com

This rarely seen (and thus relished) garage rock outfit possesses a startling sense of humor and a spastic yet smart stage presence. "The perfect thing for people who like this sort of thing," reads the website.

NECRO HIPPIES

myspace.com/necrohippies

From *Maximum Rocknroll:* "Screaming and slurring over mostly mid-paced thick and dreary riffs, and stompy drums. This is also one of those bands that are able to come up with the simplest of riffs that still make you clench your fists." A favorite at **Siberia**.

NEW ORLEANS BINGO! SHOW

neworleansbingoshow.com

A combination platter including but not limited to theremin playing, seedy clowns and mimes, original short films, a couple rounds of actual bingo with the crowd, plus quirky songs about life in the New Orleans booze-gutter. Bingo upped the ante a few years ago and gained mad crossover appeal after pairing up with the venerable **Preser-**

vation Hall Jazz Band**. The act's ringleader, **Clint Maedgen,** a conservatory-trained saxophonist, sang for Pres Hall for several years before the band lost its clarinetist, and Clint began filling in.

NOOMOON TRIBE

noomoon.net

Former curators of the local Land of Nod, providing most of the local bands at each year's Voodoo Music Experience, NooMoon's group of performers and artisans moved their stage into the French Quarter for a wild mid-October multimedia music and arts festival to benefit the **New Orleans Musicians' Clinic**. The Tribe's other events include Exotica New Orleans, a fetish model and lifestyle convention in April (exoticaneworleans.com) and NOLA **Bunarchy,** a bunny-costumed bar hop around the French Quarter and Marigny, held on the Thursday before Easter to benefit the LASPCA.

NORCO LAPALCO

norcolapalco.com

A New Orleans supergroup of sorts, this band is named after an area of the city lacking even one tourist destination. Former members of legendary local rock groups **Evil Nurse Sheila, Egg Yolk Jubilee, Lump,** and the **Black Problem** sew together new riffs nodding to Minutemen, Sonic Youth, even Van Halen. Leady lady **Alba Houston** puts melody behind a ton of New Orleans in-jokes.

Zack Smith

Anthony Cuccia leads the Other Planets when not performing his hip-hop–influenced solo electronic act, the Night Janitor.

ONE MAN MACHINE

myspace.com/onemanmachine

Alone or with a group (likely assembled that week), **Bernard Pearce** swears by a seat-of-the-pants improvisational style not seen much in rock circles. Usually based on one consistent loop and a few memorized poetic lyrics, One Man Machine's music, and the players who realize it, all vary wildly from show to show.

OPPOSABLE THUMBS

Caveman new wave.

THE OTHER PLANETS

theotherplanets.com

When people talk about New Orleans jazz, they're usually referring to the trad/Dixieland stuff you hear at venues like **Preservation Hall** or the **Palm Court Café**—but in fact, the city has been an off-and-on hub of avant-garde space-jazz weirdness for decades, helped along by proponents like **Alvin Batiste** and **Earl Turbinton**. The Other Planets continue this nontraditional tradition with bizarre cosmic explorations, sarcastic, spacey freak-rock soundscapes, and **Sun Ra**–inspired trips through the sonic spaceways. And sometimes, there's a light show.

THE PALLBEARERS

myspace.com/neworleanspallbearers

It's always Halloween for New Orleans' original sicko horror punks, the Pallbearers, who've been trafficking in loud guitars and blood since 1997. More than a couple shows have ended with the singer going to the hospital.

PANORAMA JAZZ BAND

panoramajazzband.com

The stellar local players in Panorama dress in traditional brass band captain's hats and ties, but that's as far as the band's traditionalism goes. Its signature sound is classic New Orleans street parade music mixed with a healthy, exotic dose of Balkan brass and other rare forms.

PHIL THE TREMOLO KING

myspace.com/philthetremoloking

This Belgium-born guitarist who later survived New York City's infamous 13th Street squats now lives in New Orleans, mixing Velvet Underground, tropicália, gypsy punk, Casiocore, and the kitchen sink into what he calls "Tremophonic pop." Catch him at **Circle Bar, Big Top,** or **AllWays Lounge**.

N.O. MOMENT

RATTY SCURVICS

BANDS

Ratty Scurvics and his Black Market Butchers make some of New Orleans' best groundbreaking modern music.

Jonathan Traviesa

Ratty Scurvics comes in many forms. In his one-man-band **Singularity**, Scurvic's hands pound stacks of keyboards while his feet pump the snare and bass drums. After ending Singularity in 2007 (the only one-man-band to ever break up), Ratty started the **Black Market Butchers** multimedia ensemble featuring members of **Fleur de Tease** and **Morning 40 Federation**, plus singer **Meschiya Lake**, guitarist **Rob Cambre,** and others. The band's first album, *In Time,* was produced by multiple Grammy–winner **John Porter**, an auxiliary member of Roxy Music who produced most of The Smiths' singles. These days Ratty mostly composes music for plays, some of which he acts in. He can also be seen playing guitar in his trio featuring **Microshards** on bass and **Jimmy Ford** on drums. In whatever capacity Ratty performs, the spectacle is amazing, but Ratty's powerful, thoughtful music transcends the spectacle. Ratty is emblematic of how modern New Orleans music often defies categorization.

The Mayor of New Orleans' original music scene, organist and inventor Mr. Quintron.

Jonathan Traviesa

R. Scully and his Rough 7 family spread the gospel.

Zack Smith

QUINTRON AND MISS PUSSYCAT

quintronandmisspussycat.com

All over the world, Mr. Q is beloved as a maker of strange analog electronic dance music. Swirling roller-rink organ, bleeps and bloops from his unique invention the Drum Buddy, and simple drum machine patterns complement backup vocals from his companion, Miss Pussycat, who often performs original psychedelic puppet shows before the duo's concerts. One of Q's electric pianos once belonged to deceased singer **Ernie K-Doe**, which is fitting since Q's music owes a great deal to the New Orleans R&B piano tradition (not to mention Prince).

R. SCULLY'S ROUGH 7

myspace.com/rscullysrough7

Gravel-voiced former party-boy frontman of the **Morning 40 Federation** (New Orleans' favorite drinking band, who still reform from time to time) wipes the smirk off and moves closer to the heart for songs he considers "garage gospel." **Rob Cambre** (lead guitar), **Ratty Scurvics** (piano), and singer **Meschiya Lake** (whose awesome backup wailing brings the group closest to their gospel goal) round out this supergroup of punk-influenced musicians as talented as any of the city's traditional bands.

New Orleans' preeminent frontman, Rik Slave.

Zack Smith

RHODES

myspace.com/rhodesmakesshittymusic

Pre-recorded tracks, live drum machines, and percussion toys back this one-man-band caterwauling southern electro pop, à la Britney Spears. At **Siberia** or **Saturn Bar,** Rhodes will invade your personal space. Don't attend his shows in your expensive clothes. Also see **Babes.**

RIK SLAVE

On and off since 1986, Rik Slave has been the revered frontman for numerous projects—with his brother **Greg Terry** in the bent country group **Rik Slave and the Phantoms**, and then **Rock City Morgue** with White Zombie's **Sean Yseult**. Rock City Morgue is mostly simple and to the point à la the Ramones or Misfits, with jaunts into Nick Cave territory when former **White Zombie** bassist Yseult takes to the piano. Rik's most recent by-the-books rock band is the **Cons and Prose.**

ROTARY DOWNS

rotarydowns.com

Rotary Downs is one of New Orleans' few straight-up indie rock bands, not beholden to commercial aspirations and retaining a musical purity evident in its big, sweeping compositions. The band's popularity has grown as it's developed into a slightly psychedelic but even-tempered ensemble sound, featuring eclectic instrumentation.

SECRET SOCIETY IN SMALLER LIES

Brothers **Tony** and **Corey Burgeron** and their cousin **Mark Miller**, all of Houma, Louisiana, began Secret Society in New Orleans in 2010. Miller has described their sound as "a mixture of Black Sabbath, the Cure, and the Talking Heads."

SICK LIKE SINATRA

myspace.com/sicklikesinatra

Electro-disco sex rock with a great frontman.

SLOW DANGER BRASS BAND

slowdanger.com

A large group of punkish downtowners, some of whom study music at the local university, Slow Danger plays in the brass band style, but rather than flowing free, they perform compositions, including original songs, with minimal improvisation. Unlike other brass bands, Slow Danger also switches moods: some of their music is danceable, and some is downbeat. For the brain and the booty.

THE SPECIAL MEN

The Special Men became popular years ago, playing a huge catalog of New Orleans R&B classics in a loose, rockin' guitar-based style. They returned to action in 2006 with free red beans every Monday at **BJ's** (4301 Burgundy St., 504-945-9256) in Bywater.

SPICKLE

myspace.com/spickle

Ferocious four-piece instrumental band possessing sick chops. Heavy as metal, but without any of metal's corny trappings. Spickle is one of several bands powered by guitarist **Paul Webb,** who owns **Webb's Bywater Music**.

A man of many talents, Greg Schatz is a valuable sideman on various instruments when not fronting his own band and releasing albums of truly original material.

Zack Smith

The extremely photogenic folk singer, Stix duh Clown.

Alleyn Evans

SPLIT()LIPS

This cool-headed punk version of multiband overlord **Jenn Attaway** mixes GG Allin, Butt Trumpet, Misfits, and Child Molesters into expert original bitch-anthems such as "Get Your Rosaries Off My Ovaries" and "Vagina Dentata." Meant to be an all-girl band, they reportedly use the **Pallbearers'** drummer with a wig on.

STIX DUH CLOWN

Original, bluesy folk songs. With his makeup literally tattooed onto his face, Stix strums and sings in either a Tom Waits growl or sweeter folk croon while playing bass drum on an old suitcase. Stix also fronts the bands **My Graveyard Jaw**, **Death by Arrow,** and **Michael James and His Lonesome**.

SUN HOTEL

sunhotelsounds.com

Hazy, melodious, post-gospel music featuring ambient guitar and four-part vocal harmonies singing lyrics of love and loss.

SUPAGROUP

reverbnation.com/supagroup

This established party metal group surely doesn't want to be "underground": high energy, ultra tight, big rock, never cheesy unless **Chris Lee** (husband of bassist **Sean Yseult**) and company know you'll laugh along. Check out their web TV show Amped!

SUPLECS

Fun, heavy rock, now ten years strong. Suplecs' debut album, *Wrestlin' with My Lady Friend,* was released by **Frank Kozik**'s label, **Mansruin Records,** in April of 2000, and the video for the song "Rock Bottom" played on MTV's Headbangers Ball. Suplecs does an insane, free show at **Checkpoint Charlie's** each Fat Tuesday.

TANK AND THE BANGAS

Tarriona "Tank" Ball pushed up from the city's burgeoning spoken word scene to reveal a fierce singing voice and persona, influenced by Badu but packing more than a little Aretha. The Bangas deliver tight funk.

TERRANOVA

terranovarocks.com

Catherine Terranova moved to New Orleans from Baltimore in 2008 to start a garage rock band with native **Michelle Lacayo** of **Manwitch**. The two can also be seen on a Muses parade float, playing with **Sue Ford** in the all-girl Mardi Gras party band **Pink Slip**.

THOU

noladiy.org/thou

Down-tempo stoner metal. Fucking awesome (see pages 48–50).

THE UNNATURALS

myspace.com/theunnaturals

Jenn Attaway's super-tight rockabilly surf group.

TO BE CONTINUED'S
JUICY JACKSON
ON BRASS BANDS

tbcbrassband.com

Edward "Juicy" Jackson plays tuba for **To Be Continued Brass Band,** a standout crew born from the Carver High School Marching Band. Originally famous for their sets at the corner of Bourbon and Canal Streets, TBC holds down a Wednesday night gig at **Celebration Hall** (1701 St. Bernard Ave.), where working folks go to buckjump into the wee hours. They also provide the pulse for many of the city's social aid and pleasure club parades, and pride themselves in a healthy social life. "Back when I first started, a lot of groups started infusing rap into the music," recalls Jackson. "These days we are remixing and rearranging the old music. TBC does it to transcribe and to help try to recreate the vibe that group created or made us feel when we heard their song."

When asked for tips on finding and walking in a second line, Juicy said, "Find the **Big Red Cotton** blog on Facebook or Twitter (@bigredcotton). Also **Gambit** (bestofneworleans .com) and **WWOZ** (wwoz.org) always have the best info on everything to do in New Orleans. Don't just try to roam the city for a parade or try to find the parade by word of mouth. Do your homework on what you wanna see."

In regard to brass bands, Juicy says, "I attend the **Maple Leaf** to see **Rebirth** on Tuesdays, Thursdays with the **Soul Rebels** at **Le Bon Temps,** and if I'm not playing at the **Blue Nile** with **Mainline** on a Sunday, I love to see **Hot 8** at the **Howlin' Wolf Den.**"

71

One of Walt McClements' many bands, Why Are We Building Such a Big Ship?

Zack Smith

WALT McCLEMENTS

Among the scene's most fertile musical minds, this singer and accordionist mixes widely, but he puts his distinctive part Balkan, part Steinbeck stamp on any arrangement. McClements led one of our favorite groups, the now disbanded **Why Are We Building Such a Big Ship?** but currently plays more often with the **Panorama Jazz Band** and tours with the Minneapolis-based **Dark Dark Dark**.

THE WAY

myspace.com/thewaynola

Groovy classic guitar rock with no guitars, in a new-wave vein.

THE WHITE BEACH

myspace.com/thecreamywhitebitch

Admittedly, the author's stage-name/band since 2001. Because of the White Beach's roots as a one-man indie-R&B-rock act using just drum machine beats, shreddy guitar, and high-pitched vocals, Prince comparisons continue to dog him—even now, when his new big full band (with intermittent horn section) is far heavier and more psychedelic.

WHITE COLLA CRIMES

myspace.com/whitecolla

Fun, party-rockin' white boy funk rock group with an ironic anticorporate theme.

YOJIMBO

Fronted by nerd dream girl **Carly Meyers** on trombone, this trio delivers edgier-than-usual funk in the **Trombone Shorty** mold, with a creative rhythm section and the ability to move a Frenchmen Street crowd. Their recent collaborations and roadwork equipped them with new angles.

N.O. MOMENT

ZYDECO

On-fire zydeco monster Rockin' Dopsie Jr.

Zack Smith

Sort of a Frenchified Afro-hoedown music, zydeco is a mostly fast, accordion- and washboard-driven rural Louisiana sound. Distinct from the fiddle-driven tunes of neighboring Cajuns, zydeco has along the way buddied up to the electric guitar, and worn proudly its American R&B influences. First recorded for public consumption in the '50s, the music was always meant for house parties and other more intimate gatherings. Meaning, any outsider might have a truly tough time locating live zydeco way out in the sticks. Living in New Orleans, one might assume zydeco blasts exclusively from French Quarter bead shops. The **New Orleans Jazz and Heritage Festival** does a great job of bringing zydeco to a bigger audience every year on its Fais-Do-Do Stage. But if you possess the means to drive a couple hours outside the city, consider the following events, where you'll definitely catch you some zydeco howlin':

Festivals Acadiens et Créoles (October, Girard Park, 500 Girard Park Dr., Lafayette; www.festivalsacadiensetcreoles.com). Really three free festivals in one. The Festival de Musique portion of the proceedings features fifty bands on four stages over three days—this paired up with the Bayou Food Festival and the Louisiana Craft Fair.

Lebeau Zydeco Festival (July, Immaculate Conception Catholic Church, 103 Lebeau Church Road, Lebeau, 337-351-3902). In its twenty-somethingth year now, this festival features live zydeco, games, and world-famous pork-backbone dinners.

Le Festival du Bon Temps à Broussard (April, Stine Lumber, 6501 Ambassador Caffery Pkwy., Broussard, 800-346-1958; www.bontempsfest.org). This younger festival features Cajun music and zydeco, food, drinks, dancing, and activities for the kids.

Louisiana Cajun-Zydeco Festival (Mid-June, French Quarter, French Market, 1008 N. Peters St., 504-558-6100; jazzandheritage.org/cajun-zydeco). Free, two-day festival of traditional zydeco on two stages, down by the river in the **French Market**. Given its location, it feels a bit touristy, but the music is the real deal

Louisiana Swamp Stomp (March, Nicholls State University campus, 331 Madewood Dr., Thibodaux, 985-448-4965; www.nicholls.edu/swamp-stomp). This food and music festival celebrates the culture of south Louisiana with fais-do-do contests, zydeco lessons, and more.

Zydeco Extravaganza (May, Evangeline Downs Racetrack and Casino, 2235 Creswell Lane Extension, Opelousas, 337-594-3137; www.zydecoextra.com). Started in 1987 by the Cravins family in St. Landry Parish, this is now the biggest zydeco fest in the world, featuring indoor and outdoor stages and much more.

FAUXBEAUX, GUTTERPUNKS, AND OTHER STREET KIDS

Robin Walker

New Orleans was in the 1990s famous for attracting what were called "gutterpunks," a breed of street kid buskers who combined the Blade Runner/Mad Max look with canned beers, stained white wife beaters, and soiled jeans. Often accompanied by sympathy-inducing dogs, the frequently aggressive gutterpunks leered at visitors and fell victim to nightstick-happy police. The **gutterpunk** breed came back strong on lower Decatur Street after Hurricane Katrina, begging from locals who'd just lost their homes. Luckily this was temporary, as afterwards, many mildly rebellious American kids who would have grown up to become gutter punks began evolving into what Bywater locals now refer to as "**faux-beaux**," a French Louisiana word meaning "false hobos."

These fresh-faced bards and waifs enjoy better hygiene and, from all appearances, less dependence on booze and crack than the gutterpunks. In suspenders, newsie caps, lace dresses, and clam digger pants, they harken back in dress to an imagined Depression era. Clustered on corners and equipped with washtub basses, tubas, and plaintiff voices, they draw on a musical fantasy where gypsies, slaves, and the Irish jammed in mellow slums to the works of Stephen Foster.

The Bywater and Marigny fauxbeaux snowbirds arrive in town around Mardi Gras each year, stay through festival season, then fly (or hop a train, they'd have you believe) back up north. Some of them purport to live a soulful Kerouacian existence, while most have access to credit cards to buy nicer things, but just dig the look. Locals also refer to fauxbeaux as "chimney sweeps," "Depression-era paperboys," "funkballs," and a host of other names.

Also, unlike gutterpunks, fauxbeaux rarely beg. Instead they play music, often for donations—music that sometimes makes you wish they'd just beg the normal way. Often the music is imitative of an old-timey porch-stompin' sound. But some of their female vocalists perfectly mimic beautiful old phonograph-era singers, and a few of the more ambitious fauxbeaux have honed their chops in New Orleans and worked toward well-paying gigs for the **Jazz Fest** crowd.

The group's cultural contributions are too often obscured by a well-observed xenophobia; fauxbeaux come to town, dig in with the folks who dress like them, and rarely communicate with the many other interesting creatures around them. Visually, they certainly blend into shabbily elegant New Orleans, but fauxbeaux could stand to act more local, by embracing the concept of southern hospitality. If they sound good, give them a buck. But do your best to listen for the family band near the Walgreen's on Royal, or David and Roselyn, or any of the other local street musicians trying to support themselves on your tips alone.

RAP ARTISTS

Sissy bounce superstars Big Freedia and Sissy Nobby perform at Jazz Fest.

Jonathan Traviesa

As hip-hop evolved throughout the 1980s, and before bounce came along, New Orleans rap consisted of complex rhyming and true-school MCing in New Orleans, with lyricists such as **Tim Smooth, Gregory D., Bustdown, M. C. Thick,** and **Legend Mann.** Then in 1991, "Where Dey At," allegedly the first bounce song, was recorded in two versions by both **MC T Tucker** with **DJ Irv,** and then shortly after by **DJ Jimi** as "Where They At." Bounce MCs demand responses regarding your ward, your school, and your project. The lyrics are often dirty. As with almost all other New Orleans party music, fun is stressed over art. Some of the zillions of pioneering bounce artists include **Partners-n-Crime, Ms Tee, Mia X,** and **5th Ward Weebie,** whose track "F*** Katrina" captured the local sentiment after the storm—though the only real national bounce hit was **Juvenile**'s "Back That Azz Up."

Bounce slowly gathered the steady support of radio program directors and DJs who saw hip-hop and bounce as opposing values. Today, New Orleans DJs regularly remix R&B radio hits with bounce's signature "Triggerman" rhythm (a sample from the 1986 track "Drag Rap" by New York City's **Showboys** that turns up in most bounce). Bounce pioneer **DJ Jubilee** has earned the title "King of Bounce." In 1999, Jubilee's **Take Fo'** record label (home to artists including **Choppa**) issued *Melpomene Block Party,* the first full-length release from **Katey Red**, a gay, transvestite MC from the Melpomene projects. Other gay bounce artists have followed on Katey's (high) heels, most notably **Big Freedia** and **Sissy Nobby**, both sissy bounce rappers.

But now a new generation, raised with infinite digital music at their fingertips and thus room to grow beyond radio hits, has taken a front-seat position once again in New Orleans. Today, hip-hop fans of all stripes can find the culture they love represented upstairs at **Maison** and **Dragon's Den** (both on Frenchmen Street), **Hi-Ho Lounge** (St. Claude Ave.), and many other of the city's venues. The **Supreme Street collective** headed by **Cracktracks' Law** plays host to a sizable number of shows. The **Soundclash** beat battle hip-hop variety show still goes strong. **DJ Tony Skratchere** and Poor Boy Productions sometimes promote the world-renowned **DMC DJ** battle for world supremacy in Nola. The self-congratulatory nature of hip-hop found its way to the creation of the first **Underground Hip-Hop Awards** at the **Howlin' Wolf** venue.

The following is a list of MCs suggested by local stalwarts **MC Impulss** and **Slangston Hughes** (who incidentally hosts the long-running **Uniquity** monthly, showcasing wordy MCs paired with a live band):

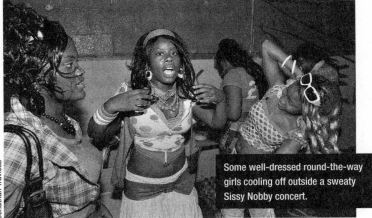

Jonathan Traviesa

Some well-dressed round-the-way girls cooling off outside a sweaty Sissy Nobby concert.

3D NA'TEE

3dnatee.com

One of New Orleans' best-ever lyricists also just so happens to be a smokin' hot female. Winner of the Best Lyricist Award at the NOLA Underground Hip-Hop Awards, 3D Na'Tee has recently performed at Jazz Fest and been written about in *XXL* mag et al.

10TH WARD BUCK

myspace.com/10wardbuck

Upstanding entrepreneurial bounce rapper and concert promoter who got the game rolling with some of the first-ever bounce concerts at the Airline Skate Center. **New Mouth from the Dirty South Press** released a coffee-table biography called *Tenth Ward Buck: The Definition of Bounce.*

ATM

myspace.com/atmneworleans

Battle-tested local lyricist and freestyler known for his fast flow and emotional stage presence. The originator of New Orleans' edition of **Grind Time**, a national rap battle competition.

CALIGULA

reverbnation.com/caligulakrycek

Throw Orwell's book *1984* into a pot along with every conspiracy theory you've ever heard, every anti-depression med Big Pharma ever produced, your pervy neighbor's porn collection, a barrel of booze, a penchant for fist-fights, and a collection of head-banging beats . . . and you've discovered Caligula.

JIMI CLEVER

jimiclever.com

Maybe New Orleans' most honest lyricist. Emotion and feeling pour alongside his high-pitched cadence, compound rhymes, and perfect beat riding.

CURREN$Y

currensyspitta.com

Known for buddha-blown lyrics and laid-back delivery, Spitta jumped the **Cash Money** ship to soar with his **Fly Society** crew and **Damon Dash**.

DAPPA

myspace.com/yaboydappa

Palmyra Street Productions MC with star appeal.

DEE-1

dee1music.com

A young but very creative and real MC, who nonetheless doesn't curse on his albums, and released a single called "I Hate Money." An impressive positive lyricist, Dee-1 made serious waves after his collaboration with famous New Orleans producer and beatmaster **Mannie Fresh**.

EUPHAM

A hip-hop movement composed of **Crummy, DJ Mike Swift, Lyrikill,** and **Mercure**, giving the masses creative, quality hip-hop music that expands the genre.

K. GATES

gateswave.com

Among his many aliases, they call him International Gates for a solid reason. The author of the "Black and Gold Saints Theme Song" has traveled the world over from Mecca to Amsterdam, building his multicontinental hustle and shining superior lyricism.

GUERILLA PUBLISHING COMPANY

guerillapublishing.webs.com

Consisting of **Elespee**, **Caliobzvr**, **D.O.N.**, **DJ Skratchmo**, **Private Pile**, **Suave**, **Juskwam**, **Prospek** (providing the sonic boom-bap landscape), plus many more who wave the flag, GPC is a hip-hop supercrew that stands apart from their contemporaries.

N.O. MOMENT

KATEY RED ON BOURBON STREET, BOUNCE RAP, AND GAY CLUBS

Katey Red at the Croissant Café.

Robin Walker

With the release of her album *Melpomene Block Party* almost fifteen years ago on DJ Jubilee's **Take Fo'** imprint, **Katey Red** staked her claim as the first-ever homosexual, transgendered bounce rap artist. She has directly inspired the careers of other so-called punk rappers or sissy bounce artists, such as **Big Freedia** and **Sissy Nobby**. We caught up with Katey to get her advice on where you should party while in New Orleans. We also asked her which bounce rap artists you should check out, and where.

Do you have friends outside of New Orleans who come to town to visit you?

Quite a few. Mostly when my friends come to town they want to go to my shows. But if they just want to have a few drinks we either go on Bourbon Street, or else sit in **Siberia.** Ian Polk, the creator of Noah's Ark, he came down and wanted to hang out with me, so I took him to a few gay clubs out here. I brought him to one of my shows at **One Eyed Jacks** and I took him to **Club Fusions** (2004 AP Tureaud Ave., 504-301-5121) because he wanted to see the drag show I was performing in.

Some people disparage Bourbon Street, but you're a fan?

You can never go wrong with Bourbon Street. I am not an everyday Bourbon Street kind of girl though, so when I am out there it's new to me, like going out of town somewhere. If I am on Bourbon I end up either by **Oz** (800 Bourbon St.; ozneworleans.com), or the **Bourbon Pub** (801 Bourbon St.; bourbonpub.com). They have pickpocketers and crime but . . . after Katrina Bourbon was the first thing poppin'. That's where New Orleans make they money at the dance clubs and strip clubs and gay clubs as well as heterosexual clubs. They got bounce music, reggae music, jazz, it's all kinds of entertainment on the side street. They got people doing card tricks, they have people doing statues, people tap-dancin', people sitting on the stoop singing live and playin' keyboards. And they also have historical things. It's nice out there. Why would they talk bad about Bourbon?

Did you actually have your pocket picked on Bourbon?

Um, I had a fight on one of my birthdays on one of the side streets off Bourbon. Some guy was for some reason like, "Don't look at me." And I was like, "Don't look at me!" And he ran up on me trying to fight me and I got him off me. That was the only thing bad ever happened to me on Bourbon Street. Normally people just wanna pictures and stuff.

Where can you hear bounce rap on Bourbon Street?

The **Bourbon Heat** (711 Bourbon St.; 711bourbonheat.com) or sometimes the **Cat's Meow** (701 Bourbon St.; catskaraoke.com). Maybe it's because when I come in the club they recognize who I am and so then they start playing bounce music. If they don't play bounce music, they play it when I'm around.

Doesn't **Chris Owens Club** *(500 Bourbon St.; chrisowens club.net) also play rap and bounce?*

I been there before. It's real wild. I wouldn't suggest my outta town friends go there. Sometimes they getting wild. I seen all kinds of things going on in the bathroom—stuff you only supposed to do at home! Wow.

What about that **Club Caesar's** *on the West Bank (209 Monroe St., Gretna, 504-368-1117)? You have always performed there quite a bit.*

Most of my out-of-town friends are Caucasians, so they don't really want to go to places like Caesar's, or **Encore** (3940 Tulane Ave., 504-382-3675), 'cause it's too wild and too rough. If they want to hear bounce music all right, but they have Caucasian clubs that play bounce music. I would suggest that for them. If they wanna be around a different kind of environment and say, "I want to hang out with some black people, I wanna see where you hang at," I take them to Club Fusions. It's a lot of bounce going on in there. My fan base is real, real high in there. They may have a fight in there but there's no gunplay.

What's your strongest musical memory of childhood?

I grew up on bounce! Recording stuff off the radio, bounce music. **Mia X** and all them kinda people!

Who are your favorite local bounce artists?

Cheeky Blakk been in the game for almost 25 years. Cheeky is a legend. She needs to be heard more. [Author's note: Cheeky once told me, "I see myself as a baby Millie Jackson. 'Cause she come with it raw and nasty."]. **Ha' Sizzle** had lil slight hit with "She Rode That Dick like a Soldier." He did it in concert at gay bars and stuff like that but he never got out with it. **Walt Wiggady,** he's a big guy, he moves around real good. He don't have a hit, but with all his moves, he is perfect for a show.

KNOW ONE

An experimental MC pushing the boundaries of creativity and musicianship. A **Media Darling** crew member, he was one of the first to arrive post-Katrina and begin to rebuild not only the hip-hop scene but also the city itself, laying brick and mortar, floating sheetrock as expertly as he floats on a beat.

KOAN

koanmusic.com

Lower Ninth Ward MC of **E.O.E.** Known for his musicianship and topical depth.

A. LEVY

Owner of **The Hut Studios** who made a name with his catchy tunes and fire stage shows.

LIL' DEE

myspace.com/lildeegodsgift504

Having gathered a well-formed fan base through thousands of mixtape downloads, well-received music videos, and a giant billboard hovering over the I-10 as you drive into downtown, Lil' Dee has burned his brand into the New Orleans hip-hop scene.

LUCKYLOU

This bounce-influenced, family-friendly rap artist and dancer is often accompanied by an amazing dance troupe including a Michael Jackson impersonator.

LYRIKILL

myspace.com/mclyrikill

Wordy linguist of **Eupham** crew and one of the founders of New Orleans' monthly beat battle, **Soundclash**.

LYRIQS DA LYRICISS

A smooth, young expert living up to his name and out-rhyming his elders.

M@ PEOPLES' COLLECTIVE

Indie rock/hip-hop fusion band brought to you by local MC, **M@ Peoples (Missing Persons)** and members of New Orleans jam band **Gravity A.**

New Orleans megastar Lil Wayne plays an intimate concert at One Eyed Jacks in the French Quarter.

The head on the right is MC Trachiotomy's. It raps.

Jonathan Traviesa

MC TRACHIOTOMY

On the scene for a decade and a half, Trach makes intentionally garbled psychedelic hip-hop funk, heavily influenced by the odd genius of bands like the **Butthole Surfers** and **Captain Beefheart**.

MERCURE

myspace.com/jonmercure

Member of **Eupham** crew, co-host of the monthly **Soundclash** beat battle, and local producer, mixing synths, old-school R&B, and witty freestyles.

NESBY PHIPS

nesbyphips.com

Hailing from **Curren$y's Fly Society**, Phips holds down regular gigs at the **Whiskey Blue** bar and is a popular beatmaker here and in NYC.

THESEKONDELEMENT

teamt2e.com

A multitalented woman also known as **KAMMs TheACE**, she is smart on the mic, nice with the graphic design, and visually precise with photography.

The "Connoisseur of Fine Rhyme," Slangston Hughes.

Taslim van Hattum

SESS 4-5

myspace.com/nuthinbutfirerecords

Ninth Ward rapper Sess 4-5's tracks sound sorta bounce-ish, with the lawn-sprinkler high-hats, but his lyrics are dense; the same combo locals loved in late, great New Orleans rapper **Soulja Slim**. Sess is also the proprietor of **Nuthin but Fire** record store (see "Shopping"), which regularly releases mixtape CDs featuring all of New Orleans' best underground rap artists, and runs the **Industry Influence** showcase with **Wild Wayne**.

THE SHOW

Mannie Fresh protégé from New Orleans East.

SLANGSTON HUGHES

reverbnation.com/slangstonhughes

The Connoisseur of Fine Rhyme, member of **Tygah Woods Crew**, and head of **P.T.E. Productions** (local hip-hop promotions/event company). Lyrical MC taking his reverence for old-school hip-hop and infusing it with contemporary elements. For six years Slangston's booked and curated the hip-hop variety show **Uniquity,** now every last Saturday at **Dragon's Den.** Uniquity is a performance opportunity for rappers, singers, and spoken-word artists both local and regional.

SOUL CAPITAL

Composed of **Ben Brubaker** and **DJ Miles Felix**, Soul Capital brings a fresh sound and style to the game with conscious, yet entertaining lyricism and beats that move the crowd.

TRUTH UNIVERSAL

truthuniversal.com

Truth has been hustling and grinding not only in New Orleans but throughout the continental United States for ten-plus years. One of the city's most respected MCs and the longtime chief of the influential **Grassroots!** series, Truth lives up to his name every time he hits the mic to rap about politics, the NOPD, and the game.

TYGAH WOODS CREW

myspace.com/tygahwoods

New Orleans' version of the Wu-Tang Clan—at least structurally: five MCs **(Slangston Hughes, Mr. J'ai, J-Dubble, Blaze the Verbal Chemist, D. Francis)** unite with **DJ Mike Swift** to bring hip-hop music back to its roots.

DJs, ELECTRO ARTISTS, DANCE CLUBS, AND RADIO STATIONS

One might argue we're experiencing a DJ renaissance in New Orleans, with more diversity and activity than ever before. While some fans of traditional New Orleans music have no time for DJs ("DJs aren't real musicians," blah blah blah), the truth is our many popular and downright important DJs improve the city. In New Orleans we have fewer DJs spinning the latest top 40, or even the hippest underground indie-rock dance music, but many more working in bounce, local hip-hop, and a wide variety of forms and niches that make the world of turntablism (digital or vinyl) an interesting landscape to explore while you're here.

DJs AND ELECTRO ARTISTS

CHRISTOPH ANDERSSON

This young New Orleans transplant has made an international name with his funk-influenced electro-pop and his world-touring monthly dance music party, **TKVR**. Prior to his success, Andersson attended the **New Orleans Center for Creative Arts (NOCCA)** and once worked as a recording assistant for **Dr. John**. His original music now combines contemporary indie electro and French house music.

JOEY BUTTONS

dance

Spins all vinyl sets of nu-disco, old disco, electrofunk, and whatever else will make young uptowners dance.

CORROSION

Three goth music DJs host this ambitious dance night decorated in bondage gear and black silk, with candles, even indoor metal fencing, plus both new and classic goth and industrial tunes.

DANCE IN DA PANTS

original instrumental; soundcloud. com/dance-in-da-pants

This live one-man band sings plus plays guitar, bass and keys, frequently collaborating with hip-hop MC **M@ Peoples**.

DJ BEESKNEES

eclectic; stingingcaterpillar.com/ dj-beesknees-stuff

A recovering hip-hop DJ, Beesknees eschews top 40 and now rocks a seamless mix of unusual funk, old and nu-disco, electro, new wave, boogie, and Italo. Check the listing in Marigny and Bywater.

DJ CHICKEN

hip-hop

Best known these days for the "Chicken and Waffle Mix," a drive-time weekday morning show at 8 a.m. on Power 102.9, as well as the throwback lunch mix, DJ Chicken has forever spun old and new hip-hop, bounce rap, and brass band music as part of the Definition crew of DJs and MCs.

DJ E. F. CUTTIN

hip-hop; djefcuttin.com

Member of **Go DJ's**, producer, and personal DJ of **Truth Universal**. As a working DJ, E. F. plays to the crowd and breaks quality records on the daily. He heads up the **Industry Influence** parties for Louisiana rap and R&B artists, and also puts together the **Nuthin but Fire** mixtape series for the record store of the same name (see "Shopping"). He currently DJs for rapper **Curren$y's Jet Lounge** night at House of Blues.

DJ FRENZI

hip-hop

Frenzi DJs hip-hop and house DVDs and records simultaneously, most notably on Friday nights at Omni Royal Orleans Hotel (French Quarter, 621 St. Louis St., 504-529-5333).

DJ JUBILEE

bounce/hip-hop

Rapper, DJ, football coach, and king of New Orleans bounce music for many years now, Jubilee pops up everywhere, from the biggest block parties to **Essence Fest** and **Jazz Fest**. His '90s tracks like "West Bank Thang" and "Do the Jubilee All" are still hot club jams today. He's always hustling; check his Myspace page for his most recent residency.

DJ KARO

soundcloud.com/deejaykaro

With roots in punk and new wave, Karo ended up a hip-hop DJ with scratching abilities, who also spins exotic tunes from Bollywood to bounce to dub reggae with partner **Maddie Ruthless**.

DJ MADDIE RUTHLESS

Known as a reggae selector relying mostly on vinyl 45s, Maddie is a musician. As a child she sang in choir and played piano, and she eventually moved to London, where she fell hard for rocksteady, a style she infiltrates now as a DJ and singer/songwriter.

DJ PASTA

classic country/undefined; myspace. com/pastapie

Pasta doesn't have a radio show, so you'll have to catch him live—but that's not hard to do, since he spins in a different bar for no cover almost every night. He's the kind of insane record savant who can play four hours' worth of your favorite songs you've never heard of, mostly on 45s. He often has a rock 'n' roll and punk night, a Louisiana swamp pop night, or a weepy country night where if prodded he will whip out his massive collection of bizarre '60s country novelty songs.

DJ POPPA

www.djpoppa.com

A member of the worldwide **Core DJ** clique, one of the city's best bounce mixers, and live DJ for bounce artists. Between intermittent spots at **Jazz Fest** or **Voodoo Fest,** Poppa holds it down at various local clubs. Check his website for dates and times.

DJ PROPPA BEAR

jungle/drum-n-bass; myspace.com/ djproppabear

The proprietor of the **Dragon's Den**—which has been heavy on DJs since he bought the place after Katrina—Proppa spins drum-n-bass and jungle, mostly on Thursdays at his **Bass Bin** Safari night, which is currently approaching its fifteenth year. Novices can come early for an open-mic style vibe, where Proppa gladly passes tricks of the trade on to DJ hopefuls.

DJ Q

Spins hip-hop. Also runs tracks for genre-bending bounce rap and dance troupe **NOLA Fam.**

DJ QUICKIE MART

hip-hop; djquickiemart.com

After representing the hip-hop/rap scene in New Orleans for many fruitful years, Quickie Mart moved to L.A. to become more of a touring national act—meaning we still see him a lot around New Orleans. Quickie has spun for **Devin the Dude, The Knux**, and the late, great New Orleans MC **Bionik Brown** among many, many others.

N.O. MOMENT

DJ RQ AWAY ON DJS AND DANCE PARTIES

whatisawayteam.com

A candidate for the "hardest-working" mantle, RQ holds down decks at several spots, keeping us abreast of what the coolest hip-hop kids are up to. His Friday "Tipping Point" parties at **Handsome Willy's** (handsomewillys.com) are a good bet for dancing all night under the shadow of the shuttered Charity Hospital. We asked him to recommend some spots for the DJ-inclined.

DJ RQAway is all business.

Sierra Hudson

BASS CHURCH at the **Dragon's Den** (Marigny, 435 Esplanade Ave., 504-949-1750). **DJs Carmine P. Filthy, Unicorn Fukr,** and **Rekanize** drag their own PA up the stairs of the Den every Sunday for their church residency, where they play electro-disco, dubstep, and other bass music.

THE BOOT (Uptown, 1039 Broadway St., 504-866-9008; thebootneworleans. com). Just off of Tulane and Loyola campuses. **DJ G Cue** has been creating a unique musical landscape to complement college life.

CURREN$Y'S JET LOUNGE (weekly event, French Quarter, House of Blues, 225 Decatur St., 504-310-4999; currensyspitta.com). The local MC with the most national shine since Dwayne Carter, Spitta delivers gauzy weed rap with effortless flow that masks his serious work ethic. A mixtape machine, he maintains a presence in his hometown with his weekly Jet Lounge at the House of Blues Parish Room: a hazy, smoke-filled environment filled with contemporary hip-hop orchestrated by **DJ E. F. Cuttin**.

HANDSOME WILLY'S (CBD, 218 S Robertson St., 504-460-7365; hand-somewillys.com). Features **DJ Otto**, a purveyor of a wide range of party-starting sounds, heard biweekly on Fridays from 5 to 10 p.m., followed by a joint set by Otto with **DJ Yamin**, an expert in reggae, hip-hop, and old-school soul, who also created **NOLA Mix** (nolamix.com), a DJ and production school for all ages.

INDUSTRY INFLUENCE (monthly event, Howlin' Wolf, 907 S. Peters St.; industryinfluence.blogspot.com). Q93 radio personality **Wild Wayne** and MC **Sess 4-5** (CEO of **Nuthin but Fire Records**), both mainstays of the local hip-hop scene, hold down this long-running open-mic and showcase, where you can catch the rawest aspirants, plus meet record execs and community activists. The performances are understandably hit-or-miss, but still a good source for the latest street sounds.

THE SAINT (Garden District, 961 St Mary St., 504-523-0050; thesaintnew orleans.com). Walk beneath the neon halo sign into a venue that hosts DJs and often gets blessed with sets from major names like Diplo, **Force Feed Radio,** and **DJ Musa**, plus a heavy rotation of locals including **Brice Nice, Pr_ck, SKB, Cousin Cav, Tuggle,** and others. **DJ Q of NOLA Fam** holds down the eclectic but rap-heavy **Wobble Wednesdays.**

SILENT DISCO (event). The new hot ticket, usually featuring the competing sounds of **DJ Datboi & DJ PK1**, the event also recruits some very talented guest DJs.

DJ SOUL SISTER

vintage soul; djsoulsister.com

Soul Sister's purview is deep funk, rare groove, and disco from the late '60s to early '80s, and she's been known to throw parties that pay specific tribute to Prince, Michael Jackson, and early hip-hop. She usually spins two to three times a week live, plus sets at **Jazz Fest, Voodoo,** and **Essence**. Her long-running "Soul Power" radio show airs from 8 to 10 p.m. Saturday nights on **WWOZ**.

RIK DUCCI

hip-hop; rikducci.bandcamp.com/

A locally known but nationally respected DJ who has spun for **KRS-One, EPMD, Busta Rhymes, Lost Boyz, Camp Lo, Naughty by Nature,** and the late **Big Pun,** among others. Ducci hosts a weekly Thursday gig at **Handsome Willy's** (218 South Robertson St.).

FORCE FEED RADIO

forcefeedradio.com

Starting as a DJ-and-production duo in high school (not terribly long ago), **Kid Kamillion (Bryan Normand)** and **Money P. (Patrick Bowden)** grew up manning the decks at anything-goes open-format electronic music parties, mashing together southern hip-hop, techno, punk rock, plus their own original songs, edits, and remixes. When in town, they can now be caught at the **Republic, Club Ampersand**, and various bottle-service clubs that can accommodate the cut-and-paste digital video show that accompanies FFR's set.

RUSTY LAZER

bounce; rustylazer.com

If you ever want to see white girls get really nasty, Rusty Lazer spins mostly New Orleans bounce music for the punk and fauxbeaux crowds in the Bywater and Marigny neighborhoods, especially at **St. Roch Tavern** every Saturday night. He has also often served as official DJ for **Big Freedia**.

ED MAXMILLION

hip-hop

An OG of New Orleans hip-hop who continues to open for national acts and special events, spinning classics as well as R&B and funk. If you're here to purchase vinyl, track down one of the city's preeminent purveyors of rare groove.

MOD DANCE PARTY

A monthly New Orleans tradition for almost fifteen years, the Mod Dance Party features **DJ Matty**'s hundreds of pre-1970 vinyl dance records from New Orleans and beyond. Cut loose and dance to the kind of upbeat '60s soul

DJ Matty/Matt Uhlman

Mod Dance Party: DJ Kristen moved away, actually, but we couldn't give up this sweet photo.

DJ Brice Nice hides behind his clean record.

Zack Smith

that the loose moniker "mod" implies. All vinyl 45s and LPs—no iPods or laptops allowed. The party, which routinely rages till dawn (attendance skews young), goes down at **Saturn Bar** on St. Claude Avenue in the Ninth Ward. Every Monday at **One Eyed Jacks,** Matty and **DJ Bunny** also host "the birthday party," spotlighting the music of famous musicians on their birthdays, whether that's Sam Cook, Johnny Cash, Iggy Pop, or Ian MacKaye.

BRICE NICE

everything; bricenice.com

Many claim Brice Nice owns the most records in New Orleans. He also hosts "The Block Party" on 90.7 FM each Saturday from 6 to 8 p.m., which is designed to fuel an actual block party with heavy funk, brass band music, disco, dancehall and other reggae, soul, afrobeat, and Latin. Brice also gigs around town, most likely on weekends at **The Saint,** and recently cofounded Sinking City Records (sinkingcityrecords.com).

PRINCE PAUPER

reggae

Reggae, dub, dancehall, and world music dominate sets by selector Prince Pauper, just as they do his Mid-City record store, Domino Sound.

BEVERLY SKILLZ

hip-hop; beverlyskillz.com

Originally from Shreveport, Louisiana, Skillz has spent the last ten years spinning dance music suited to every New Orleans crowd: electro, dubstep, hip-hop, house music, and rock 'n' roll, all garnished with Skillz's scratch routines. She won third place in 2011 in the New Orleans DMC turntablist competition and has shared the stage with artists such as Skrillex, DJ Jazzy Jeff, and MSTRKRFT. She currently hosts a weekly at **Club Ampersand.**

TONY SKRATCHERE

turntablist; tonyskratchere.com

Besides being an intelligent, experienced, in-demand hip-hop DJ, Tony Skratchere—his name a pun on the creole seasoning Tony Chachere's—is the turntablist who invented Yacht Bounce, a new genre that puts a "triggaman" beat behind famous smooth rock songs such as Toto's "Africa." Catch Skratchere anywhere from **The Saint** to the **Dragon's Den** to big main event shows at the **Republic** and **Voodoo Fest**.

RAJ SMOOVE

hip-hop; rajsmoove.com

A local legend, this hip-hop and reggae DJ and producer has appeared on **Rap City, Showtime at the Apollo,** and **Phat Phat & All That**, to name just a few shows. He's toured with **Cash Money Records, Lil Wayne,** and **Mannie Fresh**, and has done production for Lil Wayne ("I Miss My Dawgs," "Heat," "Who Wanna"). He hosts Sunday nights at **Metro** (310 Andrew Higgins Blvd.) and Saturdays at **Club NV** (1901 Poydras St.).

JIM-E STACK

Another eclectic and heavy young New Orleans bedroom artist getting national love before we even realize he's here. The *Fader* described Stack's "Bubble Boy" release like this: "rubbery woodwinds mimic a thousand expanding party balloons, while his ricocheting synths sound like what would happen if you fired a ray gun from inside an impenetrable sphere. Stack also incorporates swirling space-goddess vocal samples, sometimes manipulating them into his trademark choppy stutter."

DANCE CLUBS WITH DJ NIGHTS

BLUE NILE

*Marigny, 532 Frenchmen St.,
504-948-2583; bluenilelive.com*

New Orleans' premier reggae and dancehall selector **DJ T-Roy** has a night during the week. On the second Saturday of every month, Blue Nile hosts the hip-hop beat battle **Soundclash**.

CLUB CAESAR'S

*West Bank, 209 Monroe St.,
504-368-1117*

On the other side of the bridge, Caesar's is the place for bounce music, and a regular spot to catch sissy bounce artists **Big Freedia, Sissy Nobby,** and **Katey Red**.

DRAGON'S DEN

*Marigny, 435 Esplanade Ave.,
504-949-1750*

Electronic music parties featuring hip-hop, jungle, reggaeton, and the like dominate at the Den. Among other Dragon's Den DJ nights, Wednesday night features dancehall classics with **DJ T-Roy,** and Sunday night is **Bass Church**: dubstep, jungle, and drum-n-bass.

THE DUCK OFF

Gentilly, 2304 AP Tureaud Ave., 504-947-3633; myspace.com/theduckoff

Duck Off's regular DJ, **Money Fresh**, also curates mixtapes of local rap remixes and originals under the club's imprimatur. Stop by Sunday late afternoon, when a brass band is usually throwing down with a rapper or two. It's an awesome spot to check out the real-deal local hip-hop scene, but tourists should use street smarts and caution; it is in the hood, so park close, and don't be a jerk.

R BAR

Marigny, 1431 Royal St., 504-948-7499; royalstreetinn.com

R Bar is owned in part by former **Afghan Whigs** frontman and current **Twilight Singer** and **Gutter Twin, Greg Dulli**. For info on the R Bar's **Royal Street Inn**, see pages 221–22.

THE SAINT

961 St. Mary St; 504-523-0050; thesaintneworleans.com

As close as New Orleans ever gets to hipsterism, The Saint is an ultra-late-night, often rowdy bar (the photo booth has immortalized some of the most debauched moments in New Orleans drinking). The Saint hosts DJ and dance parties often, featuring everything from aggressive metal to booty bass; check the web for up-to-date listings.

DJs AND DANCE CLUBS

ELECTRONIC MUSICIANS

Justin Peake finds inspiration for his electronic music in nature.

Zack Smith

JUSTIN PEAKE (AKA BEAUTIFUL BELLS)

Justin Peake moved to New Orleans in 2006 and has already performed with many phenomenal musicians as a multi-instrumentalist, improviser, composer of music, and a straight(ish) jazz drummer. But since 2007, Peake has spent most of his time performing original, live electronic music as **Beautiful Bells**. Under his alias, Peake creates future jazz from homemade samples and improvised melodies fused with rich synthesized textures. His album *Managing Depth (Moodgadget)* boasts influences as disparate as Fela Kuti, Autechre, and John Cage.

In October 2012, Peake started the **Merged Music Series,** which showcases the live, original electronic music scene in New Orleans. "The sheer range and variety of music that has been bubbling up here is astounding," says Peake, who uses his connections in the jazz world to find and book some really interesting acts. In 2012, Peake also started **Articulated Works** (www.articulatedworks.com), essentially an art hub focusing on music, art, aesthetic, and experience in general. The site's podcast, Parlour, features musicians' interviews and performances.

Below are Peake's descriptions of some artists you might hear and see at his Merged night:

BIRDMAGIC. Bubbly melodies and rhythms. Really nice.

CONTEXT KILLER (Simon Lott). Solo project featuring monster drummer Lott at the helm of synthesizers and whatever other toys he chooses on a given night.

ISIDRO. Raw tribal essence. Vocals, guitar, drums, beat box, keyboard/electronics, live vocals and song looping, post-pop, post-folk, really awesome . . . He also performs with **Whom Do You Work For?**

THE MONOCLE (auroranealand.com). Saxophonist/composer **Aurora Nealand**'s solo performance project. Vocals, accordion, drums, computer, and other niceties.

SETEC ASTRONOMY. Pensive and profound textures from saxophonist **David Polk** and visual artist **Everett DiNapoli.**

TRANSMUTEO (transmuteo.tumblr.com). Lush and tranquil sounds that are often improvised by mixing analog tape and some digital sounds. Often accompanied by video.

RADIO STATIONS

POWER 102.9

modern urban; power1029.com

For fans of modern black music, a good alternative to the highly repetitive local Clear Channel urban-top 40 format, 102.9 has actual human DJs curating their own shows. The Powermix at 5 p.m. with **DJ Mike Swift** is a daily special, and the throwback lunches give you ample Eric B. & Rakim to stretch out the middle of the day.

WTUL 91.5 FM

eclectic modern; wtulneworleans.com

Tulane University's legendary radio station is one of the best in town, spinning anything and everything from indie rock to hip-hop, metal, squalling punk, and vintage country, with requisite attention to all local bands working outside the brass/jazz/funk box. WTUL plays **Quintron and Miss Pussycat** multiple times a day, and also publishes the satiric but musically informative coffee-shop zine *The Vox.*

WWOZ 90.7 FM

New Orleans/world/roots; wwoz.org

New Orleans' community radio station started more than a quarter century ago in a studio above **Tipitina's** uptown. After getting rained out of its Armstrong Park studio by Katrina, the station relocated to the French Quarter. OZ routinely wins all sorts of awards, and is an icon for roots and jazz fans worldwide, who listen on their streaming webcast. With a 24-hour schedule of volunteer show hosts, all kinds of weirdness can happen; listen in the early mornings for trad jazz and New Orleans music, and afternoon and early evening for blues and R&B. For real on-air weirdness, listen after 10 p.m., when undersupervised hosts will spin everything from **Ennio Morricone** to **Sun Ra** to tapes of the late legendary oddball **Ernie K-Doe** hosting his show in the '90s.

RESTAURANTS AND COFFEE SHOPS FEATURING MUSIC AND/OR ART

Your vacation and its menu of artistic stimulation doesn't have to pause when you sit down to eat! Many New Orleans restaurants feature music and/or rotating art exhibits, while other grubberies are attached to music venues or remain open late night for post-concert chow-down.

Some Like It Hot jazz band plays every Sunday brunch at Buffa's in Marigny.

Jonathan Traviesa

RESTAURANTS

BUFFA'S

Marigny, 1001 Esplanade Ave., 504-949-0038; buffaslounge.com

Like some odd cross between **Palm Court Jazz Café** and **Checkpoint Charlie's**, Buffa's is a dive bar in front, where you can smoke and bring your dog—but not your kids—while the back area around the very red stage is a kid-friendly, sit-down restaurant where Fido's not allowed, and you can't smoke. Seafood, fat sandwiches, and Sunday morning cocktails mark the menu while jazz artists like **Aurora Nealand** take the stage.

CAFÉ NEGRIL

Marigny, 606 Frenchmen St.,
504-944-4744

Funk and reggae populate the music menu at this low-key concert venue, its stage backdropped by a Bob Marley mural. Since there's never a cover, Café Negril is also the perfect place to pop in for affordable, late-night (i.e. drunken night) Honduran chow, including vegetarian tacos and gorditas, all on gluten-free corn tortillas. Carnivores are encouraged to try the pineapple-pork burritos or chicken tostadas. **Gypsy Elise** and the **Royal Blues Band** are regulars on the Negril stage, and blues-rock singer **Dana Abbott** and her band play most every other night.

CHECKPOINT CHARLIE'S

Marigny, 501 Esplanade Ave.,
504-281-4847

This definitive dive music club seems held together by band stickers. Checkpoint's may not seem like much at first, but the place really has everything from blues to rock to bulk burger patties (with a side of tater tots), two pool tables, pinball, even laundry machines. One of the last places in town to still serve free red beans on Mondays, Checkpoint's (open 24 hours) also hosts metal band **Suplecs'** annually sublime and tripped-out Mardi Gras show. Though little's ever changed at good ol' Checkpoint's, they now host karaoke every Monday night at 10 p.m. Don't sing with your mouth full!

CHICKIE WAH WAH

Mid-City, 2828 Canal St.,
504-304-4714; chickiewahwah.com

This homegrown music venue—a rarity in Mid-City—features local artists, mostly rootsy and a little brassy. **Anders Osborne** is a staple, but the stage regularly welcomes everyone from old-timey singers like **Meschiya Lake** and the **Pfister Sisters** to avant-jazz group **Cloud Sharp 9**, featuring guitar geniuses **Phil deGruy** and **Cranston Clements**, bass monster **James Singleton,** and drummer **Doug Belote**. Chickie Wah Wah (named after the New Orleans R&B classic "Little Chickie Wah Wah," by **Huey "Piano" Smith and the Clowns**) is also one of the few places in the city where one might hear zydeco acts like **Sunpie Barnes**. The club's sister business, **Garage Pizza**, serves from lunchtime to late night, selling not just pizzas but appetizers including feta rolls, crawfish and spinach rolls, fried green tomatoes, and crab cakes.

HOWLIN' WOLF DEN

CBD/Warehouse District, corner
of St. Joseph and S. Peters Sts.,
504-529-5844; thehowlinwolf.com/
the-den/

A veteran enterprise, the Howlin' Wolf has booked an eclectic array of touring bands for years. The Wolf Den is its smaller counterpart, which not only exponentially increases the number of shows in the Warehouse District but provides top-shelf bar grub until the wee hours. Owner **Howie Kaplan** is also famous for managing the **Rebirth**

Brass Band to Grammy status for the band's 2011 album, *Rebirth of New Orleans*. Chow on a Cuban sandwich, various po-boys, crawfish or meat pies, tacos, or jambalaya while catching the club's famous Brass Band Sundays, now helmed by the aptly named **Hot 8**. Comedy Beast every Tuesday features local, semi-polished standups, while Thursday's **Comedy Gumbeaux** serves as a weekly open mic for up-and-coming jesters.

JACQUES-IMO'S

Uptown, 8324 Oak St.,
504-861-0886; jacques-imos.com

Jacques-Imo's is sort of a musical work of funky art in itself, attached as it is to the famed **Maple Leaf** music club. It's not unheard of for the entire **Rebirth Brass Band** (who've played the Leaf every Tuesday for forever) to parade over from next door and blast the restaurant with horns and thumping drums. The wacky chef is a local personality (a mural of him in his signature Jams chef pants graces the side of the building), and his food is an unpretentious, skillfully done Creole soul food. He does the traditional favorites (barbecue shrimp and corn maque choux) but doesn't do them to death (acorn squash stuffed with mussels in curry cream).

KERMIT RUFFINS' TREMÉ SPEAKEASY

Tremé, 1535 Basin St., 504-309-5828

Icon, actor, and BBQ master, trumpeter Kermit Ruffins has invested in several venues over the years, the latest riding the popularity of HBO's *Treme,* where

he plays himself regularly. The newest joint is small, with good soul food and a tiny, anything-goes stage manned by rotating musicians and characters. The interior could use some work, but we're guessing a year or two of family-style gatherings will suitably round the edges. Located just down the block from the Mahalia Jackson Theater and Louis Armstrong Park, the venue is poised to further stake Kermit's claim as the "King of the Tremé."

LE BON TEMPS ROULÉ

Uptown, 4801 Magazine St.,
504-895-8117;
myspace.com/4801magazine

Oh, the late, loud nights you'll have at this place. One of Uptown's few music venues, Le Bon Temps still hosts **Soul Rebels Brass Band** every Thursday. Along with brass and other traditional genres, Le Bon Temps steps outside the box as well, booking rock acts such as **R. Scully's Rough 7** and veteran cosmonauts **Rotary Downs**. The menu includes basic bar food like burgers, French fries, po-boys, and quesadillas. And don't tell anyone but . . . free oysters every Friday on Le Bon Temps' much-beloved back patio.

MAISON

Marigny, 508 Frenchmen St.,
504-371-5543; maisonfrenchmen.com

This larger-than-it-seems concert venue kicks into high gear before the sun sets. Maison features a stage in the downstairs window where you can catch early-evening jazz shows by the **Courtyard Kings,** then head to the big stage upstairs for comedy nights, the mighty monthly **Soundclash** beat battle, or bigger acts like rapper **Juvenile** or members of Brooklyn's Wu-Tang Clan. Come take swing dancing lessons from the NOLA Jitterbugs, or sit down and order up a plate of Jamaican ginger-beer pulled pork, or sandwiches such as steak and brie.

MICHAUL'S

CBD, 840 St. Charles Ave.,
504-522-5517

Michaul's is a low-key gem, with great New Orleans food and drinks, plus live Cajun music and zydeco. It's as Cajun as you can get here in la ville. The waitresses teach customers to Cajun line dance. Its big picture window looks right out onto the streetcar line and grand Lee Circle a little ways up. For Mardi Gras, Michaul's sells reasonably priced wristbands that entitle the wearer to buffet food, drinks, and a nice bathroom (because as **Benny Grunch's** famous local song goes, "Ain't no place to pee on Mardi Gras day!").

MID-CITY LANES ROCK 'N' BOWL

Mid-City, 3000 S. Carrollton Ave.,
504-861-1700; rockandbowl.com

One of the most unique clubs in the world, this bowling alley and concert venue also serves food from burgers to beignets. Music fans both local and visiting for **Jazz Fest** know that Rock 'n' Bowl is one of the only places in town to catch real Cajun music and zydeco on a regular basis. Line dance with zydeco kings like accordionist and singer **Geno Delafose,** or **Nathan and the Zydeco Cha-Chas.** Organist **Joe Krown** is a regular performer, as is young fiddle player **Amanda Shaw** and the **Creole String Beans.**

MIMI'S IN THE MARIGNY

Marigny, 2601 Royal St.,
504-872-9868;
mimisinthemarigny.net

This is one of the places hard hit by Mayor Landrieu's music club crackdown, so maybe as you're reading

Bingo's Clint Maedgen and Helen Gillet shine upstairs at Mimi's.

Robin Walker

this, Mimi's hosts no bands. There is undoubtedly late-night boozing, a sexy-bohemian vibe, and a delicious Castilian menu of hot and cold tapas mostly under $8 each, served till four a.m., with a very decent wine list to boot. Upstairs the local art exhibits rotate monthly. When the city lets it, Mimi's hosts traditional New Orleans dance bands and DJs. No cover.

PALM COURT JAZZ CAFÉ

French Quarter, 1204 Decatur St., 504-525-0200; palmcourtjazzcafe.com

Open since the night **Topsy Chapman** first took the stage here in 1989, the Palm Court showcases New Orleans–style traditional jazz, with frequent performances by the city's oldest living jazz trumpeter and vocalist, **Lionel Ferbos**, now 101 years old. Enjoy the company of proprietor **Nina Buck**, who greets and entertains her guests. The menu features French Creole cuisine such as Shrimp Ambrosia sautéed in a light fennel and Pernod cream sauce over pasta and the café's famous oysters bordelaise.

PRYTANIA BAR

Uptown, 3445 Prytania St.; www.prytaniabar.com

Chances are you'll end up in the Lower Garden District at some point during your stay. This bar is halfway between the streetcar and Magazine Street, conveniently close to a hospital (we're just saying), and regularly offering indie, jazz, hip-hop, and dance music. Open round the clock with bar food, rotating drink specials, doctors, and nurses.

PUBLIQ HOUSE

Uptown, 4528 Freret St., 504-826-9912; publiqhouse.com

The first live music venue to arrive on Freret is popular with college kids, spacious and well-crafted, and features decent if slightly middle-of-the-road music several nights a week. Publiq House carries a wide variety of beer and specializes in daiquiris.

RIVERSHACK TAVERN

Metairie, 3449 River Road, Jefferson, 504-834-4938; therivershacktavern.com

The story on this remarkably colorful establishment has it that after years of business, old asbestos shingles were finally removed from the structure, uncovering classic, hand-painted advertisements from the '40s—all in mint condition. Check out obscure New Orleans rock, blues, funk, and jazz bands while munching sandwiches, seafood, a creative assortment of burgers, and an impressive selection of salads. Rivershack's sports bar vibe is accentuated by a pool table, dart boards, and video golf. Boiled seafood (and lots of shouting) available during Saints games.

SIBERIA

Marigny, 2227 St. Claude Ave., 504-265-8855; siberianola.com

Owned by **Luke Allen** from the **Happy Talk Band**, music booker **Matt Russell** of **Classhol,** and former **Mimi's** bartender **Daphne Loney**, the club they named Siberia could not feature a more apt menu. "My family's Ukrainian, so I learned a few things from [my] grandma and great aunts," says **Matt the Hat**, who cooks pierogi, kielbasa, blini, cabbage rolls, and other Slavic foods until midnight, daily.

SNUG HARBOR

Marigny, 626 Frenchmen St., 504-949-0696; snugjazz.com

Historically, modern jazz gets less attention in New Orleans than you might guess, given the Olympian status of native son **Wynton Marsalis**. Snug is the preferred home for modernists and other members of the Marsalis clan, with straight-ahead food, a cozy balcony, and a bar where you can watch the music stage on television. Not every night is exciting, but national acts tend to gravitate here, so check the calendar if you're looking to change speeds.

New Orleans' premier Frenchmen Street jazz venue, Snug Harbor, also serves a nice seafood or steak dinner.

Zack Smith

SPORTS VUE TAVERN

Marigny, 1701 Elysian Fields Ave., 504-940-1111

In the dwindling New Orleans tradition of daiquiri shop as African American meeting ground (à la the barbershop everywhere else in America), this non-smoking ultra-hangout has pizza and other bar food to munch while partaking of many arcade games, electronic basketball and darts, mad pool tables, and, on not infrequent occasions, live New Orleans bounce rap. Truly special drink specials and a chance to rub elbows with very real locals.

ST. ROCH TAVERN

Marigny/St. Roch, 1200 St. Roch Ave., 504-208-6582

This is a divey bar with food at the edge of Tremé—close enough to walk from the Marigny and Quarter, but you shouldn't. It's big-ish inside, warmly lit, cheap and dirty, but cozy, and near a couple of funky, community-run art spaces (**Homespace** and **Sidearm**). Meaning, it is indeed a block you could hang out on all evening, as long as you don't stray from where people can see you. Everything from punk bands to blues acts play any night of the week, and on weekends DJ nights featuring Nola bounce. The kitchen in back serves a variety of sandwiches and other superior bar foods.

STAR STEAK AND LOBSTER

French Quarter, 237 Decatur St., 504-525-6151; starsteak.com

The food here is good enough, but the real treat while eating steak, lobster, crab cakes, and grilled oysters is one-man-band **James Dee** (Wed. through Sun., 6 to 10 p.m.), who with his truly original music, plus his pompadour, reverb-heavy saxophone, Casio keyboard beats, and dramatic but mellow voice, will never leave your memory of New Orleans—imagine Tom Waits as a cruise ship entertainer. "**Famous Joey**" has also served as Star's doorman for over twenty-nine years.

SWEET LORRAINE'S

Marigny, 1931 St. Claude Ave., 504-945-9654; sweetlorrainesjazzclub.com

For 30-years plus, this unassuming Marigny eatery and club has featured artists as diverse as smooth jazz violinist **Michael Ward** and free jazz titan **Pharoah Sanders**. Tuesday nights' open-mic events are famous, while Thursdays feature blues with **Chucky C and Clearly Blue**. The dinner menu boasts seafood, gumbo, wings, and pastas. Sunday brunch features singer **Danon Smith**. The club now offers a late-night breakfast buffet with omelet and waffle stations every Friday and Saturday from midnight to 4 a.m.

THREE MUSES

Marigny, 536 Frenchmen St., 504-298-8746; thethreemuses.com

A $3 drink is pretty rare on Frenchmen Street anymore, but that's exactly what you'll get at Three Muses' margarita happy hour, which also features piano music daily from 4:30 to 6:30 p.m. The cramped seating areas are more than made up for with truly creative small plates of lamb sliders, stuffed pork tenderloin, and duck pastrami pizza. Three Muses' tiny front-window stage hosts several shows a night, featuring heavy hitters like cellist **Helen Gillet** and pianist **Tom McDermott**.

VAUGHAN'S LOUNGE

Bywater, 4229 Dauphine St., 504-947-5562

This classic New Orleans bar is extremely generous with food, including free boiled seafood on most Friday nights, and amazing spreads during Saints games and every other New Orleans holiday.

YUKI IZAKAYA

Marigny, 525 Frenchmen St., 504-943-1122

Yuki stands out for its décor, food, and idiosyncratic music tastes. Tokyo business chic meets Frenchmen Street and works quite well, actually. Huddle up in a booth or cozy up to a bar lined with statuettes and attractive bartenders. International-flavored DJs, string trios, regular appearances by the great **Helen Gillet**, and amazing crab dumplings make for a cosmopolitan hideout from the scrum outside, especially during Mardi Gras.

N.O. MOMENT

RED BEANS WITH KING JAMES AND THE SPECIAL MEN

The Special Men perform at BJ's.

Jonathan Traviesa

Gold-toothed **Jimmy Horn** reconvened New Orleans downtown R&B group the **Special Men** to have fun and drink beer. A residual effect represented downtown R&B like no one else in town. Every Monday night at **BJ's** in Bywater, the dance floor is packed as the horn-and-piano-driven Special Men kick out nearly forgotten New Orleans R&B hits like "Boogie at Midnight," by **Roy Brown,** and "Ice Man," by **Big Joe**—beside Horn's own original tunes, which fit right in. "We owe everything to New Orleans producer Dave Bartholomew, and everything he did at **Cosimo Matassa**'s studio," Horn says. "All that shit from the late '40s. We play 'Great Big Eyes,' by **Archibald and Dave**, 'In the Night,' by **Professor Longhair.** A lot of these New Orleans R&B cats who invented this shit are gone or they're sick and can't come out, so a lot of kids haven't heard this shit."

The original Special Men convened Mondays at the **Mother-in-Law Lounge** starting in 1999, with Miss Antoinette K-Doe and her red beans as its nucleus. Horn finally decided BJ's, with its connection to **Little Freddie King**, was the next best place to hear this neighborhood music. And with the band's return, Jimmy's red beans are back too. "I make them in Miss Antoinette K-Doe's name," he says. "I watched. I paid attention. If I don't get them exactly like hers, my goal is to get them to taste as good as hers did."

COFFEE SHOPS

BYRDIE'S

Bywater, 2422A St. Claude Ave., 504-656-6794; byrdiesgallery.com

This tea and coffee shop, which features sandwiches and other lunch fare, doubles as an official St. Claude Arts District art gallery and as a ceramics studio offering classes, as well as memberships for anyone just needing a kiln. A new gallery show opens on the second Saturday night of each month.

CAFÉ DU MONDE

French Quarter, 800 Decatur St., 1-800-772-2927; cafedumonde.com

Every visiting tourist simply must stop in the outside courtyard of Café Du Monde, across from beautiful Jackson Square, for the only thing they serve: fried and powdered beignets and chicory coffee (a wonderfully rich, almost dirty-tasting New Orleans version of joe). The live musicians who play to the courtyard for tips will never let you forget you're a tourist. We are not snobby enough to guide you away from this wonderful experience.

RESTAURANTS

CAFÉ ENVIE

French Quarter, 1241 Decatur St.,
504-524-3689

When you imagine sitting in a coffee shop in New Orleans—or France, for that matter—idly sipping espresso, watching the world go by, you are picturing Envie. This open-air café is perfectly situated on lower Decatur for tourists who'd like to hang with locals and have something to look at out the many French doors. The young baristas double as competent DJs, their iPods piping in all decades of college rock music.

CAFÉ ROSE NICAUD

Marigny, 632 Frenchmen St.,
504-949-3300

During the day, before the live music starts, Frenchmen is still a neighborhood hub for locals, and Rose Nicaud, which bookends the Royal Street end of the strip, is a popular spot for coffee, laptop work, and lazing with a newspaper by the big picture windows. Rose Nicaud offers food that is satisfying if a bit pricey, plus vegetarian options and even some live New Orleans music on random weekends and special occasions.

CROISSANT D'OR

French Quarter, 617 Ursulines St.,
504-524-4663

This airy bakery, with its azure walls, white tile, and flooding sunlight, evokes casual Euro chic à la the South of France. Homemade French pastries are sweet or savory, and the baguettes are golden, chewy, and light. Oh—and

really cheap. Beware, though: they close at 2:30 p.m.

FAIR GRINDS

Mid-City, 3133 Ponce De Leon St.,
504-913-9072; fairgrinds.com

In the extra room upstairs, Fair Grinds hosts everything from art films to yoga to book releases to folk music to potluck dinners to mellow, avant-garde noise concerts. Right down the sidewalk from the cemetery, the **New Orleans Museum of Art**, and **Liuzza's by the Track**, not to mention the **New Orleans Fair Grounds** (get it?), home of **Jazz Fest**.

FLORA GALLERY & COFFEE SHOP

Marigny, 2600 Royal St.,
504-947-8358

Flora's is New Orleans' quintessential bohemian coffee shop, located on a great little local corner of bars and restaurants. Tons of interesting fliers and other local ads decorate its front door, and there's almost always someone tinkling the piano inside, or strumming a banjo on the benches outside next to grizzled old hippies playing chess. Flora's coffee drinks are cheap, as are its Mediterranean and breakfast foods. And Flora's smells much nicer now that you can't smoke inside.

HEY! CAFÉ

Uptown, 4332 Magazine St.,
504-891-8682; heycafe.biz

Home base for **Community Records** (see pages 43–44), this is a great spot for getting news on indie shows, read-

Flora's coffee shop in Bywater.

ing in relative peace, or watching the traffic on Magazine Street. The café's neighbors are a costume shop, an oyster joint, and the 24/7 bar **Ms. Mae's**, and the police station is across the street, so you pretty much have all you need for an interesting day on one block. Plus, the in-house stereo is always eclectic and usually killer.

JUJU BAG CAFÉ

Gentilly neighborhood (north of Marigny), 4706 Mandeville St., 504-872-0969

The JuJu Bag Café, with its huge sun deck out back, supports and hosts many community events including a weekly poetry night, book signings, and Sunday brunch, plus meetings and receptions.

MOJO

Uptown, 1500 Magazine St. and 4700 Freret St., 504-525-2244

Formerly a **Rue de la Course**, this Lower Garden District shop is a throwback in both décor and prices, with good coffee and pastries. Plus, if you're looking for fliers, zines, and free papers, they have stacks. The fountain at nearby Coliseum Square is a fine place to enjoy a to-go cup.

ORANGE COUCH

Marigny, 2339 Royal St., 504-267-7327; theorangecouchcoffee.com

An upscale yet still comfy coffee shop located on a funky corner in the Marigny. Fancy coffees are served beside light Vietnamese dishes and mochi, Japanese ice cream rice balls. Orange Couch shows local artists and photog-

RESTAURANTS

raphers, and sometimes hosts community performances, such as students from nearby **NOCCA** performing arts school.

RUE DE LA COURSE

Uptown, 1140 S. Carrollton Ave.,
504-861-4343

Once a mini-franchise in the city, with funky buildings and diehards who read and conversed daily at thick wooden tables. Today, this converted bank at the corner of ever-popular Oak Street is the last outpost of those classics. The coffee's still great, the interior is vaguely continental, and you're on the streetcar line. Close to the universities, it's a little quieter and more study-based than social, but you can sit outside and rattle as loud as you like.

SOUND CAFÉ/BETH'S BOOKS

Marigny, 2700 Chartres St.,
504-947-4477

Sound Café is a pleasant little respite of a coffee shop near the Press Street tracks (the border between Bywater and Marigny), where locals sit with laptops, coffee, sandwiches, and pastries. Local musicians (who rarely work during the day) might jump on the piano in the corner and practice for the clientele. The café shares the building with **Beth's Books**, specializing in high-quality used books, plus tons of titles by New Orleans authors. The café also teams up with trumpet player **Shamar Allen** to host weekly music lessons for kids.

ST. COFFEE

Marigny, 2709 St. Claude Ave,
504-872-9798

Serves up the usual coffeehouse stuff, plus Jarritos Mexican sodas, excellent doughnuts, and fresh pastries. The tables out front provide an excellent spot from which to watch the beautifully sketchy goings-on of St. Claude Avenue.

Z'OTZ

Uptown, 8210 Oak St., 504-861-2224

Named for a Mayan glyph, Z'otz's sign doesn't bear its name—just a giant question mark. Still, it's hard to miss. The 24-hour shop is big with students, goth kids, and bohemian sorts who enjoy the unusual candies, vegan pastries, and unique offerings like bubble tea and yerba mate. Their semiregular "night market"—an after-dark crafts bazaar—is popular, as are occasional DJ nights, open-mic events, and acoustic performances.

MORE FOODS THAT NEW ORLEANS DOES REAL WELL

Trying to eat healthy while on vacation and still eat New Orleans-y food? Well, lucky for you the city hosts a huge Vietnamese population, concentrated in a "Little Vietnam" out in New Orleans East (not very far—just take Chef Menteur Highway east until you see the Vietnamese strip malls on your left). The West Bank, on the other side of the Mississippi River, is also a haven for excellent Asian chefs. Beyond Vietnamese, New Orleans hosts every Asian possibility from cheap buffets to high-priced sushi. In fact, Asian cultures have so influenced New Orleans that many of our rickety corner stores and gas stations sell fried rice dishes with their po-boys, and crawfish pies alongside (often amazing) egg rolls. Special thanks to local Jack Porobil for his expertise:

ASIAN/VIETNAMESE

CHINA WALL RESTAURANT

Chinese; CBD, 1112 Canal St., 504-522-6802

This good-enough Chinese place is most remarkable for the fact that they deliver all the way back into Bywater. A killer order of mu-shu pork (more than enough for two people) and ten big crab rangoons costs about $15.

EAT-WELL FOOD MART

Vietnamese; Mid-City, 2700 Canal St., 504-821-7730

Get off the streetcar at Broad Street and you'll see what looks like a mini-mart (they have incredibly large selec-

tions of booze, too) next to a bank building. In the rear, you'll find a full lunch counter that offers the largest, tastiest banh mi (Vietnamese po-boy) on this side of the river. Buy a tall boy and a newspaper and still get change on a $10 bill. Jump back on the street-car and picnic in City Park.

HONG KONG FOOD MARKET

All Asian; 925 Behrman Hwy., West Bank, 504-394-7075

A super local mega-mart of fresh Asian food ingredients, with a concentration on Vietnamese. Incredible produce, live seafood tanks, a deli, plus a Vietnamese restaurant area serving everything from pho (rice noodle soup with vegetables and meat) to banh mi.

MAGASIN

Vietnamese; Uptown,
4201 Magazine St., 504-896-7611;
magasincafe.com

The difference between the West Bank and the East Bank is the presence of dark meat in your pho. We recommend the former, but if you're looking for Vietnamese uptown, Magasin does a fair job and offers outside seating. It's a little pricier than its cross-river counterparts.

MIKIMOTO JAPANESE RESTAURANT

Japanese; Uptown,
3301 S. Carrollton Ave.,
504-488-1881; mikimotosushi.com

This very basic, small sushi restaurant has tons of great one-dollar sashimi and roll specials. Mikimoto also has a drive-thru window for pickup, or if you want to avoid your car altogether, it offers the fastest delivery known to man.

NINE ROSES

Vietnamese/Chinese; 1100 Stephen St., Gretna, La. (West Bank),
504-366-7665

A nice place but very affordable. The dishes wherein you grill beef, shrimp, and/or chicken at your table yourself, then wrap in rice paper, easily feed two to three people for around $15.

PHO BANG

Vietnamese; 8814 Veterans Memorial Blvd., Metairie, La.,
504-466-8742

Pho Bang serves pho and other Vietnamese soups almost exclusively. Pho is served a number of ways: tendon, tripe, beef balls, fresh eye of round, brisket, navel . . . you can get pretty much any part of the cow or pig in your bowl.

PHO TAU BAY

Vietnamese; 113 Westbank Expwy., Stumpf exit, Gretna, La. (West Bank),
504-368-9846

Specializing in pho, Pho Tau Bay also serves amazing fresh spring rolls, as well as Vietnamese-style iced coffee: New Orleans chicory coffee French-dripped over condensed milk, to be mixed up and poured over ice. The drink's French-Asian roots make it perfect for New Orleans, especially in the summer.

SAKE CAFÉ

Japanese; Uptown, 2830 Magazine St.,
504-894-0033

A little expensive, but you can't put a price on this kind of artistry. Given that Sake Café's original New Orleans-ified rolls and other seafood dishes are delicious works of art—plus the restaurant's modern décor, too, is intriguing and creative—you might expect it all to cost even more.

TAN DINH

Vietnamese; 1705 Lafayette St., Gretna, La. (West Bank), 504-361-8008

Cheap, delicious, and straightforward, Tan Dinh occupies an unadorned space next to a gas station, but it may have the best variety on the West Bank. The pho, yes, but the alligator, the goat, and the Korean short ribs are out of this world, even if you're very much in a suburban eatery. Bubble tea and a friendly staff lighten things up.

VIETNAMESE KITCHEN AT LOST LOVE LOUNGE

Vietnamese; Marigny, 2529 Dauphine St., 504-400-6145

This charming and familial new dive bar up the street from Mimi's is not only owned in part by banjo/guitar dude **Geoff Douville** from **Egg Yolk Jubilee**, but also hosts (Thurs. through Sun., 6 p.m. to late night) a great Vietnamese restaurant in the back.

WASABI SUSHI RESTAURANT & BAR

Japanese; Marigny, 900 Frenchmen St., 504-943-9433

A simple mid-range sushi restaurant that nonetheless has the power to get you high off their fresh fish concoctions and nice selection of sakes. We've had more than one meal here where we walked away agreeing that we'd just had the best sushi of our lives. If we could recommend only one sushi restaurant in the city, Wasabi is definitely it.

CRAWFISH

You can get this boiled, spicy poor-man's shrimp all year round somewhere in the city, but you will pay dearly, and they'll be puny. Crawfish are biggest and best during the chillier months—coincidentally or not, all through New Orleans' festival season. We protest anything above $2 a pound. Here are some other crawdaddy options:

BIG FISHERMAN

Uptown, 3301 Magazine St., 504-897-9907

Kind of expensive for crawfish, but Big Fisherman certainly know what they doin' in regards to spice.

CAPTAIN SAL'S SEAFOOD AND CHICKEN

Bywater, 3168 St. Claude Ave., 504-948-9990

If you're in Bywater/Marigny, Captain Sal's is the place. A big hot-deli counter with everything from egg rolls to crawfish pies to boiled shrimp and soft-shelled crabs. Grab a cheap beer and sit down, cover the dirty table with newspaper, dump out the crawdads, figure out how to crack 'em open, get into the rhythm, stare out the window onto crazy-ass St. Claude Ave., and you just may understand New Orleans.

K-JEAN SEAFOOD

Mid-City, 236 N. Carrollton Ave., 504-488-7503

Charming little Mid-City shack that rebuilt and rebounded strong after Katrina. Hard-working crawfish experts, these people.

DAIQUIRIS

Daiquiri stands are another option that locals utilize daily. During New Orleans' hot summer, especially if you're riding your bike, a frozen daiquiri to go can save your life. Though several honest-to-god drive-thru daiquiri stands still exist on the West Bank and in other suburbs (the drive-thru worker hands it down into your car, with the straw sitting across the lid; only if you drove off and poked the straw down in could you be busted for DUI), drive-thrus unfortunately went extinct inside New Orleans proper after Katrina. French Quarter daiquiris do taste good, but they're hella expensive (a medium, enough for a good buzz, should cost less than $6), and they're never as potent. Find yourself a good generous neighborhood daiquiri stand, and the only thing you'll have to worry about is drinking just one (WARNING: drink one early in the day and you may survive till nighttime, maybe, but if you drink two, between the alcohol and the sugar you will surely crash hard before sundown). Man, do we love daiquiris, though.

DAIQUIRI PLACE CAFÉ

Uptown, 1401 St. Charles Ave., 504-524-1401

Many consider this the best daiquiri stand in the city, with drinks made from actual fruit that are just strong enough. Right off of Lee Circle, amid lots of nice tony restaurants and bars, Daiquiri Place Café is a deeply local hangout where you're as certain to meet some natives as you are to have some frozen drinks.

GABBY'S DAIQUIRIS

Bywater, 3200 St. Claude Ave., 504-875-2096

The sweet owner Gabby makes fruity daiquiris that never taste like Kool-Aid. She also offers a small but potent menu of New Orleans foods, and often hosts BBQs outside of her shop.

GENE'S PO-BOYS AND DAIQUIRIS

Marigny, 1040 Elysian Fields Ave., 504-943-3861

In the hood, this is the spot. Bounce music on the radio, video poker in back, an extra-sweet older lady workin' the counter, and frozen to-go drinks. Make sure and ask to see the menu, featuring crazily named daiquiri combos made up by the neighborhood such as the Good Joog, What the Fuck, Slim Shady (all the white liquors), and our favorite, Sweet Pussy (peach mixed with white Russian).

NEW ORLEANS ORIGINAL DAIQUIRIS

10 locations; 504-524-9504

The local chain. Better than nothing, and in a pinch, still excellent for chillin' outside somewhere. If you really want a buzz, you'll have to pay a buck for an extra shot.

ICE CREAM

ANGELO BROCATO ICE CREAM

Mid-City, 214 N. Carrollton Ave., 504-486-0078; angelobrocatoicecream.com

This Italian ice cream hot spot is old-fashioned and thoroughly local. Besides incredible ice cream, Brocato's has gelato, canolis, fresh dessert pastries, and tables so you can sit down and focus on the best dessert experience in the city.

THE CREOLE CREAMERY

Uptown, 4924 Prytania St., 504-894-8680; creolecreamery.com

This kid-friendly "ice cream experience" specializes in unique flavors, from Carmel Chicory Chocolate to Cucumber Sorbet. The street it's on, Prytania, is a great shopping and restaurant street.

LA DIVINA GELATERIA

Uptown, 3005 Magazine St., 504-342-2634, and French Quarter, 621 St. Peter St., 504-302-2692; ladivinagelateria.com

Written up in the *New York Post* for the quality of its gelato, La Divina uses all locally sourced ingredients, from berries to cream, and old-school Italian methods to churn out the icy goodness. It also serves a lunch menu of salads and panini, plus espresso drinks. A French Quarter satellite recently opened near Jackson Square.

OFFICIAL SNACKS OF
NEW ORLEANS

Zack Smith

In the spring, locals go to town on heaping mounds of boiled crawfish.

Zapp's are the official (and officially perfect) potato chips of New Orleans. Our beer is the flavorful **Abita** (which comes in all types from Christmas ale to a satsuma-flavored brew), while kids and adults alike enjoy **Barq's Root Beer** or **Big Shot** red drink. Our fried snack desserts are called **Hubig's Pies** (from lemon to chocolate to peach to sweet potato). **Boiled shrimp** are also a decadent (and messy) snack, as are **boiled crawfish**; sniff around and you'll find a bar serving up the crustaceans for free at happy hour. During summer, a giant Styrofoam cup full of frozen daiquiri to-go from one of our many local **daiquiri** stands (we suggest **Gene's**, the big pink building in Marigny, on St. Claude and Elysian Fields) may mark the highlight of your vacation. During Mardi Gras, there is also **king cake** to be scarfed, but if your piece (or one of your pieces) has a lil' plastic baby hidden in it, then assuming you don't choke, you must buy the next king cake. Sorry, them's the rules.

MORE FOODS

INDIAN

HARE KRISHNA HOUSE (FREE, VEGAN)

Uptown, 2936 Esplanade Ave.,
504-304-0032; iskcon-nola.org

Every Sunday these Krishnas host a free meal of Indian food. A "Love Feast," to be exact, on Sunday evenings, with *kirtan* beginning at 5:30 p.m., followed by a special *arati* at 6, a discourse from 6:45 to 7:30 p.m., then the aforementioned Krishna *prasadam* (spiritual food) served free of charge to everyone. We wouldn't suggest you go here and eat great free vegan Indian food if you were going to be set upon by cultists; New Orleans' Krishnas are mostly non-American, very kind and sweet, and not the least bit pushy, making this a great casual environment in which to check out a different way of life while having good food—a bit of a ritual for New Orleanians who are low on cash and want some healthy dining. Plus, it's a very pretty early-evening bike ride down Esplanade Avenue.

NIRVANA INDIAN CUISINE

Uptown, 4308 Magazine St.,
504-894-9797; insidenirvana.com

The only place within the city proper that hosts an Indian lunch buffet daily, plus dinner buffet on Thursday and Sunday.

PIZZA

Not sure why you're eating pizza on your visit to New Orleans, but . . . Pizza in New Orleans is really meant to be eaten by the slice from various windows during Mardi Gras, or all year round anywhere near Bourbon Street. But if you really need a whole pie (and we certainly understand that need), here are our suggestions:

PIZZA DELICIOUS

Bywater, 617 Piety St.,
504-676-8482; pizzadelicious.com

Charmingly cramped cafeteria seating, delicious artisan pizza made with Louisiana-grown ingredients, plus salads, pasta dishes, seafood, small plates, icy draft beers, and nice wines. Bike delivery available from 4 to 10 p.m. every day.

SLICE

Uptown, 1513 St. Charles Ave.,
504-525-PIES; slicepizzeria.com

The yin to **Juan's Flying Burrito**'s yang, Slice is run by the same people, though it doesn't quite follow the hardcore aesthetic of its older brother. Whether pizza by the slice or a whole pie, Slice offers better fare than most of the city's pizza joints, including special salads and small plates.

SUGAR PARK

Bywater, 3054 St. Claude Ave.,
504-942-2047; sugarparknola.com

Some call Sugar Park's thin cornmeal-crust pizza the best in the city. The restaurant also has two nice bars and a relaxing back patio where movies are often shown.

PO-BOYS

The po-boy is a simple thing. Fried seafood or else meat on French bread, "dressed" if you like, with mayo, tomato, and lettuce, maybe some pickles. No more. No mustard even. Given its simplicity—plus the fact that New Orleans does all food so right—most po-boys you'll eat in New Orleans will be pretty damn good. Long as the bread is crunchy, the shrimp medium sized, and afterwards you're stuffed and there are still a few shrimp/oysters/hunks of roast beef left on the big white butcher paper, then that's a wrap. Out of thousands of good po-boy joints, these are just the first four that come to mind:

COOP'S PLACE

French Quarter, 1109 Decatur St.,
504-525-9053; coopsplace.net

We'd like to tell you only about on-the-corner down-low po-boy joints, but if you're in the Quarter and want New Orleans food late into the night, Coop's is the absolute best, even though it's popular. Coop's is consistently hoppin', and loud. Big fat fried oysters on French bread or a bun are sublime, but we also love the blackened redfish po-boy.

MAGNOLIA DISCOUNT

Mid-City, 1233 N. Broad St.,
504-486-0086

A not remarkably clean gas station that can nonetheless blow your mind with over-over-stuffed shrimp and other 16-inch po-boys. Meaning, roughly two giant meals for less than $10. Again, you can pop in most gas stations that sell po-boys (earlier in the day the better as far as French bread goes) and probably end up with a good deal.

PARASOL'S RESTAURANT & BAR

Uptown, 2533 Constance St., 504-899-2054; parasolsbarandrestaurant.com

Part dive bar, part po-boy shop, part community center, Parasol's is the anchor of the Irish Channel neighborhood and a great place to catch a football game and an oyster po-boy. It is also the epicenter of all St. Patrick's Day activities. 7 days, 12 p.m. till.

PARKWAY BAKERY

Mid-City, 538 Hagan Ave., 504-482-2680; parkwaypoorboys.com

Considered by many po-boy experts to have the absolute best roast beef po-boy smothered in "debris" gravy that you could possibly ever have—ever. Parkway is also a very nice family bar with a view of the water on Bayou St. John, just outside City Park.

MARDI GRAS SEASON

A Month of Love and Parties

The Secret Society of St. Anne parades through Marigny early Fat Tuesday morning. Note there are no observers, only participants.

There is just too much one could say about Fat Tuesday, and the month of parades and parties and concerts that precedes it— Twelfth Night, or the Epiphany, is the official start of Carnival season. The party peaks the night before Fat Tuesday, which is called Lundi Gras; Mardi Gras day is the drunken, still-ecstatic wind-down to the world's longest debauch.

Jonathan Traviesa

Whether you've visited New Orleans or not (especially if you haven't!), close your eyes for a moment and picture Mardi Gras. Now, know that whatever you pictured is certainly going on somewhere in the city, but so is every other celebratory thing you could dream up. Sure, you could lick hurricane drink off a stranger's bare breast on a busy street. But you could also likely have a quiet crawfish picnic if that's your scene. For most locals, Mardi Gras is an all-city love fest where folks walk and bike around in amazing, hypercreative costumes, with the simple objective of finding and hugging your also costumed, drunken friends.

The only definitive statements that can really be made about Carnival are: don't go without a costume (ideally, Mardi Gras is all participants, no observers), and BYOB (much cheaper, you can buy enough to share with folks, and you'll avoid bar lines). It must be said again: a calm, shy person will (somehow) have as good a time at Mardi Gras as an effusive alcoholic. It's really up to you how you party. If you like to drink, just remember: Mardi Gras is a marathon, not a sprint.

The greatest Mardi Gras experiences come from partaking of an odyssey without clear direction. Still, here are some of our suggestions anyway:

BABY DOLLS

Fat Tuesday

A group of women strutting through the streets in satin and lace baby doll get-ups (that look more like French maid costumes with bonnets), continuing a black female tradition with deep and distant roots. Before her recent death, **Miss Antoinette K-Doe** had resurrected the dormant baby doll tradition, and thus a good place to catch them (and Mardi Gras Indians, and many other of Mardi Gras's best weird krewes) is her **Mother-in-Law Lounge** (1500 N. Claiborne Ave.).

BACCHUS

Sunday before Fat Tuesday; Uptown around Toledano and St. Charles Ave.; kreweofbacchus.org

Since 1969, the mainstream but wild Krewe of Bacchus rolls, with many small alternative krewes in tow, including the ever-entertaining **Box of Wine** krewe, who directly celebrate the Roman god of wine.

COSTUMES

The author and his wife go all out on Mardi Gras day.

Michael Patrick Welch

If you are here participating in a festival, you will most likely need a costume. Do not under any circumstances be the person without some kind of costume, especially on Mardi Gras or Halloween.

FUNROCK'N POP CITY (French Quarter, 940 Decatur St., 504-528-8559; popcitynola.com). Usually a store for fun knick-knacks, party supplies, and pop culture paraphernalia, this shop transforms into the premier store for masks and other costume supplies.

NEW ORLEANS PARTY & COSTUME (CBD, 705 Camp St., 504-525-4744; partyandcostume.com). Nice, spacious, well-organized two-story costume shop with everything you could possibly need.

UPTOWN COSTUME AND DANCEWEAR (Uptown, 4326 Magazine St., 504-895-7969). This comprehensive costume hub is the busiest shop in town during Mardi Gras and Halloween, just packed with college kids—which is actually really fun and helps you get in the spirit! Worth checking out even if you have to stand in line outside.

BARKUS PARADE

two Sundays before Fat Tuesday;
barkus.org

An afternoon parade featuring hundreds of hilariously costumed dogs. Also some cats, and maybe a goat or two. At around 10 a.m. the animals begin gathering at Armstrong Park on Rampart Street before the parade begins at 2 p.m., heading down St. Ann Street and winding through the French Quarter. The day culminates in a costume contest and a Barkus Ball (humans only, sorry!).

CHEWBACCHUS

chewbacchus.org

The intergalactic **Krewe of Chewbacchus** walks the perimeter of the Marigny on Saturday night before Mardi Gras. Yep, wookies, R2D2s, and other contraptions, but no unicorns, elves, or whinebots—them's the rules. They claim to be "the Future of Revelry," and they welcome one and all to join them.

N.O. MOMENT

GRIS GRIS STRUT
DANCE TROUPE

Zack Smith

grisgrisstrut.com

In 2007, New Orleans witnessed the birth of a new kind of dance troupe, Gris Gris Strut. They're blazing a path as the first-ever dance troupe in the parades performing hard-hitting, full-body, "forward-motion choreography"—a term founder, choreographer, and dancer **Cherie Pitre** coined to describe the style of movement she created. "I don't believe in a rest beat," Pitre says. "I don't think that dance should ever fight for the audience's attention—it should move them, surprise them, and invite them in."

Composed of ten thrill-seeking, professional dancers, Gris Gris Strut Dance Troupe incorporates ballet leaps, jumps, high kicks, and gymnastics. While elating spectators with sassy moves and fun grooves, the dancers toss the group's signature throws, gris gris bags, to a soundtrack of Stevie Wonder, Jackson 5, and Sugarhill Gang.

Last year, the troupe upped the ante by adding a flag corps and premiering the Gris Gris Strut Marching Band, comprised of more than thirty professional musicians and the 10- to-13-year-old Upper Ninth Ward musicians they are mentoring. In 2013, GGS was featured in **Krewe of Druids, Le Krewe d'Etat,** and **Krewe of Thoth.**

KREWE DU POUX

Lundi Gras night; Bywater

A satire of the satirical parade described above, put on by bike-punks, fauxbeaux, and other colorful snowbirds and Bywater/Marigny cretins. After the parade and coronation (**Ratty Scurvics** and his wife **Ooops the Clown** of **Fleur de Tease** served as king and queen several times), the krewe meets in an alley near Franklin Street in Marigny for its annual demolition derby of creatively altered shopping carts. The carts crash and bash until only the champion is left standing—that is, if the cops don't come and break it up first. Check the Krewe du Poux YouTube documentary.

KREWE DU VIEUX

early evening on Twelfth Night, Mardi Gras's kickoff; kreweduvieux.org

For many locals, this low-budget parade of sex jokes, three weekends before Fat Tuesday, is the real kick-off of Carnival season, which, technically, began a few weeks back. Krewe du Vieux (as in Vieux Carré, the French name for the French Quarter) is a satirical, raunchy parade in nineteenth-century Carnival style, complete with small floats drawn by krewe members and mules.

KREWE OF JOYFUL NOISE, FEATURING THE NOISICIAN COALITION

Bacchus Sunday, Lundi Gras midnight, but also Voodoo Fest during Halloween, and select New Orleans Bingo! Show gigs; noisiciancoalition.org

With an array of self-styled instruments, including tubas made from drainpipes, saxophones melded with bullhorns, and guitar-pedal-accordion contraptions, this ragtag krewe dressed in red and black split the sartorial difference between steampunk, pirate, and scary clown. Begun as an expression of **New Orleans Bingo! Show** member **Mattvaughn Black**'s love of strange noises, the Noisicians hold several parades and a ball throughout the year. Their main events, however, are a trip down the St. Charles Avenue parade route, confusing spectators waiting for **Bacchus** (as part of the lewd **Box of Wine** krewe parade), and a midnight march on Lundi Gras night, assuring them billing as the first parade of Mardi Gras day.

KREWE OF KOSMIC DEBRIS

begins at noon on Frenchmen St., Mardi Gras day

Formed in 1977, this now 200-plus-person French Quarter pub crawl parade on Mardi Gras morn invites all comers in costume to join in and jam on Dixieland standards—whether or not you know how to play an instrument.

N.O. MOMENT

MARDI GRAS INDIANS

Mardi Gras Indians, resplendent in their intricately hand-beaded suits and headdresses weighed down with thousands of brightly colored feathers, are ubiquitous images in New Orleans' tourist materials. They're hired to parade through **Jazz Fest** to create ambiance, and since Katrina, nonprofits have subsidized Indian "practices" that are open to the public. These friendly presentations can contribute to a public image of the stalwart tradition bearers as sort of happy, colorful feathered friends. What most people don't talk much about is that Mardi Gras Indians can be some genuinely scary motherfuckers.

Locals say that the Indians—African American groups divided into tribes that identify as either Uptown- or downtown-based—have been around since the nineteenth cen-

129

tury. The tribal hierarchies include a Big Chief, a Big Queen, and sometimes second and third chiefs and queens, plus the "spy boys," "flag boys," and "wild men." The tradition is interesting for combining aggressive, territorial hypermasculinity with the domestic act of sewing; each man works all year to sew delicate, intricate patterns into a suit he will show off once or twice, before destroying it and starting over for next year. On Mardi Gras day and Super Sunday, which falls in mid-March, the Indians don't parade so much as roam their neighborhoods, looking for other tribes for showdowns. Spy boys (you know the song) wander out ahead of the Big Chief to spot other tribes. These days, the contest is about who has the prettiest suit, but back in the day—especially on Mardi Gras day, when confusion reigned in the streets and most people were masked—the battles were violent. As recently as the '90s, one Indian was allegedly nearly murdered by another looking to settle a score with him by a hatchet to the head. Some locals whisper that secret Indian Council meetings still have the power to decide life or death.

In the early '70s, members of the **Wild Magnolias** tribe, along with **Willie Tee**, recorded the first album of Indian songs ever put on wax (self-titled, but later put out with extra songs as *They Call Us Wild*), a deliciously raw and dirty slice of funk—one of the finest and most unique artifacts of genuine American music in existence—with the clattering tambourine and drum percussions the Indians use on actual runs.

On Mardi Gras day and Super Sunday, neighborhood bars near Claiborne Avenue or under the Claiborne overpass (e.g., the **Mother-in-Law Lounge**), or Second and Dryades Streets, Bayou St. John, and Tremé are all great vantage points to catch the Indians' awesome spectacle. Or else all year round, you can visit the **House of Dance and Feathers** or the **Backstreet Cultural Museum** (see "Art Galleries") to learn more about Indian history and custom.

Mr. Quintron's Ninth Ward Marching Band often features a celebrity grand marshal, such as dirty female electro-rapper Peaches, shown here.

MUSES

usually on the Friday night before Mardi Gras; kreweofmuses.org

While the rest of the big float parades can get a bit monotonous, this all-female Mardi Gras krewe has the absolute best throws, plus the most dynamic array of floats and live bands. Many in town say it's the parade of Carnival. In recent years the all-female krewes have joined the scene (**Nix,** former West Bank parade **Cleopatra)**, putting the all-male krewes to shame with their ladylike creativity and generosity—where, traditionally, pretty girls always end up receiving the most throws, the all-female krewes spread the loot upon everyone.

NINTH WARD MARCHING BAND

Founded by one-man-band **Mr. Quintron**, the Ninth Ward Marching Band began in the late '90s as a project for Bywater's many bohemian musician types. Inspired by the musicianship, choreography, and showmanship of the high school marching bands, Q and crew put together a team of thirty-odd artists and oddballs in clean, pressed red-and-white uniforms emblazoned with sparkly 9s. Because the Ninth Ward is largely considered a black neighborhood, many locals roll their eyes at the nearly all-Caucasian band. Still, they've got a fun dance team, cheerleaders, a gun squad, flag girls— the whole (ahem) nine yards. The now much larger underground team has recently been welcomed by the mainstream and can be seen in several big "official" Mardi Gras parades each year, including **Muses** and **Bacchus**.

131

NORTHSIDE SKULL AND BONES GANG

early morning, Fat Tuesday; Tremé

Dressed in black with papier-mâché skull masks and other spooky attire, this long-standing black krewe (established in the early nineteenth century) delivers an early morning wake-up call to the Tremé neighborhood and "brings the spirits to the streets on Mardi Gras morning," says **Bruce "Sunpie" Barnes**, the gang's second chief.

SECRET SOCIETY OF ST. ANNE

Mardi Gras morning, some house on Clouet St. in Bywater

The now not-as-secret Society of St. Anne amasses early Mardi Gras morning on Clouet Street in the Bywater and marches into the French Quarter (to Canal Street for the big boring **Rex** parade, before doubling back to the Quarter) in some of the best, most elaborate costumes Carnival has to offer.

N.O. MOMENT

PINK SLIP: MARDI GRAS'S FIRST ROCK BAND

Alongside singer **Susan Cowsill**, **Sue Ford** fronts Mardi Gras's first official rock band, Pink Slip, once an all-woman group that now includes Sue's husband, drummer **Jimmy Ford**. "There are so many different types of music in this town, all of them should be represented," says Sue Ford of her inspiration for wanting to join the brass bands and marching bands in traditional parades. Pink Slip was first let in the door by the all-female **Krewe of Muses**, who wanted all-female musicians, and not the typical jazz and blues and stuff. Jimmy Ford used his Lion's Club affiliation to procure the girls' float, and a generator to power the PA. Jimmy also ran sound, even after the original drummer quit and he took her spot. Every year the Fords invite a new cast of characters aboard to play classic rock and disco standards, plus originals like the rock tune "I Wanna Die in New Orleans." White Zombie's **Sean Yseult** sometimes plays keyboards for Pink Slip, along with guitarist **Dave Catching** of Queens of the Stoneage and Eagles of Death Metal.

'Tit Rəx is a Bywater/Marigny parade of miniature floats.

Jonathan Traviesa

'TIT Rəx

titrexparade.com

A funny thing happened to the city's only "micro-krewe," 'tit Rəx, after two years of walking the Bywater with shoebox-sized floats crafted by some of the neighborhood's greatest minds. The original **Krewe of Rex**, founded in 1870 and populated by the wealthiest, palest families in town, took exception to the use of the name "Rex" by the plucky bohemians and threatened litigation. Downtown's response to Uptown threats? Flipping the "e" upside down and moving right along. Instead of beads, the throws are handcrafted and the size of toy soldiers, and the parade takes ample time stopping at local bars.

ZULU

Fat Tuesday afternoon; Canal St., down St. Charles; kreweofzulu.com

This all-black krewe, dating back to the early 1900s, is active all year, and based out of the **Zulu Social Aid and Pleasure Club** (732 N. Broad St.). Their parade essentially consists of black people wearing blackface, making fun of the white idea that blacks are "savages." Wearing grass skirts, lard-can hats, and banana-stalk scepters, the krewe throws out much-coveted hand-painted Zulu coconuts. Zulu's history and calendar of yearly events are extremely dense and fascinating, and should be checked out on their website.

MARDI GRAS ADVICE FROM BANJO PLAYER GEOFF DOUVILLE OF EGG YOLK JUBILEE

Geoff Douville

Wanna know what Mardi Gras is like for your average New Orleans musician? Just before Mardi Gras 2008, we randomly ran into **Geoff Douville**, a native New Orleanian, local filmmaker, guitarist, educator, and banjo player in much-loved, genre-defying brass-ish band **Egg Yolk Jubilee**. Geoff is a shining example of a local artist and neighbor.

Geoff was sitting outside of **Café Rose Nicaud** on Frenchmen Street catching his breath (which admittedly smelled of a couple drinks), sweating in formalwear like he'd just come from a job—because he had just come from a job. With his shiny banjo case at his feet he told me, "I was playing at this crazy wedding with the marching band version of Egg Yolk. We play another party tonight, and had some time to kill in between, so we all took our instruments and decided let's go to the **Alpine** off Jackson Square for a Bloody Mary.

While we're in there the owner says, 'Hey, play for us, I'll buy a round, play a couple tunes!' So we end up drinking a few more." Geoff sighed and sipped. "Now the owner wants to hire us for another gig."

Geoff gave us some factoids about New Orleans, and his Mardi Gras suggestions, for you (drop a tip in Geoff's bucket!):

DOUBLOONS

"As far as the stuff they throw off of floats, people only more recently switched over to wanting beads. Beads used to be small, but the demand for bare breasts drove up the size of beads. Then 10 or 15 years ago people were crazy about cups, whereas people don't even pay attention now when cups are thrown. I am on a one-man crusade to bring the doubloons back: the gold coins. Doubloons used to be the big thing when I was little. I have even been given the black doubloon: it's covered in black enamel, very treasured, the rarest, carried only by the black-hooded marshal KKK-looking creepy guy on the horse that leads the parades. If you get that, you've been anointed. It means you've been chosen."

THE FULL GROWN MAN SOCIETY AND HAREM

myspace.com/fullgrownmansociety

"This is our parade krewe, dedicated to the promotion and preservation of the Full Grown Man Lifestyle. It's all people from New Orleans marching, people who I grew up with in the city, or that I've just known for a long, long time. The name comes from that famous blues song, 'I'm a Full Grown Man.' One way we express our full-grown manhood is that our parade route runs against the grain; we go down one-way streets the wrong way. We host an event called 'Chicks with Hula Hoops.' Musicians versed in traditional New Orleans Carnival music are encouraged to participate. I'm the king next year."

HIGH SCHOOL MARCHING BANDS

"I am a connoisseur of New Orleans high school marching bands. They are the heart and soul of any parade, and of New Orleans itself. And their sound is honed by the frequency of Mardi Gras, and the fact that band directors have been participating in Mardi Gras for years and years. A lot of high school marching bands are only now getting it back together since Katrina. I really support that Roots of Music Foundation [www.therootsofmusic.com] started by **Derrick Tabb** of **Rebirth Brass Band,** that buses kids out to learn marching band music when middle-school programs are cut."

LEE CIRCLE

"Watch the parades under the **Calliope** overpass at Lee Circle. There is this reverb under that bridge, and the high school marching bands always play at that moment. They do their best routine, to hear it in that monstrous reverb. Plus since it's a circle, you get the chance to see the bands twice."

PARADES

"I always go to **Endymion** in Mid-City, and the all-female **Muses** parade. I usually go to the **Krewe of Mid-City,** which has been moved to Uptown; they have unique floats made of tinfoil, tinfoil decorations, it's totally unique, plus they are *the* marching band parade. I always love playing in **Krewe du Vieux** with the **Ninth Ward Marching Band.** And this year I played in something called the 'tit Rǝx parade, which I agreed to knowing only that I had to dress up like a giant. Turned out all the floats were miniature, shoebox sized, and they rolled them down the street like regular floats."

About banjos, Geoff had this to say: "I play banjo, but not like the fauxbeaux. I play a real four-string New Orleans tenor banjo, just like my great-uncle who played with **Louis Prima**, who is also from New Orleans. New Orleans banjo playing is specific to here, it evolved out of here. The funkballs try to imitate it, but their banjos are the five-string Appalachian, for country bluegrass, which has an extra 'drone string.' The four-string New Orleans banjos don't have that extra string and aren't meant to be finger-plucked but strummed, like jazz chords."

OTHER FESTIVALS

Listed by month; includes some great festivals within driving distance of New Orleans

ALTERNATIVE MEDIA EXPO

Antigravitymagazine.com

Another project by *Antigravity* music magazine publisher **Leo McGovern**, who's known for turning small, simple grassroots ideas into real winners. His Alt Media Expo—usually held at the **Contemporary Arts Center (CAC)** just after Mardi Gras (March-ish)—features anything and everything wordy and visual. A stunning presentation of dozens of New Orleans and national comix publishers, literary concerns, makers of indie movies and websites and statement clothing, etc. And of course, in true New Orleans fashion, the Expo also features good food and booze, and both the pre- and post-Expo parties always feature bands.

CONGO SQUARE RHYTHMS FESTIVAL

Tremé, Armstrong Park,
901 N. Rampart St., 504-558-6100;
www.jazzandheritage.org/congo-square

Cuban, African, and New Orleans brass and gospel music. Also featuring the **Class Got Brass** competition for Louisiana middle and high school students. Free.

FÊTE FRANÇAISE

Uptown, Ecole Bilingue de la Nouvelle-Orléans, 821 General Pershing St., 504-896-4500;
www.fetefrancaise.com

French food, art, music, children's activities, and demonstrations. Free.

ITALIAN-AMERICAN MARCHING CLUB ST. JOSEPH DAY PARADE

French Quarter, parade starts at Canal and Chartres Streets in the French Quarter, 504-561-1006;
www.iamcnola.org

Sixteen floats, nine marching bands, and hundreds of members marching in tuxedos and giving women roses in exchange for a kiss. Parade starts at 9 p.m.

LOUISIANA CRAWFISH FESTIVAL

Chalmette, La. (nine miles east of New Orleans), 337-332-1414;
louisianacrawfishfestival.com

St. Bernard Parish, home of the Battle of New Orleans site overlooking the Mississippi River, also hosts the Crawfish Fest (est. 1975). For the uninitiated, crawfish (a.k.a. crayfish, crawdads, mudbugs) are pretty much poor man's shrimp. They take a lil' more work to peel, and the meat's small, but totally worth it—not to mention that crawfish bring people together, creating a whole other party scene during the winter festival season. Aside from your basic boiled crawfish, this fest offers crawfish bread, crawfish pasta, crawfish pies, crawfish rice, crawfish jambalaya—infinite crawfish options, all of them good as hell. You'll also enjoy big carnival rides, regional arts and crafts, crawfish racing competitions, and more bands than you've seen, total, over the last five years. Four nights' worth of "Cajun entertainment" builds up finally to the coronation of the Crawfish Queen. In 2012, they were exhibiting a taxidermied two-headed albino cobra, but we're not sure it was real.

SOUL FEST

Uptown, Audubon Zoo,
6500 Magazine St., 504-581-4629;
www.auduboninstitute.org

This event celebrates African American jazz, gospel, and R&B, with dancers, Mardi Gras Indians, soul food, and kids' activities.

ST. PATRICK'S DAY PARADE

Uptown; irishchannelno.org

The Irish Channel St. Patrick's Day Club holds its annual mass and drinking celebration every March 15, beginning at noon at St. Mary's Assumption Church (corner of Constance and Josephine Streets), followed by a huge parade with generous throws, that starts at the corner of Felicity and Magazine at 1 p.m. Parade goers are pelted with traditional Irish vegetables (cabbages, potatoes, carrots, etc.) by hundreds of Irish

men and women in formal attire, either riding atop Mardi Gras–sized floats, or walking in drunken groups, collecting kisses in exchange for flowers.

APRIL

FESTIVAL INTERNATIONAL DE LOUISIANE

Lafayette, La.; festivalinternational.com

You can do it in a day if you don't drink too much, and that's a big if. We recommend an overnight stay any time of year to get a suitable taste of this capital of Acadiana, where ample music venues and the distinctive Cajun lifestyle offer countless adventures. If you want to escape **Jazz Fest**, the last weekend in the Festival International is the free, Francophile alternative, featuring global stars like **Femi Kuti** and **Steel Pulse**. Food booths offer every type of alligator- and crawfish-based delicacy, and the music is outstanding.

FRENCH QUARTER FEST

French Quarter, along the Mississippi;
fqfi.org/frenchquarterfest

Still considered by some locals to be an "alternative" to the big festival, there's barely room to walk along the river and lines for food and drinks can get huge at French Quarter Fest. FQF lacks the cheesy national headliners of Jazz Fest, and is certainly more local (and free!); the musicians often overdo the "entertain the tourists" shtick since they're playing in the Quarter. Still, you will find some less self-conscious music here if you're in the right place at the right time.

NEW ORLEANS GIANT PUPPET FESTIVAL

*Marigny, Marigny Opera House,
725 St. Ferdinand St.,
415-385-3025, and Mudlark Public
Theatre, 1200 Port St.;
www.marignyoperahouse.org*

Puppetry in a variety of styles and sizes.
Check to make sure which shows are
for kids, and which are for adults only.

PONCHATOULA STRAWBERRY FESTIVAL

*Memorial Park, downtown
Ponchatoula, La. (about 50 miles
northwest of N.O.);
www.lastrawberryfestival.com*

This festival celebrating that sweet,
lusty berry features rides, games (egg
toss, sack race), bands, a cat judging
contest, a strawberry ball and coronation, a baking contest, talent show, and
a 10-K "Strawberry Strut" competitive
run. During almost no time does the
live Louisiana music stop. Also, there
are strawberries. Beware, though—the
daiquiris are non-alcoholic.

Isaac at the Strawberry Fest.

Jonathan Traviesa

ASIAN HERITAGE FESTIVAL

Uptown, Audubon Zoo,
6500 Magazine St., 504-581-4629;
www.auduboninstitute.org

The Asian Pacific American Society and Audubon Zoo present this celebration of Asian culture with traditional song and dance and arts and crafts from China, Japan, Thailand, Vietnam, India, Taiwan, and the Philippines.

BAYOU BOOGALOO

Mid-City, at Bayou St. John;
thebayouboogaloo.com

This laid-back, family-friendly fest was first organized as a morale-booster for the flooded Mid-City neighborhood around Bayou St John, which has recovered strikingly well. The Boogaloo takes place on the bayou's banks for two days on three stages, with a mix of marquee-name and neighborhood-favorite zydeco, funk, rock, and Latin music. In 2009, the festival went 100 percent green, with solar-powered stages, biodiesel generators, and organic snacks.

CHAZFEST

Wednesday between the two weekends of Jazz Fest; Bywater, Truck Farm Studios, 3024 St. Claude Ave., 504-944-7776; chazfestival.com

Conceived as a balm for the egos of a group of downtown musicians who weren't booked at Jazz Fest one year, Chazfest is the Bywater's companion piece to the monster fest. Named in honor of the prolific, quirky bluesman **Washboard Chaz**, Chazfest is organized by Chaz's sideman, singer and guitarist **Alex McMurray**. Held in the communal yard of the **Truck Farm** (a recording studio owned by **Dave Pirner** of **Soul Asylum**), this fest fea-

Washboard Chaz entertains the crowds at his namesake, Chaz Fest, which complements Jazz Fest.

Zack Smith

Keith "Deacon Johnson" Moore, late son of R&B singer/guitarist Deacon John, and the creator of NOizeFest.

Zack Smith

tures excellent downtown groups like the **Happy Talk Band**, brass bands, side projects like McMurray's sea-shanty outfit the **Valparaiso Men's Chorus,** and of course, Chaz. Admission is usually $25–$35 (about half the cost of actual Jazz Fest). You still have to pay for (cheaper) drinks and (great) food. But for those averse to huge crowds, and who want to socialize and drink with some of the city's best musicians rather than stare at them from afar, Chazfest may indeed be a better alternative.

CRAWFISH MAMBO

Uptown, University of New Orleans campus, 2000 Lakeshore Dr., The Cove on Founders Road, 504-280-2586; www.crawfishmambo.com

Reap the benefits of a mudbug cookoff with all-you-can-eat boiled crawfish

and live local music. The event supports professional development programs at UNO.

GREEK FESTIVAL NEW ORLEANS

Lakeview, Holy Trinity Cathedral grounds, 1200 Robert E. Lee Blvd., 504-282-0259; www.gfno.com

For over forty years this fest has showcased Greek food, music, and culture. Features children's activities plus traditional Greek dancers and music.

NOIZEFEST

last day of Jazz Fest; Bywater

NOizeFest's inventor, **Keith "Deacon Johnson" Moore,** was the son of **Deacon John**, the famous R&B singer who played guitar on almost every famous New Orleans record ever. Keith came up with NOizeFest out of anger at Jazz Fest for ignoring all the nontraditional/experimental/original music that is nonetheless part of the lifeblood of the city. After Keith was shot and killed uptown in 2005, his friends continued the fest in Michael Patrick Welch's backyard, which was big enough to accommodate simultaneous multiple performers, but comfy enough to allow for serious sonic overlap. NOizeFest's anti-"band" lineup runs the gamut from DJs to tape manipulators to an all-noise marching band to well-known acts like **Mr. Quintron**, doing everything but his usual dance-rock. Recently some classical musicians have braved the fest's noisy waters, taking it to a new level. But in true New Orleans fashion, all twelve hours of the fest are usually giddy, unpretentious fun.

JUNE

BACK TO THE BEACH

Laketown, Williams Blvd. at Lake Pontchartrain, Kenner, La., 504-836-2205; www.saveourlake.org

Two days of music by local bands, local food, drinks, arts and crafts, and a classic car show.

CREOLE TOMATO FESTIVAL

French Quarter, French Market, 1008 N. Peters St., 504-558-6100

Food booths offer creole tomato favorites like fried green tomatoes, creole-tomato bloody marys, stuffed shrimp with grilled creole tomatoes, creole tomato-cream crawfish pies, blooming onion on a bed of creole tomato,

and more. Plus cooking demonstrations, music, and dancing throughout the weekend.

NEW ORLEANS OYSTER FESTIVAL

French Quarter, Woldenberg Riverfront Park, 1 Canal St., 504-835-6410; www.neworleansoysterfestival.org

Twenty restaurants offer oyster dishes, music, an oyster shucking and eating competition, and a largest-oyster contest. Proceeds help to support the Louisiana oyster industry, plus security for the NOPD's 8th District. Free.

JULY

CAJUN FRENCH MUSIC & FOOD FESTIVAL

Burton Coliseum, 7001 Gulf Hwy., Lake Charles, La. (about 200 miles west of N.O.), 337-794-2541; www.cfmalakecharles.org

This Cajun culture festival includes Cajun dance contests, a live auction, a French mass on Sunday, and other activities.

ESSENCE MUSIC FESTIVAL

Various locations; www.essence.com/festival

The annual hypercorporate, four-day music festival features national and local acts on eight stages at the Superdome, plus black speakers and authors at the Ernest N. Morial Convention Center. Tickets range from $130.50 to $2,700.

SAN FERMIN IN NUEVA ORLEANS, AKA RUNNING OF THE BULLS

Various locations; www.nolabulls.com

The ladies of New Orleans rollerderby play the part of bulls in a traditional running of the bulls ceremony, aping those in Pamplona, Spain. The festival includes other traditional San Fermin parties and events, some free.

SATCHMO SUMMER FEST

Four days at the end of July and beginning of August; Marigny/French Quarter; fqfi.org/satchmosummerfest

A family-oriented, fat weekend of jazz music and food celebrating the life of **Louis Armstrong**. Again, the music is very traditional, but New Orleans mellows out dramatically this late in the summer, making Satchmo less crowded and less expensive than the other fests.

TALES OF THE COCKTAIL

Various locations in New Orleans, 504-948-0511; www.talesofthecocktail.com

Dozens of seminars, tasting rooms, competitions, awards, and concerts celebrating American drink culture. Admission runs from $40 to $695.

AUGUST

MID-SUMMER MARDI GRAS

Uptown, begins at Maple Leaf Bar, 8316 Oak St.

We maybe should clarify that sometimes when we say "parades," we mean events which lack observers—only participants. For more than twenty years, the **Krewe of O.A.K.** (acronym for "outrageous and kinky," they claim, but the parade also starts on Oak St.) has celebrated a faux Mardi Gras with this glorified pub crawl, six months after the actual Fat Tuesday. Floats in this "parade" are generally decorated golf carts, rolling between brass bands and a sweating, drunk, dancing crowd. The heat keeps the mandatory costumes skin-oriented.

SEPTEMBER

BOGALUSA BLUES AND HERITAGE FESTIVAL

Cassidy Park, 625 Willis Ave., Bogalusa, La. (about 70 miles north of N.O.), 985-294-3895; www.bogalusablues.com

A day of music celebrating the blues and other local music, featuring a juried art show, vendors, food, and more.

SHRIMP AND PETROLEUM FESTIVAL

Downtown historic district, Morgan City, La. (roughly 85 miles west of N.O.), 985-385-0703; shrimp-petrofest.org

Ah, what a delicious-sounding combination: shrimp and petroleum. This celebration of the products that keep the Gulf Coast economically afloat features rides, crafts, food, a "Blessing of the Fleet" ceremony, and a water parade.

NEW ORLEANS
DAIQUIRI FESTIVAL

OHNO cofounder Jeremy Thompson and Ryelene "Jazz" Jasmine share drinks at Gene's Daiquiris.

Zack Smith

August; Bywater; www.NewOrleansDaiquiriFestival.com

Started in 2011 by **OHNO Co** (OpenHouse New Orleans Company) founder **Jeremy Thompson**, the annual New Orleans Daiquiri Festival celebrates the tradition of the frozen daiquiri in New Orleans, and also serves as a fundraiser for the **Bywater Community Development Corporation**. Though lacking a permanent home, the newly established Daiquiri Festival is and always will be held in downtown New Orleans in August.

The fest features a variety of frozen "craft daiqs" made with local **Old New Orleans Rum** and other fresh ingredients. Daiquiri competitions are judged by local daiquiri shop celebrities and cocktail world personalities. Local DJs like **Matty** and **Pasta** spin "daiquiri music," meaning New Orleans jazz, R&B, soul, brass, and bounce.

Accompanying local vendors selling homemade daiquiri swag of all kinds, street food is provided by New Orleans' quickly growing food truck movement. Daiquiris are "street drinks"—icons of our open-container laws—and street drinks go best with street food. A pop-up "Open Container Museum" also features everything from a survey of souvenir cups over the last thirty years to educational diagrams describing exactly what a brain freeze is.

SOUTHERN DECADENCE

Labor Day weekend; French Quarter, Bourbon St.; southerndecadence.net

For many, many years this gay sex party was extreme enough to make Mardi Gras blush—everything, just everything, going on right out there on Bourbon Street!—until some religious group pointed out to the city that public sex was against the law, and made the taxpayers spend hundreds of thousands on security for an event at which no one had ever previously been arrested. Decadence still goes off every year, but is now much mellower, at least on its surface—one must assume that something kinky is still cooking behind all those tall French Quarter gates. Sunday is still alive with ultraflamboyant cross-dressers and leather studs, all culminating in an excellent drag parade that's fun for everyone.

SUGAR CANE FESTIVAL

New Iberia, La. (130-odd miles west of N.O.), 337-369-9323; hisugar.org

Every little city in America hosts carnivals of rides and family fun, in some random field or gravel lot. But trust Louisiana's population to push any celebration to its max. This 70-year-old free festival celebrating Louisiana's sugar growers (attendees are encouraged to "dress in farmer's attire") includes four days of giant rides and fair games, plus square-dancing presentations, a flower show, a boat parade, fireworks, a special southern mass and authentic blessing of the crop, and of course, "sugar artistry." Numerous Cajun bands will be on hand to honor whoever is crowned **King and Queen Sucrose**. In terms of your getting the most dynamic, crazy taste of authentic Louisiana, Jazz Fest could never live up to this lil' celebration.

OCTOBER

BLUES AND BBQ FESTIVAL

Lafayette Square Park, 540 St. Charles Ave., 504-558-6100; jazzandheritage.org/blues-fest

Free, two-day festival of big-name blues artists and food.

GRETNA HERITAGE FESTIVAL

Downtown Gretna, La.; www.gretnafest.com

This three-day West Bank get-down features seven stages of music and over 100 food choices plus an Italian village, German beer garden, and carnival rides.

Singer Meschiya Lake in the local movie *Flood Streets*.

Kim Welsh

NEW ORLEANS FILM FESTIVAL

neworleansfilmsociety.org

Even before the film industry exploded in Louisiana, the **New Orleans Film Festival** was an impressive, week-long event of screenings, parties, and panels. Celebrating its twenty-fifth anniversary in 2015, the festival continues to showcase more local films than ever.

Although the festival does not specifically seek out local film submissions, there is so much grassroots film activity here that many New Orleans–made features, documentaries, and shorts are getting into this highly selective festival. The organizers have even added an "I Love Louisiana Day" to celebrate this trend.

In addition to featuring some great local shorts like **Ashley Charbonnet**'s "The Price of Flowers," 2012's "I Love Louisiana Day" also premiered the homegrown, narrative feature *Flood Streets* (www.floodstreetsmovie.com). Lovingly shot on a shoestring budget, this character-driven pic follows a group of creative malcontents as they struggle to find love, money, and marijuana in the surreal streets of post-flood New Orleans. Written by long-time Bywater resident **Helen Krieger** and directed by her husband **Joseph Meissner**, who also plays one of the leads, *Flood Streets* shows off the new sounds of New Orleans music, bands like the **Zydepunks**, **Panorama Jazz Band**, **Debauche**, and **Meschiya Lake**. It also features New Orleans–adapted comedian **Harry Shearer** in two very funny cameos. A nuanced look at the city after the storm, this film has won awards at festivals across the country.

The **New Orleans Film Society**, which organizes the festival, schedules other film-related events throughout the year, including panels, special screenings, and drive-up "theaters" at abandoned parking lots across town. What better use for a flooded strip mall?

JAPAN FESTIVAL

Mid-City, New Orleans Museum of Art, One Collins C. Diboll Circle, City Park, 504-658-4100

A day full of energizing performances on the museum steps. **Kaminari Taiko** drummers and other demonstrations punctuate art-making activities and tours throughout the museum.

LOUISIANA SEAFOOD FESTIVAL

French Quarter, Woldenberg Riverfront Park, 1 Canal St.; www.louisianaseafoodfestival.com

Local chefs show off their seafood chops. Also features two stages of music, an arts-and-crafts village, and a children's pavilion.

PONDEROSA STOMP

ponderosastomp.com

Highlights the largely unsung architects of rock 'n' roll. What began as Stomp creator **Ira "Dr. Ike" Padnos**'s elaborate wedding party morphed into a wild bowling alley get-down, and then an ambitious nonprofit organization. Each year, Dr. Ike scrapes the far corners of his musical mind and his rolodex, and digs up obscure old rock, soul, and blues artists and puts them on stage.

ST. TAMMANY PARISH FAIR

St. Tammany Parish Fairgrounds, 1304 Columbia St., Covington, La.; www.sttammanyparishfair.info

Rides, a beauty pageant, animal exhibits, contests, food, a Friday parade, dance team competitions, live music, and even a rodeo. And the Besthoff Sculpture Garden.

VOODOO MUSIC EXPERIENCE

Halloween weekend; Mid-City, City Park, corner of Esplanade and Carrollton Aves.; thevoodooexperience.com

New Orleans' only festival of nationally famous alternative rock bands, the Voodoo Music Experience in City Park makes Halloween weekend in New Orleans just that much more of an event. From **TV on the Radio** to **Nine Inch Nails** to **R.E.M.** to **Kiss** to the **Bingo!** tent, which features the upper echelon of truly original New Orleans musicians. There's even a small **Preservation Hall** tent if you just gotta hear the standards. Voodoo's best quality, though, may be its location in City Park; whereas Jazz Fest puts you in direct contact with the sun for long hours with barely any shelter, much of City Park is shaded by giant oak trees, which also serve to break up the Voodoo crowd and dilute that claustrophobic festival feeling.

MIRLITON FESTIVAL

Bywater; mirlitonfestival.com

This important, well-attended Bywater neighborhood festival pays homage to a seasonal squashlike vegetable with little taste and little function. In **Markey Park**, most of the Bywater/Marigny's restaurants rise to the challenge of making something delectable out of the mirliton. The beer is cheap, and the fest is usually a great mix of traditional and fringe neighborhood bands. Mirliton Fest is a big deal to hundreds of neighbors and musicians, and yet always feels wonderfully mellow. Check website for location.

NEW ORLEANS FRINGE FESTIVAL

Various locations, mostly Marigny and Bywater; www.nofringe.org

The five-day festival of feral theater features almost one hundred groups per-

White Beach at Voodoo Fest.

Michael Patrick Welch

forming original theater of all stripes. Of course there's also a parade. Prices vary by event.

PO-BOY PRESERVATION FESTIVAL

Uptown, Oak St.; poboyfest.com

A seven-block party in celebration of the mammoth sandwich of French bread and fried seafood or roast beef. Of course you'll find many more dynamic variations on the cultural staple at this fest, which also hosts two stages of music, over sixty artists, a children's section with games, a po-boy photo booth, and panel discussions covering the po-boy's history.

THANKSGIVING AT FAIR GROUNDS RACE COURSE & SLOTS

Gentilly, 1751 Gentilly Blvd., 504-944-5515; fairgroundsracecourse.com

On many special occasions throughout the year in New Orleans, black people dress to the nines and go out in public. The older black gentlemen, especially, will kick your ass in the style department. But the one time of the year when a lot of white folks get equally gussied up for the express purpose of showing off is the opening day of horse racing at New Orleans' Fair Grounds (the site of our annual **Jazz & Heritage Festival**). The food is amazing, the drinks are strong, everything's pretty cheap (entry is free!), and every sector of New Orleans humanity is represented—friendship and holiday love hang thick in the air. Dress mad stylish, and do not forget a bad-ass hat of some sort.

TREMÉ CREOLE GUMBO FESTIVAL

Tremé, Armstrong Park, 901 N. Rampart St., 504-558-6100; www .jazzandheritage.org/treme-gumbo

Orleans brass band music is on display beside artists, with food vendors offering varying takes on gumbo.

DECEMBER

CHRISTMAS BONFIRE PARTY

Oak Alley Plantation, 3645 Hwy. 18, Vacherie, La. (about 60 miles west of N.O.), 225-265-2151; www.oakalleyplantation.com

Cajun and Creole food, an open bar, dance, and a band-led procession to the levee for bonfire lighting are all included in the $125 ticket price.

CHRISTMAS EVE BONFIRES ON THE LEVEE

Various locations around Lutcher and Gramercy, La. (about 45 miles west of N.O.); www.stjamesparish.com

Like a Christmas version of Burning Man, artists build large wooden structures on the levee, only to later set them ablaze as a sort of lighthouse for the Cajun Santa Claus, Papa Noël. Free.

DELCAMBRE BOAT PARADE

North Pier Marina, 307 Isadore St., Lafayette, La., 337-658-2422; www.delcambreboatparade.com

A parade of lighted boats is accompanied by live Christmas music. Free.

LITERARY NEW ORLEANS

From **Tennessee Williams** to **William S. Burroughs** (whose house at 509 Wagner Street was visited by **Kerouac** and company in *On the Road*; today it's inscribed with a plaque), from **William Faulkner** to **Truman Capote** to **Charles Bukowski** (whose first two books were published from an apartment on Royal Street), **Anne Rice, Walker Percy, Andrei Codrescu,** and poor old **John Kennedy Toole** (whose novel *A Confederacy of Dunces* was published and won a Pulitzer after Toole killed himself), New Orleans has always been a writer's mecca. If you're into books, read up:

LITERARY EVENTS

ALTERNATIVE MEDIA EXPO

March-ish?; Antigravitymagazine.com

Independently published books are just one part of this festival put on by *Antigravity* music magazine publisher **Leo McGovern**. An amalgam of indy publishers, filmmakers, webmasters, and more, the AME often occurs after Mardi Gras but has had trouble settling down into one venue and time, so check the website for specific details.

LOUISIANA BOOK FESTIVAL

November, Baton Rouge, 225-219-9503; louisianabookfestival.org

This free celebration of readers, writers, and their books features independent publishers, author presentations, readings, book signings, and more. It all takes place at the State Library of Louisiana, Louisiana State Capitol, Capitol Park Museum, and in tents on neighboring streets. Worth the short drive outside the city.

NEW ORLEANS BOOK FAIR

around Halloween; neworleansbookfair.com

One more reason to visit New Orleans as October turns into November is our great book fair, featuring big names in independent publishing, anarchist literature, zine culture, printing, plus all types of singular, handmade pieces of art that happen to be books. Most good-size cities have a book fair, but New Orleans' becomes a bit of a party, which can even get a little wild—the official annual after-party was held one year in an abandoned YMCA. As the DJ spun great rap, everyone danced and played basketball, got wasted, and rode their bikes around the gym. Somehow the cops never came. And everyone walked away with a lot of good books.

SAINTS AND SINNERS

mid-May; sasfest.org

This Marigny literary festival features the top names in the gay and lesbian publishing/literary world. Saints and Sinners is curated in part by **Otis Fennell,** owner of **Faubourg Marigny Art and Books**, who also manages the literary angle of New Orleans' **Pride Festival** (June; www.gayprideneworleans.com) in Washington Square Park on Frenchmen Street.

TENNESSEE WILLIAMS/ NEW ORLEANS LITERARY FESTIVAL

March, various locations; tennesseewilliams.net

For more than a quarter century, the city's largest literary festival has welcomed writers, playwrights, poets, and scholars for a four-day, late-March celebration of **Blanche DuBois**'s creator and the various wordsmiths who've made New Orleans home. A perpetual complaint from younger locals about the white-haired crowds and stuffy programming began to give way in recent years as festival organizers focused more on contemporary literature and diversity. As a result, TWF can be fun if you like to mix your reading with your booze. Several healthy parties and the generosity of liquor sponsors offer occasion to rub elbows with nationally known writers, French Quarter septuagenarians, and canny freeloaders. The Sunday afternoon **Stella shouting contest** on Jackson Square is world famous and worth experiencing, but be sure to hit **The People Say Project**'s (thepeoplesayproject.org) annual late-night party, where young talent explores the weirder side of Tennessee and his adopted hometown.

N.O. MOMENT

NEIGHBORHOOD STORY PROJECT

The Best New Orleans Souvenirs You Could Possibly Buy

Abram Himelstein and **Rachel Breunlin** are two young teachers who believe that New Orleans' story must be told by the people who live it. With that in mind, Abram and Rachel began the **Neighborhood Story Project**, which in 2008 opened its own office and writing workshop area in the Seventh Ward (corner of Miro and Lapeyrouse Streets). Anyone is welcome to pop in, tour the office, get free writing advice and guidance, and maybe even a book advance if you're local. NSP has published many well-received books borne from the hearts and brains of regular New Orleanians—

Neighbors gather for a block party outside the Neighborhood Story Project center, to celebrate the release of a new book by someone in the community.

Rachel Breunlin

both adults and children—most documenting the nuanced struggles and celebrations of various neighborhoods, **Mardi Gras Indian** tribes, social aid and pleasure clubs, and other New Orleans phenomena of which the outer world knows little.

The NSP's books are among the best independent, grass-roots sellers in the city. The 200-page, full-color tome *The House of Dance and Feathers: A Museum,* by Ronald Lewis, is based on the museum Lewis built in his back yard in the Lower Ninth Ward, on Tupelo Street (also see "Art Galleries"). *House of Dance and Feathers* details the world of Mardi Gras Indians: how it works, who sews patches, what those relationships are like. Lewis then takes readers through the social aid and pleasure club world and that of the **Northside Skull and Bones Gang**, and in the process maps the history of the Lower Ninth Ward.

If you can't make it down to the NSP's offices, all their books are sold at most New Orleans bookstores. You couldn't possibly buy a better souvenir of your trip to the city.

Definition of Bounce: Between Ups and Downs in New Orleans, by Alison Fensterstock and Lucky Johnson

Garret County Press

A coffee-table picture book on the beginnings of New Orleans' bounce rap craze, featuring narrative by charismatic rapper **10th Ward Buck**, as told to *Times-Picayune* music writer **Alison Fensterstock**.

Ernie K-Doe: The R&B Emperor of New Orleans, by Ben Sandmel

The Historic New Orleans Collection

The folklorist, drummer, and producer **Ben Sandmel**, author of *Zydeco!*, tells the world the dynamic story of New Orleans R&B underdog Ernie "Mother-in-Law" K-Doe. Wild archival material reflects the one-of-a-kind subject.

The Gravy: In the Kitchen with New Orleans Musicians, by Elsa Hahne

independent

A compilation of photographer **Elsa Hahne**'s long-running *OffBeat* magazine columns, which gleans recipes from local musicians of all stripes. Features an introduction by **Dr. John**.

Groove Interrupted: Loss, Renewal, and the Music of New Orleans, by Keith Spera

St. Martin's Press

Times-Picayune's head music writer **Keith Spera** chronicles **Aaron Neville** returning to New Orleans for the first time after Hurricane Katrina to bury his wife; **Fats Domino** promoting a post-Katrina tribute CD; **Alex Chilton** living forsaken in a cottage in Tremé; rapper **Mystikal** rekindling his career after six years in prison—and these are just the iceberg's tip.

The Kingdom of Zydeco, by Michael Tisserand

Arcade Publishing

Former *Gambit Weekly* editor Tisserand studied the Lomax archives in DC, worked with a genealogist, and lived in Lafayette for a year hunting down and spending time with zydeco legends at church dances and trail rides.

New Atlantis: Musicians Battle for the Survival of New Orleans, by John Swenson

Oxford University Press

In the wreckage of Katrina, widely published music journalist and author Swenson follows the paths of **Dr. John, the Neville Brothers, "Trombone Shorty," Big Chief Monk Boudreaux,** and others, touching intimately on New Orleans music genres from jazz, R&B, brass band, rock, and hip-hop.

The World That Made New Orleans: From Spanish Silver to Congo Square, by Ned Sublette

Chicago Review Press

Musician, historian, and mad scribbler **Ned Sublette** gives a dense and entertaining lesson in how New Orleans slavery culture begat all black music in America. The book is a must-read for all musicians and lovers of New Orleans music.

LOCAL PUBLISHERS

Looking for local poetry? We're fortunate to have several small presses with integrity, good taste, and smart editors.

GARRET COUNTY PRESS

www.gcpress.com

Run by G. K. Darby of UNO Press, GC Press publishes all things high quality, from the poetry of **Andrei Codrescu** to reprints of travel books by world-famous hobo author **Leon Ray Livingston,** with an emphasis on youngish New Orleans authors.

LAVENDER INK

lavenderink.org/content/

Run by literary OG Bill Lavender, this press publishes veterans and upcoming voices on the local scene, including poetry anthologies, fiction, and a "Yat Dictionary." Bill's network stretches from Scotland to Mexico, and the catalog is refreshingly experimental. Highly suggested: poet **Thaddeus Conti.**

Poet and publisher Bill Lavender.

Louis Maistros

TREMBLING PILLOW PRESS

tremblingpillowpress.com

Publisher of **Bernadette Mayer**, **John Sinclair**, **Bill Lavender**, and other important writers, Trembling Pillow was founded in 1997 by poet **Dave Brinks**.

Current publisher **Megan Burns** continues to produce chapbooks, broadsides, postcards, and the *Solid Quarter Poetry Magazine,* as well as host readings at BJs (Bywater, 4301 Burgundy St.) and other venues.

CHARLES BUKOWSKI

If not for New Orleans, Charles Bukowski may have amounted to nothing. This city played just as big a part in his career as it did **Faulkner**'s. In the documentary *The Outsiders of New Orleans: Loujon Press,* **Louise "Gypsy Lou" Webb**—now well into her nineties and currently living in the burbs of Slidell—tells how she and her husband **Jon Webb** published the avant-garde literary magazine *The Outsider* from a small apartment on the corner of Royal Street and Ursuline Avenue in the French Quarter in the early 1960s. *The Outsider* and Bukowski's first two books by **Loujon Press** (loujonpress.com)—*It Catches My Heart in Its Hands* and *Crucifix in a Deathhand*—are now rare collectibles, along with two other handcrafted books by **Henry Miller**. Bukowski cavorted around the Quarter drinking and fighting with strangers while the Webbs labored over his work in their apartment. At some point he etched "Hank was here" in the cement outside of the **R Bar** (1431 Royal St.). For the longest time, one of the guest rooms he rented upstairs from the R Bar was called the Bukowski Suite. Somehow that wasn't a big selling point, and the name was recently changed.

Graziano Origa/Creative Commons

LITERARY NEW ORLEANS

BOOKSTORES

ARCADIAN BOOKS & PRINTS

CBD, 714 Orleans Ave., 504-523-4138

Known for its pulley system that keeps a large floor fan strapped above one of the aisles, this small bookshop is crammed with an incredible selection of used books in all genres, with a focus on local history, and books in French.

BECKHAM'S BOOKS

French Quarter, 228 Decatur St., 504-522-9875

Containing an estimated 50–60,000 books, Beckham's looks like a used bookstore in a movie about New Orleans. A rolling ladder helps you access upper shelves, where you might find a book of spells—though you're more likely to find classic literature. Near the front door is always a good selection of new local novels, cookbooks, and whatnot, and the upstairs is loaded with classical music LPs for sale, and more books. Truly a gorgeous place.

BETH'S BOOKS

Marigny, 2700 Chartres St., 504-947-4477

Beth's Books shares a building with **Sound Café** and specializes in high-quality used books, plus tons of titles about New Orleans and by local authors.

BLUE CYPRESS

Uptown, 8126 Oak St., 504-352-0096; bluecypressbooks.blogspot.com

Blue Cypress buys, trades, and sells classic and contemporary fiction and nonfiction, poetry, art and photography books, science fiction, mysteries, and antiquarian and collectible books. Its claim to fame is the largest local secondhand collection of children's and young adult books. Check the website for a great schedule of author readings and other events.

CRESCENT CITY BOOKS

French Quarter, 230 Chartres St., 800-524-4997; crescentcitybooks.com

This two-story treasure trove of local, rare, used, and popular books—complete with couches upon which to read them—also doubles as a poetry hive, with frequent in-store readings. Shop owner **Joe Phillips** also curates the poetry imprint **Black Widow Press** and hosts many book releases.

CRESCENT CITY COMICS

Uptown, 4916 Freret St., 504-891-3796

Crescent City Comics reopened at an Uptown location in the fall of 2009 after being knocked out of business by Katrina but has returned with a vast selection of independent and underground comics and graphic novels, your favorite superheroes, and a friendly staff. The shop also doubles as the office for the local music magazine, *Antigravity*.

DAUPHINE STREET BOOKS

French Quarter, 410 Dauphine St., 504-529-2333

Cluttered but deceptively well organized used bookstore, complete with cat.

DEVILLE BOOKS

CBD, 736 Union St., 504-569-1016

More a bookstore for tourists, this is where you can buy your tomes on voodoo and cemetery tours, plus books on traditional New Orleans music including a pictorial history of Jazz Fest, *The Down Home Guide to the Blues,* and *Jazz for Dummies.*

FAULKNER HOUSE BOOKS

French Quarter, 624 Pirate's Alley, 504-524-2940; faulknerhouse.net

Funny to call this the most high profile bookstore in the city, since it is nonetheless small, quaint, and quiet. But located in the French Quarter's heart, Faulkner House is the force behind the **Pirate's Alley Faulkner Society,** the nationally recognized nonprofit arts organization that hosts **Words & Music: A Literary Feast in New Orleans,** as well as the **William Wisdom Creative Writing Competition,** among other organizations and contests. It even has its own literary Mardi Gras krewe, the Krewe of Libris.

GARDEN DISTRICT BOOKS

Uptown, 2727 Prytania Street, 504-895-2266

Garden District is in a building converted from a nineteenth-century skating rink. The staff actually read the books they sell, which can't be said of the nearby chain bookstore.

IRON RAIL BOOK COLLECTIVE

French Quarter, 503 Barracks St., 504-383-3284; ironrail.org

Collective-run, nonprofit, anarchist bookstore, record store, and lending library. Too small for shows, but a possible space for organizational meetings or reading/speaking engagements.

KITCHEN WITCH

French Quarter, 631 Toulouse St., 504-528-8382; kwcookbooks.com

Though specializing in rare, out-of-print, and pre-owned cookbooks, this odd and charming little store also seems to contain at least one copy of each book ever published about New Orleans.

LIBRAIRIE BOOK SHOP

French Quarter, 823 Chartres St., 504-525-4837

Pick from a good selection of new and used New Orleans–centric books, then walk around the corner and sit and read on Jackson Square or on the river. This place is owned by the same awesome guys who own the incredible **Beckham's Books** on Decatur.

MAPLE STREET BOOKS

Uptown: 7523 Maple St., 504-866-4916; Marigny, 2372 St. Claude Ave., 504-304-7115; Bayou St John, 3141 Ponce de Leon St., 504-309-9815

One of New Orleans' most famous, and tiniest, bastions of liberal thought for over thirty years. Serious **Walker Percy** fans take note: Maple Leaf had an ongoing relationship with the author, who did many readings there until his death.

FAUBOURG MARIGNY ART AND BOOKS OWNER, OTIS FENNELL

Zack Smith

The gay and straight bookstore **Faubourg Marigny Art and Books** (FAB) first opened in 1977. When in 2003 the original owner decided to call it a day, **Otis Fennell** bought the store, simply to save a cultural institution. "Now that **Oscar Wilde**'s in Greenwich Village has closed," Otis says, "FAB might be the only bookstore of its type in the States. You'll go all over the country and not find anything like this."

Though thoroughly gay-seeming from the outside, FAB carries one of the city's best selections of both straight and gay New Orleans-bred literature, alongside a nice selection of new national releases and worn classics. Otis also hosts readings by nationally famous, mostly gay authors, almost weekly. Regardless of sexual orientation, you'll want to stop in and talk to Otis, who has lived in (and actively participated in) New Orleans for fifty years. Especially since buying FAB, Otis has become the don of Frenchmen Street, standing beside the rainbow Napoleon statue outside his shop on the corner of Chartres every single day from noon to midnight. "I'm open late because the street is a late-night spot," he smiles, watching the crowds pass.

Otis has added much more local art to the store; under his reign, FAB has become essentially the only de facto art gallery on Frenchmen. "I also represent Frenchmen's musicians by selling their music in my store," says Otis. "Mainly the classic CDs and albums. I have a 30-year-old **Dr. John** LP, but I also have bands like **Why Are We Building Such a Big Ship?**—who, incidentally, got their start on the corner across the street. That corner continues to attract music all day and night."

FAB becomes more and more important as Frenchmen becomes more like the French Quarter; if Otis were to give up for some reason, Starbucks would surely pay stacks for such prime real estate. But for now, "FAB is the cultural anchor of Frenchmen Street," Otis brags. "My goal is to make the bookstore responsive to this street and the people who live in this neighborhood. So that even if people are only coming to New Orleans to drink and eat and shop and hear music, at least they're doing it in a real New Orleans neighborhood."

When asked—not only as a gay man but as a longtime New Orleans resident—to outline his idea of the perfect visit to the city, Otis replied, "I would start the day off early at **Croissant d'Or** coffee shop on Ursuline in the Quarter, the most authentic French coffee shop in the country—then head immediately back to Frenchmen Street! Stopping along the way, of course, for some alternative furniture shopping on lower Decatur Street, which has amazing antique shops and second-hand stores. I'd stroll up and down Frenchmen, then maybe order food from **Verte Mart** (1201 Royal St., 504-525-4767): a major 24-hour French Quarter deli with excellent delivery—their 24-hour liquor delivery has killed more than a few people. Then I'd maybe head into the Bywater to go for a dip at the **Country Club** on Louisa Street if it's the weekend; weekends are the best times to visit the oldest clothing-optional pool in the South. Then at night I would just stay on Frenchmen St. hopping from club to club hearing who knows how many live bands."

Otis also recommends visiting near Halloween for the giant **New Orleans Book Fair**, featuring all the biggest names in independent publishing. Otis himself helps curate the **Saints and Sinners** literary festival (www.sasfest.org) in mid-May, featuring the top names in the gay and lesbian publishing/literary world, as well as the literary aspects of the **Pride Festival** (www.gayprideneworleans.com) in June, in Washington Square Park on Frenchmen Street.

McKEOWN'S BOOKS AND DIFFICULT MUSIC

Uptown, 4737 Tchoupitoulas St.,
504-895-1954; mckeownsbooks.com

A wide selection of used books from novels to interesting math texts, plus local releases both literary and musical. McKeown's also hosts mostly acoustic concerts by New Orleans' more scholarly abstract/noise musicians. Noon to 8 p.m. daily.

MORE FUN COMICS

Uptown, 8200 Oak St., 504-865-1800

The first comic shop to open on the entire Gulf Coast, run by **D. C. Harbold**, who leads the musical ventures **Dr. A-Go-Go** and **Clockwork Elvis** (see "Bands").

OCTAVIA BOOKS

Uptown, 513 Octavia St. (corner of Laurel), 504-899-READ;
octaviabooks.com

As eclectic and "local" as anything in the French Quarter, but also a tad smarter and classier than your local chain bookstore. The staff works tirelessly to keep up with local titles and small but amazing titles from national indie presses. At great readings featuring well-known and local authors, Octavia never forgets the wine and cheese. The shop is a wee bit tricky to find in what at first seems like too residential an area, but it's so worth the effort.

Along with being a top-notch used bookstore, McKeown's also hosts small concerts of experimental and avant-garde music, tending toward the scholarly.

Jonathan Traviesa

LITERARY NEW ORLEANS

ART GALLERIES

New Orleans' visual art scene may have long played second fiddle, recognition-wise, to attractions like music and food—but the same playful, liberated, indulgent attitudes that created the conditions for those pleasures have also encouraged a vibrant arts community. The city's art can sometimes be too self-referential, pandering to touristy notions of "outsider art." But with a push from international art biennial **Prospect 1**, which called New Orleans home in 2008, the city's underground art scene has come out fighting. The tons of new high-quality, big-personality galleries in Bywater/Marigny call themselves the **St. Claude Arts District** (scadnola.com), and provide a much welcome complement to the already existing Julia Street galleries in the CBD, which are nice, but maybe a 'lil too "professional." Between the two districts, though, New Orleans can now proudly brag on its art scene.

ST. CLAUDE ARTS DISTRICT (SCAD)

ANTENNAE

Bywater, 3718 St. Claude Ave.; press-street.com/antenna

Via its 501c3 literary and visual arts umbrella Press Street, Antennae produces an array of risk-taking solo and group exhibitions, special events, educational programming, and artist talks. Press Street also hosts the 24-hour arts education extravaganza **Draw-a-Thon** (each December); **Room 220**, a blog dedicated to the literary life of New Orleans; free public film screenings; and the publication of books focusing on the relationship between the visual and literary arts.

BARRISTER'S GALLERY

Bywater, 2331 St. Claude Ave., 504-525-2767/504-710-4506; barristersgallery.com

Barrister's maintains a permanent collection of strange folk, outsider, and ethnographic art from Africa, Haiti, and Asia. The gallery also brings in a monthly featured contemporary exhibit in keeping with its focus on the eclectic, unorthodox, and freaky.

The Front art gallery is as close as the St. Claude Arts District comes to "professional."

Jonathan Traviesa

COMMUNITY PRINTSHOP

Bywater, 1201 Mazant St.; nolacommunityprintshop.wordpress .com

This print-making collective provides public access to affordable equipment, training, and services. Designed to help independent artists and entrepreneurs grow their business through screenprinting, the Community Printshop also provides adult education, youth education, and outreach. It also has public art shows of print work by local artists. Open Tuesday and Thursday evenings, 6 to 10 p.m.

THE FRONT

Bywater, 4100 St. Claude Ave.; nolafront.org

This talented collective gallery is spearheaded by **Kyle Bravo**, who also runs **Hot Iron Press**, a printing company specializing in gorgeously original chapbooks. The modern-leaning art can certainly get wacky, but The Front is the most meticulous high-quality gallery in the SCAD. Open noon to 5 p.m. Saturday and Sunday.

GOOD CHILDREN GALLERY

Bywater, 4037 St. Claude Ave., 504-975-1557; goodchildrengallery .com

This more laidback space features high art with personality, and often a sense of humor. The Good Children collective includes the duo **Generic Art Solutions (GAS)**, who continually enact a performance piece called "Art Cops," where they roam the more highfalutin' local art world arenas in cop uniforms, handing out tickets for bad art and other offenses. Saturday and Sunday, 12 to 5 p.m., and special nighttimes.

HOMESPACE

Marigny/St. Roch, 1128 St. Roch Ave., 917-584-9867

A casual space intermittently open for local art shows and other community gatherings (i.e. drinking events). Expect everything from photography and paintings to original clothing and sculpted soaps. Call for hours or a private tour.

RUSTY PELICAN ART

Bywater, 4031 St. Claude Ave., 504-218-5727; rustypelicanart.com

Out of their big, beautiful funky St. Claude home next to Good Children Gallery, the artists **Travis** and **Lexi Linde Wolf** fix motorcycles and other vehicles, and then make giant birds and other sculptures out of the leftover parts. A pretty interesting, fun little place.

SECOND STORY GALLERY CO-OP AT THE NEW ORLEANS HEALING CENTER

Marigny, 2372 St. Claude Ave., 504-710-4506; neworleanshealing center.org

This collective of roughly a dozen artists hosts rotating local and national exhibits in the New Orleans Healing Center.

SIDEARM GALLERY

Marigny/St. Roch, 1122 St. Roch Ave., 504-218-8379; sidearmgallery.org

This community-based, not-for-profit collective hosts avant-garde performance art, theater, dance, fashion shows, and film as well as visual art on the Marigny end of the St. Claude Avenue Arts District (which means if you're

gallery-hopping on the other end of the avenue, where art spaces are more densely distributed, you'll need a bike or car to get here). Opened in 2003, it was one of the earliest art spaces to develop along the now-vibrant St. Claude strip.

STAPLE GOODS

St. Roch, 1340 St. Roch Ave., 504-908-7331

Located in a former corner grocery in the St. Roch neighborhood, Staple Goods is an artist collective dedicated to innovative programming of contemporary visual art by its members and invited guests from the United States and abroad. Open weekends noon to 5 p.m.

UNO GALLERY

Lakefront, 2429 St. Claude Ave., 504-280-6493/6401

An exhibition space dedicated to showing the work of University of New Orleans MFA candidates and faculty as well as exhibitions in conjunction with district and community events. Open Fridays, Saturdays, and Sundays from 12:00 p.m. to 5:00 p.m. and by appointment.

OTHER NEIGHBORHOOD ART

BACKSTREET CULTURAL MUSEUM

Tremé, 1116 Henriette Delille St., 504-522-4806; backstreetmuseum.org

Located in New Orleans' Seventh Ward (just a hop from the Quarter, though you may not want to go on foot), the Backstreet Cultural Museum is the genuine article. The museum's holdings, curated by "self-motivated historian" **Sylvester Francis**, are an overflowing repository of artifacts documenting New Orleans' amazing African American urban cultural traditions. Items from the museum are shown each year on the grounds of **Jazz Fest**, but it's better to dig them in their home, in the historic Tremé. It's a unique window into the venerable worlds of Mardi Gras Indians, social aid and pleasure clubs, traditional jazz funerals, and Carnival groups like the **Northside Skull and Bones Gang** and the **Baby Dolls**. On Mardi Gras day, it's a good place to spot some downtown Mardi Gras Indians out showing off the pretty.

THE BIG TOP

Uptown, 1638 Clio St.,
504-569-2700; 3rcp.com

The Big Top is a multipurpose gallery space, operated by the **Three Ring Circus** arts collective, just over the border in what locals refer to as vaguely as Uptown—upriver of the business district in a part of town where not much goes on after dark except at the **Circle Bar**. Still, the Big Top is a worthwhile spot to see quirky local art, theater, and bands in a nonsmoking venue (they also do yoga classes and, often, a Friday-afternoon music "camp" for kids, with cocktails for grownups), and during Mardi Gras season, its location just off the St. Charles Avenue parade route makes it a hopping home base for marathon bead-catching.

DR. BOB'S ART GALLERY

Bywater, 3027 Chartres St.;
drbobart.net

If, during the course of your visit to New Orleans, you do something like eat in a restaurant, drink in a bar, or shop in a store, the odds are you'll see a quaint, hand-painted sign with a bottle-cap frame that says "Be Nice or Leave." These are the work of Dr. Bob, a local character and self-styled folk artist whose Ninth Ward warehouse is almost always open to the public. Visit as much for his personality as for the color-splashed, rough-hewn art.

HOUSE OF DANCE AND FEATHERS

Lower Ninth Ward, 1317 Tupelo St.,
504-957-2678;
houseofdanceandfeathers.org

The beautifully named House of Dance and Feathers is a tribute to New Orleans' urban cultural groups, specifically Mardi Gras Indians and social aid and pleasure clubs, and the social history of the Lower Ninth Ward. The museum was started as a personal archive (and barbershop) in a backyard shed. Curated by **Ronald Lewis**, a former streetcar repairman and union rep, the collection was completely rebuilt after Hurricane Katrina and now does double duty as a meeting spot for community organizers working to rebuild the neighborhood. In 2009, Lewis and the excellent documentary/education group the **Neighborhood Story Project** (see "Literary New Orleans") published a full photo catalog and history of the museum. Call for an appointment.

PEARL GALLERY

Uptown, 4421 Magazine St.,
504-322-2297

Not to be confused with the bizarre
Ninth Ward speakeasy of the same
name, Uptown's Pearl is a recent addition to the Magazine Street corridor.
Its latest show, at press time, featured
the lowbrow rock 'n' roll poster-style
work of local artist **Stevie Williams**.

POETS GALLERY

Uptown, 3113 Magazine St.,
504-899-4100

This framing shop shows local artists
with a decidedly goth bent, like **Hazard
County Girls** front-gal **Christy Kane**—
who makes creepy, delicate Victorian-
looking dolls—and **Chris Slave**, whose
canvases depicting New Orleans
scenes are awash in rich, jewel-like
swirls of deep, dark color.

MUSEUMS

OGDEN MUSEUM OF SOUTHERN ART

CBD/Warehouse District,
925 Camp St., 504-539-9600;
ogdenmuseum.org

The Ogden has a great collection of
contemporary and classically important pieces from below the Mason-
Dixon. The museum also hosts **Ogden
after Hours** ever Thursday from 6 to
8 p.m., a popular concert series with
the after-work, white-wine-in-plastic-
cups crowd. Southern musicians play
two short sets broken up by a twenty-
minute interview conducted by a local
music writer. Once a month, the **Pon-
derosa Stomp** (see "Other Festivals")
sponsors the event, so there's a one-in-
four chance you'll see a ninety-year-old
blues or soul legend playing the museum lobby and sharing some amazing

Ogden after Hours, as seen from the museum's third floor.

Jonathan Traviesa

life stories. The **New Orleans Museum of Art** (NOMA) (Esplanade Ave. at City Park, 504-658-4100; noma.org) also holds its own against any national museum, and is in a nice park. And the **Contemporary Arts Center** (CAC) (900 Camp St., 504-528-3805; cacno.org) hosts a cool, eclectic year-round program of films, music, and other events amid their fine permanent collection.

N.O. MOMENT

JULIA STREET

Jonathan Ferrara on Julia Street.

Jonathan Traviesa

Some locals feel Julia Street's art is too safe, or at best too professional, especially compared to the ragtag St. Claude Arts District downtown. The free booze that once flowed down Julia during its annual **White Linen Night** (first Saturday in August) and other events has been stemmed to a slow trickle by the line you now stand in to buy drink tickets. Many feel the good, raw art (and the free booze) are downtown in the **St. Claude Arts District (SCAD).**

A fan of more contemporary, cutting-edge work and SCAD, gallery owner **Jonathan Ferrara** sees the bright side of Julia Street, where he moved his long-running gallery in 2007. "Julia Street has really turned around in the last ten years," Ferrara says. "When I moved to the Warehouse District in 2000, Julia was a lot of designer-esque stuff. And with my moving here and spicing things up, shaking things up, the market has definitely changed to a more contemporary, less designer, more artistic-driven emphasis, which is a good thing. Before it was boring. Now it's much more exciting. It's not as exciting as St. Claude," he adds. "The edgier stuff is not gonna take place on Julia Street, but the work here is overall better, presented better."

Ferrara took us on a tour of Julia Street and attempted to objectively describe each gallery:

LE MIEUX

332 Julia St., 504-522-5988; lemieuxgalleries.com

Started over twenty years ago by **Denise Berthiaume**, a local who does great things, focuses on a lot of colorful work, landscapes, still lifes, a lot of craft-based works as well. Very good local content.

SOREN CHRISTENSEN GALLERY

400 Julia St., 504-569-9501; sorengallery.com

Specializes in local artists. Mainly sells work to designers and stuff that will go over your couch. A lot of animals and things like that.

ARTHUR ROGER GALLERY

432 Julia St., 504-522-1999; arthurrogergallery.com

He is the grand-daddy, the old standard bearer, a mixture of older and younger artists, some exciting, some not so exciting, very much engages with the designer world. He also has his project space at 434 Julia Street, where he showcases younger artists.

BLAKE BOYD SATELLITE

440 Julia St., 504-581-2440; www.boydsatellitegallery.com

Not sure what he's doing here, no one is really sure. His first show was called "Meglomania" and it was all images of him, so that tells you how that starts. If you look at the letters on the building it says "Boyd Satellite" and the initials on the door are "B.S." Something might be up with that. He likes to operate in the shocking end of things.

A band plays for revelers at one of Julia Street's many big art events.

CALLAN CONTEMPORARY

518 Julia St., 504-525-0516; callancontemporary.com

Formerly Bienvenue, this one's run by **Boris Slava** and **Steve Callan**, who also have a gallery in the Quarter, both specializing in works that are ethereal and vary from sculpture to painting and everything in between. They have a very clean and precise aesthetic, stuff you can hang in your house as well, and fit into the aesthetic you're looking for.

ARIODANTE CONTEMPORARY CRAFT GALLERY

535 Julia St., 504-524-3233; ariodantegallery.com

Contemporary crafts, a lot of great glass, and jewelry, not necessarily the fine art end of things.

JEAN BRAGG GALLERY

600 Julia St., 504-895-7375; jeanbragg.com

The spaces on this end of the street are different because they're older buildings, so smaller spaces, a little more artist-driven. It's not an open, N.Y.-style antiseptic cube, instead segmented like an old French Quarter house with rooms a little smaller, so the works are more intimate in nature. Jean's been here at least around fifteen years on this corner doing a lot of Newcomb pottery, and landscapes and figurative works, kind of classical in nature.

ART GALLERIES

THE FOUNDATION GALLERY

608 Julia St., 504-568-0955

I'm still learning about this new entrant into the Julia Street scene, but it looks pretty cool. Somewhat of a clean aesthetic.

MALLORY PAGE

614 Julia St., 504-866-4287

Also new in 2012, they have solo artist shows.

STEVE MARTIN FINE ART

624 Julia St., 504-566-1390; stevemartinfineart.com

His gallery is mostly upstairs, where he shows his own work more than other artists, though he does incorporate others. A lot of bright colored works, sculptures. He's been on Julia Street for easily ten years and had a gallery in Miami for a while after Katrina.

GEORGE SCHMIDT

626 Julia St., 504-592-0206; georgeschmidt.com

Schmidt's the quintessential artist-in-residence painter, jack-of-all-trades, renaissance man. He is one to speak his mind continually. He's "The Sheik of Julia Street." And he will be the one to tell you not to build or change anything on Julia Street.

N.O. MOMENT

THE GREY GHOST: ANTI-ART

The Grey Ghost is haunting my hood
But I don't think his graffiti's very good.
"The Grey Ghost," by Miss Pussycat and Quintron

A plethora of "street art," much of it not very ambitious, can be found in and around New Orleans. The famous muralist Banksy even came down during one of our hurricane evacuations and left some presents for us upon our return (look for the girl holding the umbrella just outside the Quarter, where Rampart St. meets St. Claude). But in recent years, the sheer amount of graffiti has doubled in both amount and ambition, thanks to one of the city's more peculiar "artists." **Fred "Grey Ghost" Radtke** gets his name from the dull, industrial color of paint he uses to roll over the work of every other graffiti artist in the city. And it's not just errant art he despises; Radtke slathers grey over lost dog fliers, heavily stickered stop signs, and in more than a few instances, commissioned artwork on private property. Our professional opinion? Dude's nuts. You'd think art killed his mama. But an overwhelmed and overburdened city government praised his vigilante efforts—which he masks with a nonprofit organization called "Operation Clean Sweep"—and in turn gave Radtke a huge sense of entitlement. But rather than quiet his rivals, Radtke's broad canvases of grey have ironically encouraged and inspired more graffiti than ever, especially in the postapocalyptic period after Katrina. Over the past several years, this back-and-forth has turned into a culture/art/street war and a fascinating visual conversation, violent at times (a claim both sides have made), but mostly entertaining. One of Banksy's aforementioned evacuation works depicted old sour-faced Radtke in a rocking chair, waving a tiny American flag, until Radtke of course greyed it out. You'll probably even see Radtke's face stenciled over some of his own work by a wry artistic responder, with a word balloon begging to be filled.

THEATER AND DANCE

With all the actual drama around the city, of course New Orleans would also possess a thriving theater scene. We've always been famous for our plays, and our dancing (in whatever odd form it takes). Here, however, burlesque is taken as seriously as Shakespeare. As with all other events in New Orleans, the dance scene strives to, above all, entertain; almost every entertainer in the city, no matter how self-serious, puts the crowd's pleasure on par with his/her own. Meaning, even the most "arty" or "postmodern" dance or theater production here will likely be energetic, smart, and fun.

N.O. MOMENT

NEW ORLEANS' BURLESQUE TRADITION LIVES ON

Fifty or sixty years ago, Bourbon was populated with swankier nightclubs where well-dressed couples hit the town to hear music and watch burlesque dancers such as **Blaze Starr**, **Lilly Christine the Cat Girl**, **Tajmah, the Jewel of the Orient,** and exotic, green-haired **Evangeline the Oyster Girl**. New Orleans' renaissance burlesque scene was nurtured in the late '90s in the club at 615 Toulouse Street (once the **Shim Sham**, now **One Eyed Jacks**). Today, several revivalist troupes exist in New Orleans and perform fairly frequently, including **Reverend Spooky & Her Billion Dollar Baby Dolls** (www.myspace.com/billiondollarbabydolls) and **Bustout! Burlesque** (bustoutburlesque.com). **Rick Delaup** also hosts his own burlesque festival: check his site for future dates (www.neworleansburlesquefest.com).

And yet there is no one in town like the mighty **Fleur de Tease** (fleurdetease.com). A ballet dancer before moving to New Orleans in 2001, Fleur de Tease's leader **Trixie Minx** didn't realize she wanted to dance burlesque until she evacuated for Hurricane Katrina and began to fear she might never get the chance. "I remember in my big heavy evacuation backpack," says Trixie, "I had no real change of underwear or clothes, just my pictures and journals and a pair of pasties that I was given, to learn how to twirl with." When finally allowed back into her city, Trixie founded Fleur de Tease burlesque variety show, which rocks one Sunday night a month at One Eyed Jacks. "Our themes are well-rounded," Trixie explains. "We are more of a vaudeville variety show, meaning not just girls getting naked but equal amounts fire, aerial acrobatics, hula-hooping, music, and magic. And all of our girls are power players in the New Orleans burlesque community. Almost all of them have their own solo shows." Fleur de Tease member **Roxie LeRouge** also hosts

New Orleans burlesque star Trixie Minx.

Zack Smith

the revolving monthly **A Night at the Roxie**. **Natasha Fiore** and **Madame Mystere** run the **Storyville Starlettes** troupe, while aerialists **Sarah Bobcat**, **Niki Frisky**, and **Ooops the Clown** guide the **Mystic Pony Aerial Troupe**. Fleur de Tease's former kinkiest member, **Bella Blue**, founded the **New Orleans School of Burlesque** at **Crescent Lotus Dance Studio** (3143 Calhoun St., 504-382-5199); seasoned students perform in the Burlesque 101 Showcase series at **AllWays Lounge**. This venue also plays host to Bella's **Dirty Dime Peep Show** which, Trixie adds, "is way more naked than any other show in town, way more alternative."

Trixie herself (or, if she's on tour, a sexy stand-in) can be seen, backed by a live band, each Friday at midnight for free in the cast of **Irvin Mayfield's Burlesque Ballroom** (French Quarter, Royal Sonesta, 300 Bourbon). "The weekly Ballroom show is a modern take on a classic show, and a very good introduction to burlesque, with live jazz from musicians such as **Meschiya Lake**, **Linnzi Zaorski**, or **Gerald French**."

ALLWAYS LOUNGE/ MARIGNY THEATRE

Marigny, 2240 St. Claude Ave., 504-218-5778; theallwayslounge.net

There's no telling what to expect at the wildest, most colorful little club and theater in the Marigny. Once a Western-themed gay bar called Cowpokes, AllWays now hosts a beautiful music stage with a grand piano in the front room, and a small professional theater for readings and intelligently bawdy plays in the back. Actually there's a lot of bawdiness in the front room as well. During Mardi Gras and other busy times, they'll even squeeze bands into a third outdoor performance area/atrium.

ANTHONY BEAN COMMUNITY THEATER

Mid-City, 1333 S. Carrollton Ave., 504-862-PLAY; anthonybeantheater .com

Community theater in the truest sense. Anyone who's ever had theatrical ambition, people from the true crevices of New Orleans, come to light and shine in original productions tackling issues unique to the city. Not the flashiest thing to do on vacation, but you'll certainly get a glimpse into what New Orleans is really like.

ART KLUB

Marigny, Michalopoulous Studio,
513 Elysian Fields Ave., 504-943-6565;
artistinc.org

Founded in 2007, **Artist International Connection, Inc. (Artist Inc.)** is an artistic community creating collaborations that enhance and promote artistic expression and opportunity. The group utilizes Artist Inc.'s giant theater space as a resource for both emerging and seasoned artists by presenting affordably priced theater productions for adults and children. The **Reese Johanson Collective** is Artist Inc.'s multidisciplinary performing arts ensemble. The organization's **Art Klub** is a regular Wednesday night series of gatherings in the theater, each with a different theme: poetry, visual art, author readings, etc.

ARTSPOT

CBD, 6100 Canal Blvd.,
504-826-7783, 866-ART-SPOT;
artspotproductions.org

New Orleans is not big on modernity, or on thinking too hard in general, but **Kathy Randels** is an exception. In 1995, Randels founded ArtSpot, an ensemble of artists dedicated to creating original, "meticulously LIVE theater" that blends and bends disciplines. Original multimedia works are codeveloped among the cast, music is written, and rehearsals are painstaking and physical. ArtSpot also bolsters the **LCIW Drama Club**, a theater company of inmates at the Louisiana Correctional Institute for Women in St. Gabriel, Louisiana, founded by Randels in 1996.

ASHE CULTURAL ARTS CENTER

Uptown/Central City, 1712 Oretha
Castle Haley Blvd., 504-569-9070;
ashecac.org

Also a community gathering place and conference center, this performance space promotes African, Caribbean, and African American art and artists with frequent live concerts, dance recitals, movies, etc.

BACKYARD BALLROOM

Bywater, 3519A St. Claude Ave.,
504-473-6819

The Backyard Ballroom is a theater project conceived by **Otter**, a flamboyant local performance artist with a marquee name in Ibiza clubland and roaring flame tattoos on her personal orifices. Over the past year or so, she's re-imagined her sprawling Ninth Ward mansion and the garden beside it into a funky performance venue for original musicals and theater written and performed by a collective of neighborhood artists. The end product is much more legit than our description belies.

CONTEMPORARY ARTS CENTER (CAC)

CBD, 900 Camp St., 504-528-3800;
cacno.org

This is no funky shotgun art shop. In two separate auditoriums and a main multiroom gallery, the CAC hosts music of all kinds—from brass bands to avant orchestration to huge bands like **Death Cab for Cutie** and **Ween** during Jazz Fest—plus theater, local and national touring dance companies, and film festivals. $5 general, $3 students and seniors. 11 a.m. to 4 p.m., Thursday to Sunday.

ANDREW VAUGHT OF CRIPPLE CREEK THEATRE COMPANY

The rise of a vibrant theater scene is one of the more positive cultural developments in the post-Katrina era. Previously home to a few stalwart companies and university departments, New Orleans today boasts a robust crop of inventive, ambitious groups, none of them more ambitious than **Cripple Creek Theatre Company** (cripplecreekplayers.org), led by artistic director **Andrew Vaught**. Born and raised just across the lake in Covington, Vaught returned home in 2006 to what he calls "a pretty raw environment," both creatively and financially.

"The hardest thing was connection. There were multiple groups starting and making work, but not a lot of channels to communicate with each other," he says. "There was a sense that lots of spaces were available, but it seemed a little tricky to find one, especially for a theater company with no connections and very little capital."

The result was an improvisational approach that fostered edgy if fragile productions of politically shaded works by Gogol, Wilder, Dario Fo, and others that seemed to shadow the events taking place in the city. Along the way, Vaught's own writing evolved (his original country songs are terrific, too), as did the company's partnerships with other new groups. Past partners include many of the new scene's brightest lights, including **Goat in the Road Productions,** the **NOLA Project, Mondo Bizzarro, Skin Horse Theatre,** and **Keen Amity Productions**, as well as more established **Southern Rep** and **Tulane Dance**. Inspiration remains ripe in the city, new talent continues to arrive, but funding is another matter.

"Well, I think the key to survival along those seven years was a certain amount of brand consistency, at least for us,"

Andy Vaught of Cripple Creek
Theatre levitates.

Zack Smith

177

says Vaught. "Smaller companies and new companies haven't reached that point where they can start going for and receiving the big money from national sources. What's nice is that's a more practical realistic model. You can only spend what you have, it's like paying cash and not having a credit card. The down side is you aren't gonna buy a home anytime soon."

More recently, Vaught and crew took up a residence at the **AllWays Theater**, located behind the lounge of the same name on St. Claude Avenue and a good bet if you're in town and it's . . . open. "You literally don't know if you are gonna see a nudie Mario Brothers burlesque or a Tennessee Williams oldie," Vaught advises. Or, as New Orleans theater continues to experiment, a little bit of both.

DRAMARAMA PERFORMING GROUP

CBD, Contemporary Arts Center, 900 Camp St., 504-528-3800; dramarama.org

This group curates an open-call minifestival of all things theatrical (entry forms on the website), which for six hours in April fills every inch of public space in the **Contemporary Arts Center** with new works of comedy, dance, and theater from nationally known artists and most of the local dance/theater companies detailed in this section. Its offshoot, **DramaRama Junior,** features new works by teenagers, while **DancerRama,** in March at the CAC, is a six-hour sampler platter of dancers from New Orleans and beyond.

FRINGE FESTIVAL

venues all around the city, mostly in Bywater/Marigny, 504-941-3640; nofringe.org

A vast buffet of amateur and professional New Orleans performers producing, concurrently all over the city, multimedia cabaret, comedy, dance, drama, magic shows, musical theater, performance art, puppetry, storytelling, burlesque, spoken word, you name it. The organization books all of the venues, rents all the chairs, handles all of the promotion, solicits the volunteers, even buys the drinks, so that performers need only worry about their 30- to 60-minute performances. Entry forms on the website.

HAPPENSDANCE

offices at 129 University Pl., 504-523-6530

Founded by **Louisiana Philharmonic** cellist **Jeanne Jaubert**, this is one of those postmodern, experimental, but fun dance troupes we mentioned.

LE PETIT THÉÂTRE DU VIEUX CARRÉ

French Quarter, 616 St. Peter St., 504-522-2081; lepetittheatre.com

One of the nation's oldest continuously operating theaters. Meaning, it's beautiful but don't expect any envelope-pushing; they're slaves to schlocky musicals, and to Tennessee Williams — much of the **Faulkner** and **Tennessee Williams** festivals are held at Le Petit.

LOUISIANA PHILHARMONIC ORCHESTRA (LPO)

offices at 129 University Pl., 504-523-6530; lpomusic.com

The LPO is America's only musician-owned and -operated symphony — meaning they can play their classical music and pops favorites wherever they choose, from New Orleans' small First Baptist Church to the huge Morial Convention Center.

MAHALIA JACKSON THEATER OF THE PERFORMING ARTS

Tremé, 801 N. Rampart St., in Armstrong Park, 504-529-3600; mahaliajacksontheater.com

Located inside **Louis Armstrong Park**, and named for the famous New Orleans–born gospel star, this mainstream but beautiful theater was creamed by Katrina and only reopened in January 2009. Though famous as a place to hear opera and the Louisiana Philharmonic, the theater also hosts mainstream Broadway fare like *Cats* and *The Color Purple,* plus a smattering of famous comedians and black theater productions.

MID-CITY THEATRE

Mid-City, 3540 Toulouse St., 504-488-1460; midcitytheatre.com

Intimate comedy, drama, and caberet music club run by director of operations **Su Gonczy**, of the legendary **Le Chat Noir**.

THE MUDLARK

Bywater, 1200 Port St.; themudlarkconfectionary.com

This down-home crushed-velvet hot-box of a theater, located on a flood-ragged street, features very small plays, puppet shows, and other progressive performance art, including a good deal of experimental and noise music.

NEW ORLEANS BALLET ASSOCIATION (NOBA)

Uptown/Garden District, 104 Dixon Hall, Tulane University, 504-522-0996; nobadance.com

Open from September to May at Tulane University's Dixon Hall, the NOBA dance institute is the largest dance classroom on the Gulf Coast, providing thousands of recitals, concerts, lectures, workshops, and classes. Check website for schedule.

NEW ORLEANS
BALLET THEATRE

various venues, 504-210-0222;
nobt.org

This company's founders, **Gregory Schramel** and wife **Marjorie Hardwick**, danced in Miami, Cincinnati, Atlanta, and Dallas before returning to their home town. They claim as influences George Balanchine, Maurice Béjart, and Twyla Tharp. Recent programs include the comedy *Yes Virginia* and *Thick as Thieves,* with music by U2.

NEW ORLEANS CENTER FOR
THE CREATIVE ARTS (NOCCA)

Marigny/Bywater, 2800 Chartres St.,
504-904-2787; nocca.com

This school for creative high school students (which counts **Harry Connick Jr., Wynton** and **Branford Marsalis,** and **Terence Blanchard** as its graduates, among many others) hosts performances of all kinds, from around the globe. Artists come to teach NOCCA students and give stage performances that are open to the public. Ticket prices are very reasonable.

NEW ORLEANS
OPERA ASSOCIATION

CBD, 1010 Common Street, Ste.
1820, 504-529-3000;
neworleansopera.org

The New Orleans Opera Association, founded as the **French Opera House,** is the oldest opera in North America. Performances are held at the Morial Convention Center and Tulane University's McAlister Auditorium.

RUNNING WITH SCISSORS

norunningwithscissors.com

This newer but well-loved troupe presents mainly farce and high-camp productions. Their performance locations vary from small theaters like **Le Chat Noir** to even bowling alleys, so check the website.

THE SHADOWBOX

Bywater, 2400 St. Claude Ave.,
504-298-8676;
theshadowboxtheatre.com

Among an increasing number of galleries and performance spaces on St. Claude, the intimate Shadowbox welcomes all types of shows from musicals to improv comedy by heady local troupe the **New Movement.**

SOUTHERN REPERTORY
THEATRE

French Quarter, 365 Canal St., 3rd
Floor, 504-522-6545;
southernrep.com

Just outside the French Quarter in what looks like a mall (because it is), Southern Repertory presents both classic and modern American and regional drama, featuring experienced local thespians as well as Broadway and Hollywood performers.

TRUE BREW COFFEE HOUSE

Warehouse District/CBD, 200 Julia
St., 504-524-8441

This coffee shop is also a small theater continually hosting grassroots plays, poetry readings, improvisational comedy, cabaret, and of course music.

TSUNAMI DANCE COMPANY

tsunamidance.com

Since 2002, this New Orleans–based modern/multimedia dance company has incorporated athletic, innovative movement with a dynamic contemporary style. In fall 2008, Tsunami created an innovative, edgy take on **Bruno Schulz** imagery and philosophy for *Street of Crocodiles.* They can be seen at most of the events detailed in this section.

TULANE UNIVERSITY'S SHAKESPEARE SEASON

Uptown, Lupin Theater, Tulane University, 504-865-5101

Shakespeare performances presented around the city in awesome park settings as well as on campus.

UNO DOWNTOWN THEATRE

CBD, at the Scottish Rite Temple, 619 Carondelet St., 504-539-9580

Home to cutting-edge and emerging theater companies (**Running with Scissors, ArtSpot,** etc.) as well as UNO student and faculty productions.

ZEITGEIST MULTI-DISCIPLINARY ARTS CENTER

Uptown/Central City, 1618 Oretha Castle Haley Blvd., 504-352-1150; zeitgeistinc.net

Famous for its "theater experiments," Zeitgeist, considered one of the premier alternative arts centers in the South, also presents modern film, video, performance and visual art, and literary events six nights a week, year-round, plus many small festival-type events in between. Support this amazing place!

NEW ORLEANS COMEDY

Since Katrina, there is a whole new breed of open-mic comedians in New Orleans, and they bring in strong audiences. Comedy in this city used to be more underground, but it's in the forefront now with comedy shows every night of the week.

CARROLLTON STATION

Uptown, 8140 Willow St., 504-865-9190; carrolltonstation.com

Every Wednesday at 8 p.m. for seven-plus years, **Mike Henehan** and **Scotland Green** have hosted "You Think You're Funny," a high-quality comedy open-mic night. Packed audiences. Cheap drinks. Free entry.

HI-HO LOUNGE

Marigny, 239 St. Claude St., 504-945-4446, hiholounge.net

Comedian **Just Jason** runs this weekly Sunday showcase, which features up-and-coming locals and a live band.

HOWLIN' WOLF DEN

CBD, corner of St. Joseph and S. Peters Sts., 504-529-5844; thehowlinwolf.com/the-den/

Every Thursday, comedian **Red Bean** hosts "Comedy Gumbeaux" (comedygumbeaux.com). This comedy night with an urban edge features the best in the city, plus the occasional national star. 8 p.m.

LA NUIT COMEDY THEATRE

Uptown, 5039 Freret St., 504-231-7011; nolacomedy.com

On Monday and Friday, La Nuit hosts a stand-up open mic with **Jonah Baschle**. The rest of the time it's mostly improv troupes, but they also host comedians and comic plays, even comedy classes for kids and adults.

Comedian Mark Caesar hosts "Laugh n' Sip," where he hopes to make you "piss yo' pants" with laughter.

Mark Caesar

LAUGH N' SIP

Uptown, Wine Bistro, 1011 Gravier St.; themarkcaesar.com

Host **Mark Caesar**'s star continues to rise, with film appearances, YouTube hits, and some national touring. He's turned the Thursdays at Therapy into a stop for other touring comedians, as well as a proving ground for locals. A lively crowd and a backing band give the shows a party vibe. His Wednesday radio show on pissyopants.com is also a good place for comedy news.

LOST LOVE LOUNGE

Marigny, 2529 Dauphine St., 504-949-2009; lostlovelounge.com

Not only great Vietnamese food, but on Tuesday night, **Cassidy Henehan** and **Scottland Green** host "Comedy Catastrophe," which usually starts late, 10:30 p.m. at the earliest.

NATIONAL COMEDY COMPANY

French Quarter, 727 St. Peter St., 504-523-7469; nationalcomedycompany.com

For over five years, the National Comedy Company has entertained visitors and locals just off of Bourbon Street across from **Preservation Hall** with its "Usual Saturday Night" improv comedy jam on, you guessed it, Saturdays.

NEW MOVEMENT THEATER

Bywater, 1919 Burgundy St., 504-302-8264; newmovementtheater.com

These Austin transplants hit the ground running in 2010, with well-received improv and sketch comedy shows, popular classes, and a space in the Marigny. They also have a growing video presence online. New Movement hosts events almost nightly. Check the website.

No matter where you go, from San Francisco to Spain, the guide-books always make it seem like consuming goods in a strange new place is one of life's more important cultural experiences. We propose that when you visit New Orleans, it's better to first buy beers and food, and spend your time talking to people you meet and hearing live music. After that, however, here are some locally owned shops that will supply you with souvenirs while also giving you a feel for the true nature of the city:

RECORD STORES

For a city that loves its music, New Orleans doesn't boast a real abundance of record stores the way, say, Austin does. The ones we do have, though, are of course funky.

DOMINO SOUND RECORD SHACK

Mid-City, 2557 Bayou Rd., 504-309-0871

In a small Rasta corner of Mid-City near Esplanade and Broad, Domino Sound houses a well-curated selection of old LPs, cassette tapes, and local bands' releases. The owner is **DJ Prince Pauper**, one of the city's best dub reggae selectors. The shop even has pressed vinyl records of local groups such as **Why Are We Building Such a Big Ship?**

EUCLID RECORDS

Bywater, 3401 Chartres St., 504-947-4348; www.euclidnola.com

This sister store to the famous shop in St. Louis boasts an extensive, well-

curated, and organized collection of pretty much every type of music. New and used vinyl, a gorgeous collection of hand-screened posters, a good selection of music books, and a stage in the corner for free in-store performances by great local bands (and sometimes secret afternoon shows by whoever's playing a big venue that night) make this one of the best record stores in town.

JIM RUSSELL'S RARE RECORDS

Uptown, 1837 Magazine St., 504-522-2602; jimrussellrecords.com

Some people consider Jim Russell's, now in its fortieth year, the last of the real record stores in New Orleans. Others complain that it's too expensive and unorganized. Either way, they sell tons

Euclid record store in Bywater along the river.

Zack Smith

of records in every possible condition, from old New Orleans zydeco to '60s psychedelia to brand-new techno, hip-hop, and rock. They also sell new and used turntables and other DJ equipment, blank reel-to-reels, picture-discs, famous New Orleans 45s, even video games of all eras. Mon. through Sat., 11 a.m. to 5 p.m.

LOUISIANA MUSIC FACTORY

French Quarter, 210 Decatur St., 504-586-1094; louisianamusicfactory.com

Though they do have a "metal" section, they don't sell rap, and mostly don't allow any of the nontraditional bands featured in this book to play the store's very fun, free, afternoon in-store concerts. But somehow we still dig Louisiana Music Factory for its vast, two-floor collection of (almost) all things Louisiana.

THE MUSHROOM

Uptown, 1037 Broadway St., 504-866-6065

This is the obligatory funky college record store. Bongs and black-light posters, plus a fun selection of new and used music. Plus it's near **Audubon Park** and the daiquiri shop.

MUSICA LATINA DISCOTECA

Uptown, 4714 Magazine St., 504-895-4227

This jam-packed, one-room shop sells all things Latin, from the musical traditions of Cuba to Argentina, to mambo greats, plus mariachi and salsa artists.

NUTHIN BUT FIRE

Marigny, 1840 N. Claiborne Ave., 504-940-5680; nuthinbutfirerecords.com

Proprietor **Sess 4-5**, also a rapper, got his start rhyming with 504 boys like the

L.O.G. and **Shine Baby** back in junior high. He graduated to slinging burned CDs out of his trunk and, just after Katrina, opened his bona fide storefront across from the North Claiborne Avenue exit ramp. Nuthin but Fire burns its own series of local rap CD compilations featuring everything from vintage bounce to the latest hits on the urban charts. It's also a great spot to pick up flyers for relatively underadvertised New Orleans hip-hop shows. Sess is also the promoter behind the **Industry Influence** (www.industryinfluence.blogspot.com), a hip-hop networking concert series.

Skully'z Records: one of the only worthwhile destinations on Bourbon Street.

Zack Smith

ODYSSEY RECORDS & TAPES

CBD, 1012 Canal St., 504-523-3506

Founded in 1984, Odyssey finally reopened after Katrina on Canal Street, amid tourist-focused t-shirt shops and ghetto-focused jewelers. The shop peddles mostly hip-hop vinyl and CDs. Great vintage local stuff can be found if you dig, as well as info about upcoming rap shows.

PEACHES RECORDS & TAPES

French Quarter, 408 N. Peters St., 504-282-3322

Store owner **Shirani Rea** has been instrumental in the New Orleans rap and hip-hop scene since 1975, when she opened her original Peaches record store (which used to be a branch of the now-defunct national chain; the Nola outpost, which keeps the original sign, is now indie and, as far as we know, the only one left). Apart from a store, it functioned almost as an office and community center for everyone from **Mystikal** to **Souljah Slim** to the **Cash Money Crew**. The '90s queen of **No Limit Records, Mia X**, was supposedly discovered while working at Peaches. Katrina forced Peaches' relocation into the French Quarter, but with a similar vibe.

SKULLY'Z RECORDZ

French Quarter, 907 Bourbon St., 504-592-4666

The only worthwhile attraction of Bourbon Street that doesn't serve booze, tiny little Skully'z stocks a mountain of new and used vinyl, and is a great place to pick up releases by New Orleans' alternative musicians.

N.O. MOMENT

THRIFT SHOPPING WITH ACTRESS VERONICA RUSSELL

New Orleans actress and thrift store maven Veronica Russell. Damn, girl.

Scott Stuntz

Veronica Russell has been an active member of New Orleans' theater and performance community since 1990-something. She has won numerous awards for acting and costume design, performs burlesque and variety under the alias **VeVe laRoux,** is an original member of the **Noisician Coalition,** and a founding member of the **Big Easy Rollergirls.** She's needed a lot of different clothes for all of those jobs, so we asked her where you should go thrift shopping while in town:

STRAIGHT-UP THRIFT STORES

Bloomin' Deals

Uptown, 4645 Freret St., 504-891-1289; jlno.org

Twice-annual "bag sales" where $10 buys you a garbage bag full of whatever fits inside!

Bridge House

Lower Garden District, 1160 Camp St., 504-522-4476; bridgehouse.org

Red, White, and Blue

6001 Jefferson Hwy., Harahan, La., 504-733-8066; redwhiteandbluethriftstore.com

A little far afield, you gotta trek to Harahan, but the biggest and best on the East Bank of the river. Worth the drive!

VINTAGE/COSTUME SHOPS

Tend to be slightly funky, hipster hangouts, with the attendant price increases . . .

Funky Monkey

Uptown, 3127 Magazine St.,
504-899-5567

Pop Shop

Bywater, 3212 Dauphine St.

Miss Claudia's Vintage & Costumes

Uptown, 4204 Magazine St., 504-897-6310; missclaudias.com

CONSIGNMENT

A last-minute evening-gown emergency is more common than you think during Carnival season! These will be the most expensive, but still good spots for scoring discount designer duds offa Uptown debs and their moms.

On the Other Hand

Uptown, 8204 Oak St.,
504-861-0159;
ontheotherhandconsignment.com

Prima Donna's Closet

Uptown, 1206 St. Charles Ave.,
504-522-3327;
primadonnascloset.com

Swap

Uptown, 7716 Maple St.,
504-522-3327; swapboutique.com

Trashy Diva

Uptown: 2048 Magazine St.,
504-299-8777, dress boutique;
2050 Magazine St., 504-265-0973,
shoes

Downtown: 829 Chartres St.,
504-581-4555, lingerie;
831 Chartres St., 504-522-8861,
shoes; trashydiva.com

Begun as a vintage shop in the French Quarter in the mid-'90s, Trashy Diva is now the showcase for owner **Candice Gwinn**'s lovely, retro-inspired dresses. Done in silk and cotton in a variety of midcentury-style prints, the designs are brand-new versions of the amazing 1940s- and '50s-era styles that are now impossible to find, or cost a grand on eBay. There's also jewelry and a carefully curated selection of bags and shoes (Trashy is the only Frye shoe retailer in town). The French Quarter store also has a boutique dedicated to lingerie and corsets.

JUNQUE & ANTIQUES

Usually a mixture of furniture, bric-a-brac, and the odd rack of vintage clothes here and there.

Everything

Marigny, 2236 St. Claude Ave.

No Fleas

Uptown, 4228 Magazine St., 504-324-4727; nofleasmarketnola.com

San Claudio

Bywater, 2718 St. Claude Ave., 985-445-6005

This is just the tip of the berg as far as places you can go to find costumes for Halloween, Mardi Gras, and any wild New Orleans event in between.

BARGAIN CENTER

Bywater, 3200 Dauphine St., 504-948-0007

Bargain Center is one of the coolest junk shops you'll ever visit. Everything from nice clothes to slightly damaged musical equipment to a comprehensive collection of Mardi Gras costumes and paraphernalia.

CREE MCCREE

Uptown, 3728 Laurel St., call for appt., 504-269-3982

Cree McCree became a professional flea in 1975, and has taken her cheap but wearable assemblage art, using found objects, garage sale items, and vintage hats, around the country. Author of the how-to guide *Flea Market America: The Complete Guide to Flea Enterprise* (available on amazon. com), McCree also maintains the blog **Flea Queen of Planet Green.** Several times a year, Cree opens her home to sell her own line of Halloween cocktail couture (bat bustiers, skeleton bras, and vintage hats festooned with bats, spiders, ravens, and snakes) plus fabulous Mardi Gras headpieces. Otherwise, her wares can be found at Freret Street Market (first Saturday monthly, September to June), Broad Street Flea Market & Bazaar (second Saturday monthly, September to June), Blue Nile Boo-tique (Sunday before Halloween), and the Blue Nile Mardi Gras Costume Sale (Sunday before Mardi Gras).

FIFI MAHONY'S

French Quarter, 934 Royal St., 504-525-4343; fifimahonys.com

Owned by **One Eyed Jacks** club owner **Ryan Hesseling** and his wife **Marcy**, Fifi's is a temple to all things glamorously over-the-top. Need a rhinestone ring the size of a doorknob? Perhaps a bubblegum-pink wig covered in glitter, done up in a three-foot bouffant? Pancake makeup that'll cover your five o'clock shadow? A favorite of burlesque dancers, drag queens, and Carnival revelers of all stripes, Fifi's is your spot.

FUNKY MONKEY

Uptown, 3127 Magazine St.,
504-899-5587

Divided into men's and women's sides, Funky Monkey sells gently used cool clothes and accessories of mostly recent vintage, plus some new pieces, sunglasses, and costume jewelry. The men's side also prints t-shirts to order or with logos of beloved local businesses like **K&B** (R.I.P.) and **Hubig's Pies**.

LE GARAGE

French Quarter, 1234 Decatur St.,
504-522-6639

On the funky strip of Lower Decatur, dominated by punk dive bars and service industry locals' favorite pubs, there are also several intriguing antique and junk shops of which Le Garage—so named because of its garage door that yawns open like Aladdin's cave—is one of the longest standing. It has a large stock of Carnival costumes and odd military surplus, plus various quirky objects including movie posters, ceramics, and other treasures and relics.

For Mardi Gras—
themed costumes,
see page 125.

PIETY STREET MARKET

Bywater, second Saturday of every
month, 11 a.m. to 4 p.m.,
612 Piety St., 504-782-2569;
612piety.com/piety-street-market

Located at **Old Ironworks**, home of **Piety Street Sno-Balls**, the market features 40-plus vendors in an expansive indoor/outdoor setting with live acoustic music and great local food. Vendors include creative artists, crafters, vintage and flea market dealers, mix-and-match booths, and sellers of handmade art and garage sale finds. The family-friendly market hosts a lively kids' activity area beneath a shady tree in the courtyard, where a miniature train built by Old Ironworks owner **Gilbert Buras** enchants shoppers of all ages.

SOLE STARR COSTUMES

Bywater, 3000 St. Claude Ave.,
504-948-4440

This is the sister store to Sole Starr Boutique on lower Decatur Street in the Quarter, except it's not really a store. No words at all out front, just some spray-painted stars. The place is only "open" Wednesdays and Thursdays, plus all week before Halloween, and all through Mardi Gras season—still, though, you MUST call first. If she's around, **Dee Dee** herself will invite you over and give you a private tour of costumes, tights, eyelashes, face paint, stage blood, plus regular thriftwear, streetwear, vintage underwear, and pseudo-lingerie.

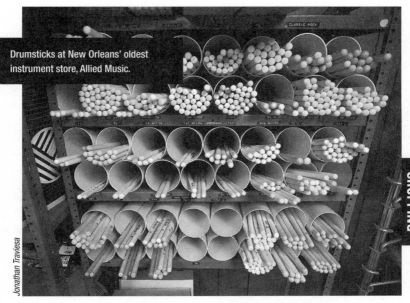

Drumsticks at New Orleans' oldest instrument store, Allied Music.

SHOPPING

MUSICAL INSTRUMENT SHOPPING

The best-case scenario for you on vacation would be having such a good time that you drink a large daiquiri and end up impulsively buying a new guitar to take home. Visiting musicians, please patronize these independent music shops:

ALLIED MUSIC

Mid-City, 4417 Bienville St., 504-488-2673

Before the flood, the oldest music store in New Orleans (est. 1966) had a bigger inventory. Now Allied features a very slim, basic collection of rock, jazz, and marching band gear for sale, with a concentration on drums—Allied's owner **Carlos McInerney** is also a passionate drummer and a partner in the **Crescent City Drum School** for kids.

INTERNATIONAL VINTAGE GUITARS

229 Pelican Ave., Algiers, La., 504-524-4557

You won't find many deals here, but there's a lot of gear to drool over, all of it well maintained.

Brass at the New Orleans Music Exchange, Uptown.

Jonathan Traviesa

NEW ORLEANS MUSIC EXCHANGE

Uptown, 3342 Magazine St.,
504-891-7670;
neworleansmusicexchange.net

Stacks of speakers by the front door, rooms stuffed full of equipment, a constantly rotating stock of guitars, basses, brass instruments, and DJ equipment is available for purchase, rental, or trade. Owner **Jimmy Glickman** and his staff, all working and performing musicians, are (mostly) happy to help, whether you're buying a guitar pick or renting a full backline.

WEBB'S BYWATER MUSIC

Bywater, 3217 Burgundy St.,
504-232-5512

The first music store in recent mind to take up residence in the musicians' haven that is Bywater. **Paul Webb**—of metal bands **Spickle, Hawg Jaw, Mountain of Wizard,** and **Classhole**—worked for many years at the New Or-

leans Music Exchange, which didn't fix guitars. Now at his own shop, Webb will do anything for any musician. We have a distinct memory of Webb, one Mardi Gras, dressed as Jesus, carrying an electric guitar he'd built, shaped like a raw wood crucifix—so, surely he could do whatever simple thing you needed. Open at noon.

Zack Smith

Paul Webb does it all at Webb's Bywater Music.

NEW ORLEANS T-SHIRTS

DEFEND NEW ORLEANS

Uptown, 1101 First St. at Magazine St., 504-941-7010; defendneworleans.com

Prior to the flood, Defend New Orleans was just a tongue-in-cheek logo. But imbued with a new, stronger meaning post-flood, Defend New Orleans garnered mad success, and soon hundreds of bathroom mirrors, walls, and cop cars all bore the appropriated Mohawk skull graphic. Defend New Orleans clothing can be purchased at various locations around town in addition to its own store. DNO's website doubles as a community sounding board, hipster video blog, music and events calendar, and ongoing documentary of the same types of local culture featured in this guidebook.

Ashley and Hannah of ska band the Local Skank model shirts by Dirty Coast.

DIRTY COAST

Uptown, 5631 Magazine St. and 329 Julia St., 504-324-3745; dirtycoast.com

Founded in 2004, Dirty Coast is the premier brand for clever New Orleans in-jokes printed on t-shirts and stickers sold at many local stores, including Rouses grocery and two different Dirty Coast shops. The company's print styles are sort of reminiscent of the Urban Outfitters aesthetic but depict

SHOPPING

jokes about beignets, absinthe, and the West Bank. Since Katrina, founders and New Orleans "exceptionalists" **Blake Haney** and **Patrick Brower** have turned Dirty Coast into a brand with a mission, using their high local profile to celebrate and start a national conversation about the region. Mostly, though, Dirty Coast's products serve as simple billboards of New Orleans pride, encouraging locals and visitors alike to "Be a New Orleanian wherever you are."

FLEURTY GIRL

Uptown, 632 St. Peter St., 3117 Magazine St., and elsewhere; fleurtygirl.net

A sort of cuter, feminine version of Dirty Coast, with expanded New Orleans inventory beyond t-shirts, including original "Bywater rain boots" graced with fleur de lis, and galvanized buckets adorned with our city's memorable Sewerage and Water Board meter logo. The brand's various locations also offer New Orleans music, books, and other souvenirs.

MAGAZINE STREET (UPTOWN)

Jonathan Traviesa

Though we'd rather you focus on New Orleans music and art, there are a few lovely and highly walkable strips of shops here, of which Magazine Street uptown is the most notable—for clothes, antiques, cool odds and ends, and snacks. The businesses are almost exclusively owned by New Orleanians. There are several definable chunks of Magazine where stores stand shoulder to shoulder, and the distance in between is safe to stroll and quite pretty. This path will also take you through the Garden District, heavily stressed in other guidebooks for its sprawling mansions, lush foliage, and former residents **Trent Reznor** and **Anne Rice**.

BRANCH OUT

2022 Magazine St., 504-371-5913; branchoutshop.com

Branch Out is New Orleans' first "green" shopping alternative. Its sustainable clothing and accessories for men and women, however, are more stylish than one would expect. This new and much-welcomed shop also carries hand-selected, quality vintage pieces and locally made designer goods—all green.

EARTHSAVERS

5501 Magazine St., 504-899-8555; earthsaversonline.com

This New Orleans mini-chain (there's another store in Metairie) has a focus on green products and living; they sell a line of organic cotton t-shirts whose proceeds go to various locally based ecoconscious rebuilding efforts. Earthsavers carries most salon and upscale beauty lines, like Bumble and Bumble and Dr. Hauschka, and a chalkboard outside indicates which spa services are available for walk-ins.

FROCK CANDY

3112 Magazine St., 504-301-9864

Frock Candy makes its boutique eye candy by organizing cute, cheap, and super-trendy dresses by color, making the store into a fluffy jewel box that's somehow extra shoppable because of it.

HOUSE OF LOUNGE

2044 Magazine St., 504-671-8300

Fancy-schmancy sexy underwear and stockings plus glamorous costume jewelry and a few naughtier selections, like sequined pasties and discreet, um, toys. HoL is designed like a luxe boudoir and carries everything from the sassy Jezebel line to Aubade and La Perla's pricey scanties.

RETRO-ACTIVE

5414 Magazine St., 504-895-5054

This tiny shop is jam-packed with carefully selected mint-condition clothes, accessories, and ephemera from the middle of the twentieth century. The collection of Bakelite and Lucite jewelry is especially impressive. No junk-shop bargains here, though; the owner has been in this spot for over a decade and is ridiculously knowledgeable about his collectibles.

While shopping, eat and get drunk at:

BEE SWEET

5706 Magazine St., 504-891-8333

A tiny storefront that sells giant cupcakes. The "Chubby Elvis" is a banana cupcake topped with peanut butter cream frosting (no bacon). All-natural "pup cakes" are also available for the dog.

CHEZ NOUS CHARCUTERIE

5701 Magazine St., 504-899-7303; gotocheznous.com

Despite a ginormous Whole Foods Market across the street, tiny Chez Nous—located in a shotgun house catty-corner to the superstore—plugs away selling its own wines, gourmet items, and prepared foods. Daily menus showcase local ingredients and New Orleans–style dishes.

JOEY K'S

3001 Magazine St., 504-891-0997; joeyksrestaurant.com

This stick-to-your-ribs diner is a neighborhood institution for home-style New Orleans soul food. Think po-boys, fried soft-shell crab, and split pea soup with smoky slabs of bacon, oven-roasted turkey with stuffing, and homemade bread pudding with ice cream for dessert.

JUAN'S FLYING BURRITO

2018 Magazine St., 504-569-0000; also 4724 S. Carrollton Ave., 504-486-9950; juansflyingburrito.com

This punk-rock burrito shop stuffs huge California-style burritos for cheap with loud rock 'n' roll in the background and lowbrow local art on the walls. There's a branch on Carrollton Avenue in Mid-City that lacks some of the hipster appeal of the original.

LILETTE

3637 Magazine St., 504-895-1636; www.liletterestaurant.com

Simultaneously fancy and casual French bistro. Huge selection of unique and adventurous gourmet options. Open for lunch.

MS. MAE'S

4336 Magazine St., 504-895-9401; msmaeswallofshame.blogspot.com

Ms. Mae's is not only open 24 hours but has $1 drinks and beers AT ALL TIMES. There's no official Web page, but they do have a "Wall of Shame" site featuring photos of people who have fallen victim to their dangerous drink special.

TEE EVA'S

5201 Magazine St., 504-899-8350; tee-evapralines.com

Good snowballs and tasty pies and praline candy. Try the miniature pies—pecan, sweet potato, or creole cream cheese; just enough for a snack. Mon. through Sat. 11 a.m. to 6 p.m.

FRERET STREET

Leo McGovern mans the counter at Crescent City Comics while publishing *Antigravity* magazine out of the shop's back office.

Zack Smith

thenewfreret.com

In recent years, the commercial corridor of **Freret Street** has experienced a renaissance of small businesses and new food options. Old-timers can tell you of visiting Freret for all your shopping needs. Today, a walk from Jefferson Avenue to Napoleon offers snowballs, garden supplies, haircuts, auto repair, coffee, cocktails, and two types of pizza. Couched in a diverse Uptown neighborhood, Freret continues to evolve. This historic street took on much water during Katrina but bounced back in unique fashion. After some promised post-flood aid money failed to materialize, entrepreneurs in the area decided to rebuild their community themselves. Zoning as an arts-and-entertainment district allowed locals to start a monthly market that quickly brought a lot of positive attention to the area, along with a slew of independent, locally owned restaurants, bars, and other shops. **Freret Market** of crafts, food, and bands happens on the first Saturday of the month, while the all-day **Freret Street Festival** (first

Saturday in April, freretstreetfestival.com) that began in the 1990s still hosts food and beer vendors, puppet shows, kids' activities, and truly local music. Today there's still something essentially soulful and a little bit Caribbean about these blocks, even if Tulane and Loyola kids are ever-present.

Antigravity magazine publisher **Leo McGovern** set up shop on Freret after Katrina in an office out of **Crescent City Comics**. Witness to Freret's latest incarnation, Leo was our first choice for recommendations:

BEAN'S FORMAL WEAR

4900 Freret St., 504-891-4675

You never know when you'll need a tuxedo in New Orleans. Mr. Bean will do you right, with various colors and styles.

BEAUCOUP JUICE

4719 Freret St., 504-430-5508

During the New Orleans summer, little stands pop up everywhere selling shaved ice drowned in colored high-fructose corn syrup. Beaucoup Juice is the first place to pour organic fruit juices on its snowballs. Smoothies, vegetable juice, even an assortment of panini sandwiches are also available.

BLOOMIN' DEALS

4645 Freret St., 504-891-1289; jlno.org

A huge consignment shop draped with new and used adult and children's clothing and shoes, housewares, furniture, books, and more, run by the Junior League of New Orleans, an organization of women committed to developing the potential of women and improving communities through educational and charitable means. Meaning, tons of cool old-lady dresses!

COMPANY BURGER

4600 Freret St., 504-267-0320; thecompanyburger.com

Known for their buttered pickles, the folks at Company Burger defy you to use the condiments they provide. The burgers are served on locally baked, buttered buns and, combined with cheese and the aforementioned pickles, are a treat off the grill. Try the tater tots but beware the weekday afternoon break, as they're closed between 3 and 5 p.m.

CRESCENT CITY COMICS

4916 Freret St., 504-891-3796; crescentcitycomics.com

Without a doubt, the best selection of comics and graphic novels in the city.

CURE

4905 Freret St., 504-302-2357; curenola.com

Pricey little craft-cocktail lounge for "mixology" fans and celebrity spotters.

DAT DOG

5030 Freret St., 504-899-6883; datdognola.com

Expanded to include grotto-style outdoor seating, this gourmet hot dog stand includes a fine selection of draft beers and a large screen for watching sports. They've also opened a satellite at 3336 Magazine Street.

FRERET STREET PO-BOYS AND DONUT SHOP

4701 Freret St., 504-872-9676; freretstreetpoboys.com

The most down-home of Freret eateries offers well-sized po-boys, fresh donuts, and deliciously unhealthy breakfasts. Friendly staff and a great view of the street.

MIDWAY PIZZA

4725 Freret St., 504-322-2815; midwaypizzanola.com

Specializing in deep-dish, Midway is the rare noncorporate pizza joint with a lunch buffet. Open till midnight.

OLLIE ON FRERET

5035 Freret St.; ollieneworleans.tumblr.com

Given our propensity for cracked sidewalks and deadly potholes, skate-boarding is problematic in New Orleans. Still, Ollie is your best bet uptown for boards, apparel, and the latest info on the skate community.

SARITA'S GRILL

4520 Freret St., 504-324-3562

The owners are Cuban, but the menu tackles all foods Latin from tacos to rice bowls to pressed.

TATTOO PARLORS

Veteran guitarist **Tony Barton**, late of psych-rap act **MC Trachiotomy** and downtown R&B group the **Special Men**, opened **Hell or High Water Tattoo Shop** (Uptown, 2035 Magazine St., 504-309-5411) in September 2009. "Mine is more of an old-style New Orleans street shop," says Barton, a Louisiana native. "We do appointments but also walk-ins." His artists vary in style. "They cover all the bases: **Daniel Barre, Jimmy the Saint** (of heavy rock band **Endall**) are more neo-traditional, with a new-school edge. **Jordan Barlow** (who plays in black metal band **Ritual Killer** and has an eagle inked on his forehead) does more realistic portraits, all evil black and gray shit. **Eric Huffman** does straight, traditional old-school, looks like it came from the '50s, with simple shading and bold outlines." Hell or High Water is open every day from 11 a.m. to 11 p.m. But if something worse than high water or hell has them closed during your visit to New Orleans, Barton suggests his impressive competition:

ELECTRIC LADYLAND

Marigny, 610 Frenchmen St., 504-947-8286; electricladyland.net

Located among Frenchmen's many awesome music clubs, this is a real clean, laid-back den of talented people, named "Best Place to Get a Tattoo" ten times by *Gambit Weekly*.

TATTOO GOGO

Uptown, 4421 Magazine St., 504-899-8229; tattooagogo.com

This art-focused custom shop draws designs for each client. The school-educated artists vary in style from traditional to Americana to Japanese.

UPTOWN TATTOO

Uptown, 575 S. Carrollton Ave., 504-866-3859; uptowntattoos.net

Near the university, this place is old-style traditional. Worth a visit just to see the attached machine shop, which creates fancy, handcrafted, custom-built tattoo machines.

Guitarist Tony Barton shreds the flesh, as well, at Hell or High Water Tattoo Shop.

Zack Smith

201

HAIR SALONS

AIDAN GILL

Garden District, 2026 Magazine St., 504-587-9090; aidangillformen.com

A sort of manly beauty shop for the refined gentleman, Aidan Gill is a haven for men to repair to while their lady friends shop the block. The barbershop in the rear offers haircuts and hot-towel shaves with a gratis Scotch on the rocks. The boutique in the front sells high-end shaving products like bone-handled brushes and razors, plus cologne, cufflinks, ties, and small books on etiquette and other masculine pursuits.

BOUFFANT BEAUTY

Uptown, 802 Nashville Ave., 504-894-8099

Fair prices, good conversation, precision haircuts, custom color, event styling, texture management, and barbering.

GOLDEN SHEARS

Uptown, 6008 Magazine St., 504-895-9269

The oldest barbershop currently operating in New Orleans features classic buzz cuts, straight razor shaves, and shoe shines.

IN THE MASTER'S HANDS SALON AND SPA

Gentilly, 3810 Elysian Fields Ave., 504-943-8873;
inthemastershands.com

This multicultural neighborhood hair salon has been owned and run by **Jean Lewis, Dana Perry**, and **Carlyn Early** for the past thirty-five years.

LUX SALON BLENDS

Mid-City, 3141 Ponce de Leon St., 504-301-2953; lux-salonblends.com/

In a cute shopping area close to the Fair Grounds, this day spa features not just haircuts and styling but also manicures, pedicures, waxing, and the like.

MAGAZINE ST. BARBER SHOP

Uptown, 4224 Magazine St., 504-267-7823; magazinestbarbershop.com

A comfortable, laid-back atmosphere with friendly service, providing clients with a current take on the classic hot-towel shave, haircut, or beard trim.

Aidan Gill salon sells more than just snazzy men's haircuts and shaves.

Jonathan Traviesa

ROCKET SCIENCE BEAUTY BAR

Marigny, 640 Elysian Fields Ave., 504-218-8982; rocketsciencenola.com

If you want to treat yourself, this funky, hip Marigny shop offers every service imaginable for both men and women.

SAVAGE BEAUTY

Bywater, by appt. only. Call or text 347-342-2426.

In the early 2000s, **Jo Starnes** learned hair and makeup working at **Fifi Mahony's** in the Quarter before training at a high-end Manhattan salon. Feeling that New Orleans street fashion provided a better home for her individual voice, she moved back to cut hair at **R Bar** (1431 Royal St.) and **Pals Lounge** (949 N. Rendon St.)—where $10 gets you a Jameson shot and a haircut every Monday—before breaking off on her own in 2010 to operate out of her house next to **Bacchanal** (600 Poland Ave.) wine bar and jazz club. Starnes offers personalized and affordable hair coloring, texture-changing processes, and manicures. Women's cuts are $30, men's $20. Cash only.

STARDUST SALON

Uptown, 1904 Magazine St.; stardustneworleans.com/

Almost twenty young, hip stylists to choose from, including owner **Jerry Miller,** who ten years ago walked away from a management position at a clothing store to open his dream salon. Stardust hosts events and sells Bumble and Bumble hair products.

TWISTED

Uptown, 4824 Prytania St., 504-309-7791; twistedsalon.com

Fun and diverse hair services for men, women, and children since 2002.

PARKS AND OTHER FAMILY FUN

Some of New Orleans' parks are very elaborate and fun (and sell booze), while others are simple places to lie in the grass and chill (and drink booze). Or else ride horses, paddle canoes, and other forms of relaxing play.

Louis Armstrong Park on Basin and Marais Streets (with access across from the French Quarter) hosts tons of concerts and parties all year round.

Jonathan Traviesa

AUDUBON PARK

Uptown, 6500 Magazine St., 1-866-ITS-AZOO; auduboninstitute.org

Designed by the same fellow who did Central Park, this bird-oriented jogging park (where people ride horses!) leads you around a beautiful moat full of giant white egrets, ibis, and other feathered species. Or if captive animals are more your thing, there's a zoo, and **Cascade Stables**, where the kids can take a riding lesson, or just gawk at the show ponies.

CITY PARK

Mid-City, 1 Palm Dr. (corner of Esplanade and Carrollton), 504-482-4888; neworleanscitypark.com

This grand old park, which houses the **New Orleans Museum of Art** (beside an amazing sculpture garden) and more beautiful horse-training stables, is also home to many gigantic oak trees—though not near as many as before Katrina. Also on the vast shady grounds: tennis courts, an old but operating minitrain, and the kiddie park **Storyland,** with its antique merry-go-round and miniature rollercoaster, among other rides (plus low-key to-go beers and drinks for the parents).

THE FLY

Uptown, Riverview Dr., Audubon Park

In back of **Audubon Park**, this Uptown river levee, known as The Fly, hosts a series of picnic areas and sports fields, where on nice days hordes of college students (i.e. cute girls in bikinis) play Frisbee, sunbathe, drink, and smoke weed. During mellower times it's one of the city's nicest breezy places (New Orleans don't get many breezes) to view the Mississippi, sip wine, and watch the giant barges float by.

LAFAYETTE SQUARE PARK

CBD, 500 St. Charles Ave., 504-881-9861; lafayettesquare.org

A beautiful patch of foliage and public art amid New Orleans' tallest buildings. This is where the free Concert in the Park series is held Thursdays in the spring, as well as the Harvest the Music free concert series each Thursday in the fall. Both series cater to more touristy notions of New Orleans music (you will almost surely hear "When the Saints Go Marching In"), even though most concert attendees are locals just getting off work. If you're simply visiting, however, it may be the best part of you and your kids' trip.

WASHINGTON PARK

Marigny, corner of Frenchmen and Royal Sts.

This "no dogs allowed" park functions as the Marigny's official dog park. Go figure. Along with some intermittent small literary and music fests (**Saints and Sinners** literary fest in May, **Pride Fest** in June; see "Literary New Orleans") and truly interesting public art (including **Marcus Brown**'s interactive sound sculpture, HUMS), one can also witness **fauxbeaux** practicing juggling, hula-hoop tricks, and other mild acrobatics.

FUN FOR THE WHOLE FAMILY

Do we recommend you bring your kids to New Orleans? Yes, if 1) you've already been here at least once before to enjoy it as an adult; 2) you're okay with not getting as drunk as that time; and 3) if the only time you flash folks is when you're breastfeeding.

Robin Walker

Great Nola photographer Shannon Brinkman and her daughter watch Luke Allen and the Happy Talk Band perform in Bywater's Markey Park.

If you meet these requirements, then, yes, your kids can get as much of a kick out of this weird crazy place as you do—if your trip is tightly curated. Here's a head start:

ALGIERS FERRY

French Quarter, at the foot of Canal St. next to the Aquarium

Since 1827, the Algiers ferry has conveyed folks across the Mississippi to Algiers Point, a quiet but fun neighborhood of beautiful New Orleans architecture sans wild nightlife or much crime. This 15-minute scenic budget cruise on the river features a panoramic view of the city. Temporarily closed to cars; free for bikes and pedestrians.

AQUARIUM OF THE AMERICAS

French Quarter, 1 Canal St., 504-565-3800; auduboninstitute.org/visit/aquarium

Not a very New Orleansy thing to do on your trip to New Orleans, since every city that wants tourist action has

an aquarium. Still, ours is pretty nice, with a focus on Gulf Coast wildlife—you can't argue with albino alligators and big sharks. To Mom and/or Dad, we recommend hitting the downstairs IMAX snackbar at the start of your aquarium tour, so you'll have a daiquiri to sip while walking around.

AUDUBON INSECTARIUM

CBD, 423 Canal St., 504-410-BUGS; auduboninstitute.org/visit/insectarium

This insect attraction opened in 2008 and has been heartily embraced by New Orleans parents. Along with learning about bugs, you can touch some, walk among them in a butterfly garden, even eat crispy Cajun crickets and grasshopper chutney in the Critter Café. Just don't lead off with, "Hey kids! Wanna go eat bugs?!" Closed on Mondays.

CELEBRATION IN THE OAKS

December; Mid-City, City Park,
1 Palm Dr., 504-483-9415;
neworleanscitypark.com

During the holidays, the already gorgeous City Park is thoroughly decked out with acres of illuminated Christmas tableaux (some with hilarious Cajun themes), various schools' displays, and sporadic live music. **Storyland** is open at night featuring its usual kiddie rides and food, with the addition of hot buttered rum and wine for moms and dads.

FAUBOURG MARIGNY HOME TOUR

Mid-May; starts at Washington Square Park, 700 Elysian Fields Ave., 888-312-0812; faubourgmarigny.org

This big, fun self-guided walking tour lets you into the Marigny neighborhood's most magnificent historic and post-Katrina renovated homes and gardens. The event starts at 10 a.m. with a kids' activity area (kids under 12 tour free) and an art market showcasing local art, photography, jewelry, home furnishings, and more. The tour now also stops in the **Den of Muses,** where visitors can see colorful and bawdy floats being made and painted. Tickets are $15 in advance.

FRERET STREET FESTIVAL

Uptown, intersection of Freret St. and Napoleon Ave.; freretstreetfestival.com

The first Saturday of each month (except July and August). If the petting zoo in the elaborate Kid Zone isn't enough, the Humane Society also brings dozens of cute dogs and cats. Somewhere in there is usually some free roller derby as well! Two hundred local vendors and restaurants are represented, plus four stages of local music like **Big Sams Funky Nation, Tin Men, Debauche,** and **Free Agents Brass Band**.

IMAGINATION MOVERS

Check website for dates and venues: imaginationmovers.com

This Emmy-nominated, primary-colored rock band for kids can be seen on Disney TV and heard on Disney Radio. Imagination Movers' concerts teach kids fun dances and games, and blow their friggin minds. Parents will be impressed by how hard "the Movers" actually rock, on modern-day classics like "The Medicine Song," "What's in the Fridge?" and "I Want My Mommy (Time for Bed)." These days the band can be seen on national television far more often than at home, but check the website while you're in town.

LOUISIANA CHILDREN'S MUSEUM

CBD, 420 Julia St., 504-523-1357; lcm.org

Smack in the middle of the **Julia Street Arts District**, this 30,000-square-foot playground for kids' bodies and minds is an essential part of any child's visit to New Orleans. Among a million other things, LCM offers a kids' spelunking wall, astronomy demonstrations, a miniature New Orleans grocery store, live children's music, plus continuous art and music classes and other special events such as Winnie the Pooh's birthday, done New Orleans–style.

MARDI GRAS WORLD

CBD, 1380 Port of New Orleans Pl., 504-361-7821; mardigrasworld.com

The ferry mentioned above takes you pretty darn close to Mardi Gras World, where all of Carnival's mainstream floats are built at the incredibly colorful, outsized studio of **Blaine Kern,** the world's leading makers of float sculptures and props. Giant grinning heads, giant mythological beings, giant crabs and crawfish—everything GIANT. As close as a kid may come to Charlie's Chocolate Factory, and pretty interesting if you don't know much about Mardi Gras (or have never worked in a float den for $8 an hour).

MUSÉE CONTI WAX MUSEUM

French Quarter, 917 Rue Conti, 504-581-1993, or 800-233-5405; neworleanswaxmuseum.com

Founded in 1963, Musée Conti tells the story of three hundred years of New Orleans history from her founding to the present day, via 154 life-size figures displayed in historically accurate settings.

NOMA EGG HUNT

March; Mid-City, City Park, Sculpture Garden at the New Orleans Museum of Art, One Collins C. Diboll Circle, 504-658-4121; noma.org

The **Sydney and Walda Besthoff Sculpture Garden** at NOMA should be on your list anyway. The garden's Easter egg hunt draws hundreds of friendly local families to its petting zoo, spacewalks, face-painting booths, and other arts and crafts activities.

RIPLEY'S BELIEVE IT OR NOT MUSEUM

French Quarter, 620 Decatur St., 504-586-1233

Wax statues and other replications of phenomena you may or may not believe to be true.

RUSSIAN FESTIVAL FOR CHILDREN

April; Rivertown Theaters for the Performing Arts, 325 Minor St., Kenner, La., 504-461-9475; www.rivertowntheaters.com

Little princesses will love this event's several **Jefferson Ballet Theatre** performances of the 1938 version of *Cinderella,* by Russian writer Evgeny Shvarts.

SUMMER STAGES

CBD, 225 Baronne St., 504-598-3800; summerstages.org

A theater featuring a wide array of contemporary musicals and other original New Orleans productions for child performers.

ZOO TO DO FOR KIDS

April; Uptown, Audubon Zoo, 6500 Magazine St., 504-581-4629; www.auduboninstitute.org

You wouldn't think kids would need even more to do while at the zoo, but when the weather is nice, Audubon Zoo spends a couple days transformed into a giant playland with face painters, live music, inflatable structures, crafts, and a video game center.

Scott Stuntz

BIG EASY ROLLERGIRLS

www.bigeasyrollergirls.com

New Orleans' highly popular contribution to the now well established national trend of that extreme girlie sport—describe their brand of flat-track roller derby racing as "burlesque meets the X Games meets WWE." They even have their own pinup calendar of big leggy blondes in short shorts crashing against petite redheaded schoolgirls, and every other foxy female archetype on eight wheels.

The league consists of three teams: the **Confederacy of Punches**, the **Crescent Wenches**, and the **Storyvillains**. Several hundred New Orleanians fill the bleachers at the girls' brawls. A top-quality local rock band begins every event, and also provides entertainment for halftime, when most of the audience is drunk and howling for chick blood.

For the women, roller derby is not unlike being in a band—except way more work, with less drinking. The girls' intensely athletic practices occur early on weekend mornings, meaning the skaters can't really party much. If they miss practice, they're canned. The national Women's Flat Track Derby Association, of which the team is a satellite, also requires teams to complete a certain number of community service hours. "We've cleaned up the lakefront," brags **Sally Asher** (skate name **SmasHer**), who plays "pivot" for the Confederacy of Punches. "We've polished statues in **City Park**, ran adoption drives for the Humane Society, you name it. We were even awarded a proclamation from the city for aiding the city's post-Katrina comeback."

On the days bouts occur, the ladies spend entire mornings and afternoons decorating the venue and laying down their own special track. Then they skate and fight at top energy for a couple of hours. And when the huge crowd finally leaves, having been totally rocked, the girls remove their skates to load everything back into the truck. All this to say: in no way is roller derby for wimps. Sit in the front row and maybe you'll get some of their hard-earned sweat on you.

Season runs almost all year round. Bouts take place at University of New Orleans' Human Performance Center, by Lake Pontchartrain, on the corner of Leon C. Simon Drive and Elysian Fields Avenue.

FRIDAY NIGHT FIGHTS (BOXING)

Central City, 1632 Oretha Castle Haley Blvd.

Mike Tata has trained fighters around the globe and carries the swagger of a man unafraid to set up shop and put on a spectacle. Originally based out of a gym on Freret Street, his Friday Night Fights change locations but take place monthly. Ring girls, live bands, BYOB—there's a lot of show biz surrounding the above-average amateur bouts. Tata's running banter from the DJ table is well worth the ticket price.

His gym on O. C. Haley Blvd. serves as headquarters for this traveling circus of pugilism.

NEW ORLEANS LADIES ARM WRESTLING (NOLAW)

www.nolaw.org

When's the last time you arm-wrestled? Grade school? Other than pride, what was at stake? NOLAW hosts tournaments every other month that combine WWE-style entourages, costumed performers who try to tear their opponents' arms off, and serious postmatch dance parties. The best thing about all these feats of strength: all the proceeds benefit worthy causes in the metropolitan area. We asked NOLAW's Katie Hunter Lowery for the lowdown:

"New Orleans Ladies Arm Wrestling hosts raucous performance-based competitions that empower women and provide monetary support for women-focused projects. As a collective we resist and reject sexism, ageism, homophobia, transphobia, classism, and racism.

Anything boys can do girls can do hotter: New Orleans Ladies Arm Wrestling.

Katrina Arnold

Jonathan Traviesa

"NOLAW brawls are tournament style with three rules: two feet on the floor, two cheeks in the chair, and one elbow in the square. Eight wrestlers (each with persona, theme song, and entourage) battle in the first round and are eliminated or move on through single, sudden-death matches. The second round is best two out of three matches. Those winners then move on to the third/final round, which is also best two out of three. Stalemates are decided by various tiebreakers, and wrestlers' entourages hustle throughout the night taking bets and bribes.

"Money from the crowd supports the beneficiary and gives the generous audience chances to win sweet prizes. Serving half-time shows, celebrity judges, dance parties, and feats of strength for a full night of Matriarchal Mayhem."

NEW ORLEANS PELICANS

CBD, New Orleans Arena, 1501 Girod St., 504-587-3663; neworleansarena.com

October through April, watch New Orleans' own NBA team, the **Pelicans** (formerly the New Orleans Hornets), shoot hoops at the New Orleans Arena. Tickets range from $15 to $1,700.

NEW ORLEANS SAINTS

Win or lose, New Orleanians love dem Saints, our formerly beleaguered boys in black and gold. Even if you dislike sports, Saints games are a great excuse to party Nola style. Outside of the completely refurbished Superdome, you'll be swept up in a parade of football-frenzied fans, some in elaborate costumes, almost all toting beer and daiquiris. Inside, you'll be treated to impromptu performances by jazz bands that roam the stands and a crowd that so completely understands what it means to lose that its ability to celebrate victory is unparalleled. Add in a ticket price below the NFL average plus the cheapest beer in the league and you win, whether or not the Saints do.

ZEPHYR BASEBALL

6000 Airline Dr., Metairie, La., 504-734-5155; zephyrsbaseball.com

From April to August, watch New Orleans' baseball team play—not in the city but in the not-far-away burbs of Metairie. Zephyr tickets are cheap, with lots of special deals and giveaways and live bands, plus fireworks after every game.

DAY TRIPS JUST OUTSIDE NEW ORLEANS

The combination of Louisiana's temperate weather and vibrant regional culture means that throughout spring and fall, each weekend offers a multiplicity of food and music festivals and other attractions within a day's drive of New Orleans. Festing goes on year-round, really, but on a good May or October weekend it's possible to hit three or four good ones on less than half a tank of gas. And the French Quarter has nothing on those people in regards to music and food. The burbs also host some amazing markets and shops. Here are a few fun places you can go for an afternoon, a day, or if you're forced to evacuate:

BAYOU SAUVAGE NATIONAL WILDLIFE REFUGE

New Orleans East;
fws.gov/bayousauvage/

Fifteen minutes from the Quarter, you can take a stroll along a boardwalk that carries you into the bayou. Yes, there are gators and wild boar lurking, but mostly you get the feeling of life in the odd world of Louisiana swamps. Birders and kids love it, and the road there carries you past **Versailles**, the Vietnamese village that offers great bakeries and banh mi joints.

DORIGNAC'S FOOD CENTER

710 Veterans Blvd., Metairie, La.,
504-834-8216; dorignacs.com

Going to a grocery store doesn't sound like much of a field trip, but in the afternoon, Dorignac's bakery and seafood deli are both stacked with French breads and fresh shrimp and home-made crabcakes and remoulade—plus an insane wholesale booze selection, from European-priced wines that taste great to a thousand kinds of vodka in an icy wonderland of over-ambitious bottle designs. If you're having a cookout in New Orleans, or maybe thanking the friends whose floor you're staying on by cooking a meal, Dorignac's is pretty much the New Orleans equivalent of the meat, cheese, and booze markets of France and Spain.

FESTIVAL INTERNATIONAL DE LOUISIANE

Lafayette, La.;
festivalinternational.com

The capital of Acadiana offers ample music venues and Cajun culture. During Jazz Fest in the last weekend in April, the **Festival International** celebrates all things French, Cajun, and Louisiana.

JEFFERSON FLEA MARKET

5501 Jefferson Hwy. in Jefferson Parish, 504-733-0011

Jefferson Flea Market, open on weekends only, has long been the go-to spot for inexpensive antique furniture for New Orleanians—particularly armoires, since because of strange taxation laws, traditional New Orleans shotgun houses don't have closets. So if you want an armoire, New Orleans is a good place to get one. We have lots. But the many booths in the flea market complex are also full of more portable curiosities, many with local flavor; world's fair souvenirs and promotional items bearing the names of beloved but defunct New Orleans brands like **K&B** drugstore, **Jax** and **Regal** beer, and **Krauss** and **Maison Blanche** department stores are all still in steady supply.

JEFFERSON VARIETY

239 Iris Ave., Jefferson, La., 504-834-2222; jeffersonvariety.com

You say there's no reason you can think of to have to visit a fabric store on vacation? Apparently, you've never been to New Orleans, where parties, parades, festivals, and other various and sundry occasions demand a costume. And Jefferson Variety, with its rainbows of costume satin, yards of shimmering taffeta, and what look like endless miles of strips of braided sequins, rhinestones, and multicolored fringe, will make you want to find a reason. It's also where, they claim, Mardi Gras Indians buy their feathers, and big-time Carnival krewes buy the elaborate sequined appliqués and fake stones that give their royal robes sparkle.

MIDDENDORF'S

985-386-6666; middendorfsrestaurant.com

Head west on I-10 and enjoy the view as you skirt the edges of **Lake Pontchartrain,** then take Hwy 51 to this isolated eatery on the water. Middendorf's slogan is "We're with you through thick and thin," a reference to their own storm-ravaged history and their famous paper-thin catfish fillets. You can eat fried anything here while gazing out at the water. You're also almost to **Ponchatoula,** so combining the two makes for a full Louisiana experience.

Living in New Orleans as we do, the authors of this book formerly knew little about where to stay. We had to do a lot of research and make many calls in order to find the nice places that aren't too expensive—and in the summer, you need a pool! We also included a couple fancier, special bed-and-breakfasts. The prices of all New Orleans B&Bs fluctuate depending on festivals and such (except at Annabelle's House), so at the end of each of the following blurbs we've listed the absolute lowest price (always during summer) for the smallest room and each place's highest rates (during Mardi Gras or Jazz Fest) for their nicest room.

1870 BANANA COURTYARD

French Quarter, 1422 N. Rampart St., 504-947-4475/800-842-4748; bananacourtyard.com

Each antique-appointed room has its own name in this 1870s house a half-block from the Quarter. The back relaxation area is tropical, and the veranda hosts a hammock and a porch swing— stoop-sitting being a big New Orleans pastime. $69–$169.

AAE BOURBON HOUSE

Uptown, 1660 Annunciation St., 504-644-2199; bourbon.aaeworldhotels.com

This hotel/hostel in the Garden District a block off of Magazine Street is perfectly situated for shopping and house-gawking, but pretty far from the French Quarter. The main mansion offers a party-hardy environment, and dorm beds start at $20 a night. Deluxe single rooms and other affordable private abodes house up to six guests.

ANNABELLE'S HOUSE BED AND BREAKFAST

Uptown, 1716 Milan St., 504-344-0938; wix.com/randal1000/ bed-and-breakfast

This 52-room Victorian mansion has three guestrooms. Continental breakfast includes fresh waffles. Their lowest rate ($99) is certainly not the lowest in town, but their highest rate ($149) never fluctuates, even for Mardi Gras and other holidays.

AULD SWEET OLIVE BED AND BREAKFAST

Marigny, 2460 N. Rampart St., 877-470-5323; sweetolive.com

The former owner, an artist who worked in set design on many famous movies shot in New Orleans, also transformed the Sweet Olive into a work of live-in art. The website brags: "around each corner is another visual treat." Others now thoughtfully curate the former owner's works. $65–$150.

AVENUE INN
BED AND BREAKFAST

Uptown, 4125 St. Charles Ave.,
1-800-490-8542; avenueinnbb.com

This 1891 Thomas Sully mansion is located in the shopping district that Magazine Street has become. It's steps from the streetcar line and just off Lee Circle, home of the Circle Bar, one of the best (and smallest) clubs in the city.

B&W COURTYARDS
BED AND BREAKFAST

Marigny, 2425 Chartres St.,
800-585-5731; bandwcourtyards.com

This award-winning restoration job consists of three nineteenth-century buildings connected by courtyards, and features a Jacuzzi, massages if you need them, and a continental breakfast.

BISCUIT PALACE

French Quarter, 730 Dumaine St.,
504-525-9949; biscuitpalace.com

This underadvertised, funky guesthouse in the heart of the Quarter has very reasonable rates and can't be beat for its geographic centrality. It's located inside a historic Creole mansion with a fading, ancient ad for Uneeda biscuits painted on the side—hence the name. Rooms are old-style New Orleans Storyville swank, and some have wrought-iron balconies looking out on Dumaine Street. You won't dig it if you're into

W Hotel–style modernity. You'll love it if you think you're Tennessee Williams.

BURGUNDY
BED AND BREAKFAST

Bywater, 2513 Burgundy St.,
800-970-2153; theburgundy.com

The Burgundy welcomes straight folks, but it is definitely gayish. Meaning it is nice, and clean, with fascinating southern antiques, and though you can't smoke inside, outside you can sunbathe nude—an option that really should appeal to anyone. $70–$150.

BYWATER BED & BREAKFAST

Bywater, 1026 Clouet St.,
504-944-8438; bywaterbnb.com

This rose-colored double shotgun offers, among the usual amenities, a library of books about New Orleans and a CD collection of Louisiana music, plus a sweet back patio with ceiling fan—perfect for reading whilst drinking. $70–$125.

CHEZ PALMIERS
BED AND BREAKFAST

Marigny, 1744 N. Rampart St.,
504-208-7044; chezpalmiers.com

Just two blocks from the French Quarter and four blocks from Frenchmen Street, Palmiers provides an experience like staying with friends. Meaning, you make your own bed. Breakfast is included but otherwise you're left to your privacy. Rooms go for under $100 during nonevent times, but even during high-demand times like Jazz Fest, the rates don't break $200 a night.

THE CHIMES BED AND BREAKFAST

Uptown/Garden District,
1146 Constantinople St., 504-
899-2621; chimesneworleans.com

Each room boasts a private entrance, a private bath, and grand French doors opening onto a tropical courtyard. Following a continental breakfast of freshly baked local pastries, walk two blocks and hop the St. Charles streetcar, or grab the Magazine Street bus line through the shopping district and directly to the French Quarter. $120–$400, including tax and parking.

A CREOLE COTTAGE

Marigny, 1827 Dauphine St., 504-
948-4517; bbonline.com/la/creole

This circa-1810 Creole cottage sits just one block from Bourbon Street and two blocks from Frenchmen. The one rental unit boasts a living room, bedroom, bathroom, and kitchen with a refrigerator for all the leftovers you will inevitably have after visiting our gluttonous restaurants. Price for one or two people: $70–$115–$130.

CREOLE GARDENS AND GUESTHOUSE BED & BREAKFAST

CBD, 1415 Prytania St.,
866-569-8700; creolegardens.com

More like a hotel, with 24 guest rooms; large enough to host weddings. Located a block from the streetcar, and dog friendly with a dog park around the corner, Creole Gardens also provides a full southern breakfast. $69–$129.

CREOLE INN

Marigny, 2471 Dauphine St.,
504-941-0243; creoleinn.com

In this unassuming little Marigny cottage, the double suites all have two private bedrooms, rather than just one room with two beds like a hotel. No breakfast, but the beds are memory foam. Oooh. "Quiet hour" after 9:30. $49 (for five nights), $70–$249 otherwise.

CRESCENT CITY GUEST HOUSE

Marigny, 612 Marigny St.,
877-281-2680; crescentcitygh.com

This pet-friendly guesthouse is sweetly located in the Marigny, and so close to the Quarter you can hear the calliope playing on the Mississippi from your hot tub (actually, you can hear that thing's drunken hoot from almost anywhere in the city). Also features an enclosed sunbathing area, and gated off-street parking. $69–$159.

DAUPHINE HOUSE

Marigny, 1830 Dauphine St., 504-
940-0943; dauphinehouse.com

Not the most bohemian of places, just your basic, excellently restored two-story pre–Civil War house with 12-foot ceilings and hardwood floors. Rooms each feature a private bath, small refrigerator, microwave, wireless internet, yadda yadda. Continental breakfast is left in your room. $65–$125.

HOTELS

DIVE INN

Uptown, 4417 Dryades St.,
504-895-6555/1-888-788-DIVE;
thediveinn.com

Located in a residential neighborhood, the Dive Inn is not especially convenient without a car or at least a bike, but it does provide some special, um, lifestyle amenities, namely a clothing-optional guesthouse. Dive Inn is quirky, homey, obviously quite relaxed, and centered on an indoor pool done up in watery tones with tropical plants and a stately mahogany-and-ivory island bar. Rooms are inexpensive, cozy, and funky. No kids and no overt sexual themes; just good, old-fashioned, possibly naked fun.

EMPRESS HOTEL

Tremé, 1317 Ursulines Ave.,
504-529-4100;
empresshotelneworleans.com

The bare minimum (see the works of Bukowski for similar boarding houses). But all 36 rooms are just a very short (and sketchy) two-block walk from the French Quarter. This may be the place if you like unseemly adventure.

FAIRCHILD HOUSE BED AND BREAKFAST

Uptown, 1518 Prytania St.,
504-524-0154/800-256-8096;
fairchildhouse.com

Courtyard for small weddings, with a minister available if you get that drunk during your visit. Walking distance to the streetcar, which will take you right to the Quarter. Proprietor speaks Portuguese, English, French, Italian, and Spanish. $79–$149–$199.

GREEN HOUSE INN

Lower Garden District,
1212 Magazine St.,
504-525-1333/800-966-1303;
thegreenhouseinn.com

Tropical gardens surround a heated saltwater swimming pool, huge Jacuzzi hot tub. Clothing optional, so adults only. Three blocks from streetcar. $89–$139–$189.

HOTEL STORYVILLE

Tremé, 1261 Esplanade Ave.,
504-948-4800; hotelstoryville.net

Nine rooms boast colorful, almost Floridian décor as well as private dining areas. The grand backyard garden features a lighted bamboo patio bar and a reflecting pool. Or else chill and drink and people-watch on the front porch facing gorgeous Esplanade Avenue. Efficiencies now available for single travelers at $69 in summer, whereas a six-person room during Mardi Gras runs $359.

INDIA HOUSE HOSTEL

Mid-City, 124 S. Lopez St. (corner of Canal St.), 504-821-1904;
indiahousehostel.com

Unfortunately, only American students and foreign travelers are allowed to stay in this amazing big yellow house with its seasonal crawfish boils and "Indian Ocean" swimming pool. Communal rooms start at $17, while private "Voodoo" and "Bayou" Cajun cabins, which sleep two (communal bathrooms), are $45, as are private double rooms.

JOE & FLO OLD CANDLELIGHT

Tremé, 1129 N. Robertson St.,
504-581-6689

This hostel hasn't gotten too many rave reviews (they charge for toilet paper and "rent" towels) but should satisfy students and travelers on tight budgets, looking for just a roof over their head and a lock on their door. The staff makes up for the shortcomings in hospitality, though, and they offer cheap car service.

LA DAUPHINE BED AND BREAKFAST, RESIDENCE DES ARTISTES

Marigny, 2316 Dauphine St.,
504-948-2217; ladauphine.com

La Dauphine's Alec Baldwin Suite features the Louisiana cypress four-poster bed in which Alec made love to Kelly Lynch in the movie Heaven's Prisoners, filmed locally. The innkeepers speak Danish, Norwegian, Swedish, Spanish, English, French, and German, and yet state on their website, "We steer clear of the formal, pretentious crowd. We love to host nice, relaxed people who can 'go with the flow.'" Couples or singles only, no children or pets, and a three-night minimum stay is required.

LAMOTHE HOUSE

Marigny, 621 Esplanade St.,
800-367-5858; lamothehouse.com

This architectural wonder built in 1839 now has a heated Jacuzzi and pool and serves a continental breakfast. 24-hour front desk. $99–$299.

LIONS INN

Marigny, 2517 Chartres St.,
800-485-6846; lionsinn.com

Your basic pool, hot tub, and breakfast kitchen, but with a communal piano, wedding facilities, "wine hour" every afternoon, and best of all: free use of house bicycles to pedal around town. Between the wine and the bikes, we fully endorse Lion's Inn. $50–$165.

LOOKOUT INN—
This place is for sale. Call.

Bywater, 833 Poland Ave.,
888-947-8188;
lookoutneworleans.com

Located by the Naval Annex, Lookout Inn is named for its tower, where the Navy/lady boys would keep lookout on the Mississippi during World War II. Upon request, the staff will arrange yoga instruction, oyster and shrimp parties, wine tastings, and other good times. Lookout also has an awesome little saltwater pool and Jacuzzi. Though you're deep in the neighborhood (you will surely be the only tourist), it's a great spot for killer restaurants (The Joint BBQ, Jack Dempsey's fried seafood) and dive bars like B.J.'s and the inimitable Vaughan's (free food and live music Thursdays, holidays, and intermittently in between). Rooms start at $59.

MAISON DE MACARTY GUESTHOUSE

Bywater, 3820 Burgundy St.,
504-267-1564; maisonmacarty.com

One of Bywater's few guesthouses, this historic Victorian-style building across

HOTELS

the street from the country's first World War I monument was once part of the Chevalier de Macarty plantation. In January 2012, new owners expanded to host weddings and other events with a new 1,000-square-foot deck and stage. A full sit-down breakfast is included. Unregistered guests are not allowed to join you for a swim in the sweet little pool, nor are children under ten. $129–$259.

MARIGNY MANOR HOUSE

Marigny, 2125 N. Rampart St.,
504-943-7826;
marignymanorhouse.com

An affordable, quaint, restored 1840s Greek revival house located super close to Frenchmen Street's music clubs and restaurants (as well as Gene's Po-Boys and Daiquiris, the bright pink building on Elysian Fields and St. Claude: highly recommended).

MARQUETTE HOUSE HOSTEL

Uptown, 2249 Carondelet St.,
504-523-3014

A bare-bones, grungy hostel with $25 beds. But it also has a bar, and is near other bars such as Igor's, and after a bloody mary or two, it's fun to stumble out into the street and onto the streetcar and relax on a long slow ride through half of the city.

NEW ORLEANS GUEST HOUSE

Tremé, 1118 Ursulines St.,
800-562-1177

This salacious pink building on the Rampart Street side of the French Quarter is an 1848 gable-sided Cre-

ole cottage with a tiny, funky-quaint garden. Its insides are as funky as its outside. Rooms start at $79.

PARKVIEW MARIGNY BED AND BREAKFAST

Marigny, 726 Frenchmen St.,
877-645-8617;
neworleansvisit.com/bed_breakfast/
parkview_marigny.html

A 135-year-old Creole townhouse, the owner of which is a great breakfast cook. Laundry on site. $125–$160.

RATHBONE INN

Mid-City, 1244 Esplanade Ave., 504-
309-4479; rathbonemansions.com

Two mansions across the street from each other on gorgeous Esplanade Avenue bordering the French Quarter. One mansion features a pool and Jacuzzi, the other a lush courtyard for chillin'. Cheapest rooms are $59 during summer, while the most expensive during Mardi Gras cost $250 for a courtyard suite with kitchenette and three beds (sleeps six).

ROYAL BARRACKS GUEST HOUSE

French Quarter, 717 Barracks St.,
504-529-7269; rbgh.com

The bunk room, garden room, gothic room, and peacock room with ten-foot chandelier were each designed by a different local artist. The pool is temporarily out of service, but the courtyard wet bar is open. $69–$149–$299.

SCHIRO'S BALCONY GUEST HOUSE BED AND BREAKFAST

Marigny, 2483 Royal St.,
504-945-4425;
balconyguesthouse.com

You couldn't ask for a better locale than this B&B above Schiro's grocery, laundry, and restaurant, which serves New Orleans–style breakfast, lunch, and dinner along with a short menu of Indian dishes. Tucked into the neighborhood, it's also right smack in the middle of two coffee shops, a bookstore, half-a-dozen great nighttime hangouts (some with live music), and other plusses. So much entertainment, you may forget about Frenchmen Street and the Quarter just a few blocks away. $79 during the summer, and $129 during peak season.

ST. PETER HOUSE

French Quarter, 1005 St. Peter St.,
504-524-9232/800-535-7815

Aside from its nice price, this tropical brick courtyard with broad iron-lace balconies is exactly what one would expect of a French Quarter hotel. Continental breakfast included. $59–$79–$199.

ST. VINCENT'S GUEST HOUSE

Uptown, 1507 Magazine St.,
504-302-9606; stvguesthouse.com

This 70-room hotel boasts an onsite restaurant, bike rental (all New Orleans hotels and B&Bs should loan bikes to their clientele!), and private rooms, plus male, female, and coed dormitories with 3 to 6 beds. Dorms run from $20 to $45, while hotel rooms hover around $69 all year.

·N.O. MOMENT

ROYAL STREET INN/R BAR AND ITS ROCK STAR OWNER, GREG DULLI

Provocative songwriter Greg Dulli mans the R Bar downstairs from his small, funky inn.

Zack Smith

More of a "bed and beverage," owing to the R Bar downstairs—a place essential to any New Orleans visit anyway, with its intermittent free shrimp and crawfish boils, and DJs spinning everything from old New Orleans R&B and garage rock to weird ancient country to whatever rock is cool in Brooklyn. On Monday nights, $10 will get you a shot, a beer, and a haircut by a semiprofessional stylist. R Bar is now owned in part by former Afghan Whigs frontman and current Twilight Singer and Gutter Twin Greg Dulli. Upstairs the rooms are decorated for maximum "sleazy luxury." One room was formerly named the Bukowski Suite for the author who stayed there and etched "Hank was here" in the cement outside the bar door. The name was changed after the rooms were upgraded.

BIKES AND PUBLIC TRANSPORTATION

New Orleans' public transportation is just okay. Choose to rent a car and drive yourself, and parking can be nightmarish. Rely only on your feet, and risk missing chunks of the Quarter. A nicer way to put this would be: rent a bike. On a beach cruiser, you can pedal from one end of the remarkably flat city's heart

Zack Smith

to the opposite end, in about one hour if you need to. On a bike you'll cover the most ground, see the most sights, and always find parking.

Nolacycle.com provides great information on New Orleans' bike culture (not sports-oriented "bike culture," more like bikes with cup-holders on the handlebars, Mardi Gras beads, and fake flowers), with listings of bicycling events and downloadable New Orleans biking maps. The following local shops are also fighting the good two-wheeled fight—they'll rent you a bike:

A MUSING BIKES

Lower Garden District,
1818 Magazine St., 504-208-9779;
amusingbikes.com

If you are on the other side of Canal Street and want to cruise the Garden District, rent here.

BICYCLE MICHAEL'S

Marigny, 622 Frenchmen St.,
504-945-9505; bicyclemichaels.com

As far as legitimate professional (but still a tad funky) bike shops go, Michael's has a monopoly over the Marigny/Bywater. They're kinda pricey on some things, and sometimes the staff's kind of gruff, but they do set aside a gate outside of their shop for bands to post fliers. Bike rental is $25 a day.

BIG EASY BIKE TOURS

504-377-0973; bigeasybiketours.com

This company hosts the Esplanade Avenue of the Creoles tour, and the American Sector tour of the Garden District. Or, if you prefer a longer ride that might seem like exercise, BEBT hosts a 20-mile trip around the city.

BIKE EASY

Marigny, 1024 Elysian Fields Ave.,
504-861-4022; bikeeasy.org

Bike advocacy and safe bike route maps.

THE BIKE SHOP

Uptown, 4711 Freret St.,
504-265-8071; thebikeshopnola.com

Features new and used bicycles for adults and children. They also repair, buy bikes, and have records for sale. Pick up all your bike accessories including baskets, bells, racks, helmets, and more! Featuring new Sun-brand bikes Big Shot and SE.

GERKEN'S BIKE SHOP

Bywater, 2803 St. Claude Ave.,
504-373-6924; gerkensbikeshop.com

A down-home, cheap bike shop across the railroad tracks from the **Green Project** (an architectural salvage spot that's a junk collector's dream), Gerken's caters to the neighborhood boho bike crowd. They're not afraid to utilize used parts, Plan B, but they'll fix stuff for you. Gerken's doesn't directly rent bikes, but call them and they'll figure something out for you.

CONFEDERACY OF TOURS
BIKE TOURS AND A BICYCLE
NAMED DESIRE RENTALS

Zack Smith

Some lucky visitors to New Orleans plop down on a random bar stool and happen to sit beside a drinking, parading, gumbo-cooking historian who wants to spend the next three hours talking about the city they love. **Confederacy of Tours** and **A Bicycle Named Desire Rentals** aspire to give you that same funky educational experience, but while riding comfy cruisers (often equipped with drink holders).

Tours for those who don't usually take tours, CoT's excursions are easy riding through quiet, flat streets. The guides are the owners' friends and drinkin' buddies, who all share an obsession for the city's history. The stories they tell—both historical and what they did the night before—paint a great picture of how New Orleans remains apart from America to this day. CoT offers tours of the Creole side of New Orleans, neighborhood eating tours, the history of drinking tours (with bar stops), and a Ninth Ward tour that focuses on the

OTHER INFO

importance of the neighborhood's culture, and why rebuilding is still so important.

Confederacy of Tours partners with **A Bicycle Named Desire** (whose office is located at an address used in *A Streetcar Named Desire*) to provide rental bikes, maps, and ideas for those who'd rather set out on their own. But either way, biking is the most efficient and exciting way to see the Quarter, for sure. If you aren't staying in Marigny, the crew at CoT suggests these other, mostly bike-oriented businesses:

KAYAK-ITI-YAT

985-778-5034 or 512-964-9499; kayakitiyat.com

Kayak right up the middle of a community filled with little neighborhood parks, great food, fun bars, and sometimes music festivals or Mardi Gras Indians.

LAID-BACK BIKE TOURS

Mid-City, 1815 Elysian Fields Ave., 504-400-5468; confederacyofcruisers.com

Comfortable beach cruisers rent for $25 a day, including free delivery and pickup, plus helmet, lock, and basket. The shop is right on Bayou St. John, an amazing bike route with almost no car traffic. Pedal around the water or through Mid-City's gorgeous residential streets. Confederacy also gives great three-hour, eight-mile tours that expose tourists to non–French Quarter neighborhoods and provide insight into neighborhood architecture, Mardi Gras Indians, and New Orleans R&B music.

PLAN B: THE NEW ORLEANS COMMUNITY BIKE PROJECT

Marigny, 1024 Elysian Fields., 504-272-7266; bikeproject.org

The mission of Plan B is to "rescue useful bikes and parts from the trash and reuse them to counter the extreme wastefulness of industrialized nations." They won't fix your bike for you, but rather will provide free workspace, tools, and maybe advice, plus used and new parts for small donations. For the cost of a regular three-day bike rental elsewhere you can build your own Plan B bike alongside smart, strange, fun New Orleanians, ride the bike all through Mardi Gras or Jazz Fest, then donate it back to Plan B. Weird hours, so call ahead.

RUBARB

Bywater, 2239 Piety St.; rubarbike.org

Its name an acronym for Rusted Up Beyond All Recognition Bikes, this is another community bike shop where you can learn to build or repair a bike, obtain a bike through work, trade, or a suggested donation of $40–$75, or just volunteer. They even host field trips! Unlike Plan B, Rubarb also offers some rentals during major New Orleans holidays, with all donations going back into the shop to purchase tools as well as art supplies (because your bike has to costume on Mardi Gras too!). Mon. 10 a.m.–2 p.m., Wed. 3:30–6 p.m., Sat. 1–6 p.m.

MIKE THE BIKE GUY

Uptown, 4411 Magazine St., 504-899-1344

This particular Mike worked fixing bikes for others for twenty years before opening his own place. Bikes rent for $30 a day, $120 for a week, but once one of the bikes has been used for a week, Mike sells them for around $180.

CITY BUSES (RTA)

504-248-3900; norta.com

After flying into the Lil Wayne International Airport, you can take the $1.25 city bus into town, rather than wasting $30-plus on a cab ($30 can mean a lotta drinks in New Orleans' better dive bars!). Once you're in town, though, you'd only choose a bus over bike for A/C, or to dodge rain, or when shopping on Magazine Street, where they run straight and efficiently up and down miles of shops and cafés. Otherwise, our city buses are mostly only good for meeting interesting local characters, which you will, indeed. (From the airport, for $15 you can also get the airport shuttle, which will drop you at any hotel or guest house.)

GREYHOUND BUSES

CBD, 1001 Loyola Ave, 504-525-6075; greyhound.com

When you need to flee New Orleans at a moment's notice, Greyhound provides economic getaways for lawless fugitives, and for fauxbeaux utilizing Mom's gold card for an air-conditioned break from train-hopping.

MULE BUGGIES

French Quarter, 504-944-0366

Especially during the hell-hot summer, those poor animals don't want to drag you around the French Quarter. All summer the poor things sweat, their tongues twisting and writhing trying to spit the bits out of their mouths. No matter how well the mules are supposedly treated, they'd surely be much happier if you just rode a bike.

STREETCAR

504-248-3900; norta.com

Same as our city buses: $1.25, every fifteen minutes, though you can often, on foot, out-pace the streetcar to your destination. Of course that's not the point; all visitors should ride the streetcar once. Especially if one of the cooler drivers lets you sneak your daiquiri onboard, it's great to ride slow and long through the CBD, staring out the window at all the poor suckers working, before snaking around Lee Circle, through the Garden District and into the big trees and mansions of Uptown. The streetcar ain't meant for reaching important destinations on time, but then again, you might realistically end up sharing a streetcar with a brass band practicing on their way to a gig. Runs 5 a.m. to roughly 2 a.m.

TAXIS

United Cab, 504-522-9771; unitedcabs.com

In New Orleans you'll need to phone for a cab unless you're on Frenchmen Street, Esplanade, Decatur, or Canal, where you can maybe flag one down. United is the local favorite.

N.O. MOMENT

PEDICABS

nolapedicabs.com; needaridenola.com; neworleansbiketaxi.com

Claims of progress never go uncontested in New Orleans, and nowhere was this more visible than in the process that recently brought **pedicabs** to the French Quarter and CBD. Buggie drivers and cab companies opposed the new competition, while proponents of rickshaws argued that every other city already allowed them—never a trump card in Big Easy arguments.

The battle raged for a decade until 2011, when three pedicab companies won city council approval and took to the streets. Today you can stand on most corners in the Quarter and hop aboard within minutes. We have a fondness for local taxi drivers, but they're not always necessary or available, particularly below Canal Street. The supple legs of youth are your best bet, typically charging $1 per block and running late into the evening. Tips are welcome and rates seem, well, negotiable. Drivers are mostly young and willing to talk while they pump pedals. If you need to get from, say, Café Du Monde to the Superdome, pedicabs are quick and easy.

Of course, if you want to know more about city politics, take a regular cab, mention pedicabs, and prepare for a treatise.

HELPFUL LOCAL PUBLICATIONS

Here are some printed publications you can pick up while you're in town.

ANTIGRAVITY

antigravitymagazine.com

If you like this guidebook, you'll probably dig *Antigravity*. Printed black and white, tabloid-sized *AG* gives a street-level view of Nola's alternate musical universe of punk, metal, indie, and other underground sounds you won't find in the publications listed below.

GAMBIT WEEKLY

bestofneworleans.com

Gambit focuses on local politics, bar and restaurant guides, and A&E coverage, giving almost equal space to both traditional and edgy happenings both in its print publication and at its blog: blogofneworleans.com. This book's author Michael Patrick Welch has contributed music coverage to *Gambit*.

OFFBEAT

offbeat.com

This 25-year-old-plus music magazine doesn't always have its ear to the streets, but *OffBeat* extensively covers Jazz Fest and other mainstream local events and artists. It reviews almost every Louisiana CD released, and at times can take you deeper into Louisiana roots music than any other local publication. Author Michael Patrick Welch wrote for *OffBeat* for ten years, beginning with his monthly "alternative music" column, which ran from 2003

until the flood. Co-author Brian Boyles writes for the magazine still.

TIMES-PICAYUNE

nola.com

Besides having a truly great name, the *Times-Picayune* newspaper is a Pulitzer-winning paper that unfortunately now publishes only three days a week. Friday's Lagniappe pullout features the mainstream arts, music, and culture picks for the week ahead. *The Pic* is where you'll now find the best music writer in town, **Alison Fensterstock**.

WHERE Y'AT?

whereyat.com

Where Y'At? magazine is a slim little tabloid full of ads, bar guides, ads, some music coverage, and some ads. Great reading for when you're at a bar and your date goes to use the bathroom and is there a long time.

NEW ORLEANS WEBSITES

Here are informative and fun websites you can check for New Orleans entertainment and culture news.

THEAMERICANZOMBIE.COM

Blogger **Jason Brad Berry** was an essential truth-seeker after the storm, with particular dedication to corruption in public contracts. When the feds indicted former mayor **Ray Nagin**, local media credited American Zombie for digging up key dirt.

OTHER INFO

ARTSNEWORLEANS.ORG

Run by the **Arts Council of New Orleans**, this site keeps a strong calendar of events, as well as profiles of venues and cultural organizations.

BESTOFNEWORLEANS.COM

Gambit's website with news, reviews, and listings; an online version of the paper. Blogofneworleans.com is *Gambit*'s blog site, with extended interviews from the print version, news bits and bytes, plus more colloquial tidbits on local goings-on.

DEFENDNEWORLEANS.COM

Maker of now-iconic shirts and throwers of parties, their site features blog entries and videos of hipster antics, such as what happens when a bounce rapper plays a debutante party.

GONER-RECORDS.COM

The New Orleans section of its lively message board is great for garage and punk show listings and entertaining scene gossip.

HOMEOFTHEGROOVE .BLOGSPOT.COM

An exhaustively informative music blog that digs deep into New Orleans R&B and rock 'n' roll history.

HUMIDCITY.COM

A smart, snarky blog of news-driven commentary and colorful musings that gives great context for this strange city and its goings-on.

THELENSNOLA.ORG

This nonprofit site started by preservationists and led by former *Times-Picayune* editors is dedicated to investigative journalism in the region, breaking big stories about local government, preservation issues, and the ongoing upheaval of public school education. If you want an in-depth look at the issues facing locals, the Lens is a great place to start.

MYSPILTMILK.COM

Editor **Alex Rawls** of this music site offers a robust source of interviews and think pieces dedicated as much to touring indie bands with upcoming New Orleans gigs as to local music.

NEWORLEANS.ME

Good aggregator of Nola-related content, with constant updates on events, shows, and festivals. Same crew that designs the **Dirty Coast** t-shirts.

NOLA.COM

The *Times-Picayune*'s site—real-time breaking news and live-blog coverage of crimes and music festivals.

NOLADEFENDER.COM

Community journalism, entertainment listings, and free mixtapes by famous locals.

NOLADIY.COM

Incredibly thorough, simple listings for all punk, metal, and otherwise underground bands and shows, including house parties and the like. This website was invaluable for putting together this book you're now reading.

NOLAFUGEESPRESS.COM

Sarcastic but often informative news. They've self-published a few books of essays that dealt primarily with life after the 2005 flood.

NOLAUNDERGROUND .WORDPRESS.COM

Focusing mainly on the hard, loud, and/or fast, this blog was, in its words, "created as a tool for understanding the truth and reality of the best music scene spawned from the pits of NOLA." They also put on the Raise the Dead festival.

OFFBEAT.COM

Music news, reviews, and listings. Fairly catholic music coverage and more general musings on the music world, and music news that paints a little more well rounded picture of the city.

PELICANBOMB.COM

Art site that runs features, portfolios from local artists, and gallery listings.

THEPEOPLESAYPROJECT.ORG

These guys crank out quality video and long-form writing, much of it dedicated to the cool live events they produce regularly.

UPTOWNMESSENGER.COM

Though dedicated to the area above Canal Street, **Robert Morris** and company regularly break stories on crime, zoning, and school issues.

WWOZ.ORG

Streaming real-time audio from the station, plus DJ blogs, playlists, and community news.

OTHER INFO

S.O.S.:
HELP POST-KATRINA
NEW ORLEANS!

Nine years after Katrina, most of New Orleans is still in dire need—honestly, a lot of New Orleans' infrastructure was screwy before the storm. The following groups have specifically helped New Orleans and/or our musicians in one form or another, and all of them are worthy of your donations:

Brad Pitt is a cool person who did a lot for New Orleans after Katrina. This is one of his housing projects.

Jonathan Traviesa

HABITAT FOR HUMANITY

habitat-nola.org

This national organization dedicated a block of houses—the **Musicians' Village**, in the Upper Ninth Ward—for New Orleans musicians who qualified for the program.

HANDSON NEW ORLEANS

handsonneworleans.org

This volunteer aggregator partners eager volunteers with needy causes in New Orleans. Since Katrina, they've mobilized over tens of thousands of volunteers.

MAKE IT RIGHT FOUNDATION

makeitright.org/see/new-orleans/

Brad Pitt's cause célèbre builds green housing in the areas most ravaged by the flood. Said houses are all odd but cool twists on traditional New Orleans architecture. Drive down to the Lower Nine and check 'em out.

ROOTS OF MUSIC

therootsofmusic.org

Founded to fill a void in local music education, Roots of Music teaches students the basics of marching band music while focusing on academic achievement. Some of the city's best brass band musicians lead the after-school classes, which have even marched in the Rose Bowl Parade and Jazz Fest.

SWEET HOME NEW ORLEANS

sweethomeneworleans.org

One-stop shopping for musicians in need, Sweet Home's comprehensive caseworker system hooks up musicians with housing, legal, medical, and cash grant assistance.

N.O. MOMENT

NEW ORLEANS MUSICIANS' CLINIC

3700 St. Charles Ave., 504-412-1366; neworleansmusiciansclinic.org

Musicians are broke because you forgot to tip them, then went and downloaded their music for free. Luckily, the **New Orleans Musicians' Clinic (NOMC)** provides comprehensive health service dedicated to sustaining New Orleans' musicians and others of nonconventional employment by providing access to affordable medical care, mostly via LSU's medical school.

The New Orleans Musicians' Clinic's nurse practitioner Catherine Lasperches makes sure the author is okay.

NOMC is under the umbrella of the **New Orleans Musicians' Assistance Foundation (NOMAF),** the brain-child of retired **Jack McConnell,** M.D., whose son played piano with jam-band numero uno, Phish. Though relied upon by New Orleans to help generate tourist dollars, musicians were woefully lacking a health safety net until, in 1995, McConnell set out to design a system specifically to treat musicians. Today, the Musicians' Clinic is an American anomaly, and possibly the only thing in New Orleans that makes sense.

We spoke with the clinic's beloved nurse practitioner Catherine Lasperches about how she got involved with the Musicians' Clinic nine years ago, and how you can get involved today.

What's your title here?

I'm a family nurse practitioner. I treat all the musicians. I am the primary care. Since Katrina we opened up to like Mardi Gras Indians, and writers, dancers, photographers, so now we're more open to anyone who is helping with the arts in the city. We treat the whole family, the wife, and if they are 18 years old the children too.

Oh wow, so you all have really broadened your focus!

Yes, we see the patient as a whole. We're also a foundation, which means we have a social worker, we help patients find a place to live, we help them pay their bills if they cannot pay their energy bill or mortgage. We can connect them to a lot of organizations like Music Cares. We have a diabetic educator and other outreach programs. So we do a lot of work outside the clinic.

Did you start working here because you were always a fan of musicians?

I'm not a groupie. Sorry [laughs]. I grew up playing the piano, but I came to New Orleans twenty years ago with my boyfriend who played piano on a Fulbright scholarship from Loyola. I got a master's at UNO and was teaching French, but I'd come here to study the history of jazz; I was writing a thesis about jazz for my master's back in Paris. I did know a lot of New Orleans musicians and had another boyfriend who was a drummer. But then I started working at Oschner and went to nurse practitioner school. I used to go out a lot to shows more than I do now because now I am too tired, but yes, some of my friends have become my patients.

Among our circle of friends you have saved a lot of lives!

No, we don't save lives [laughs]! We do facilitate access to care a lot faster. Being in the LSU system, we can refer musicians to the public or private LSU access. If there is a surgery needed, we can make it happen at the university hospital the next day.

Though nonresidents cannot utilize the clinic, what would you tell folks who want to donate to the Musicians' Clinic?

There's a donation area on the website where you can use your credit card. Right now we are not sure what's going to happen with the Medicaid—we have a lot of Medicaid patients right now and that's helping the clinic a lot, so I don't know if we're going to lose that [because of Gov. Bobby Jindal's reforms]. If you donate, you have to be specific on the website if you want the money to go to the clinic or the foundation, which helps pay for nonmedical needs.

Bru Bruiser of Gov't Majik retains hope.

Zack Smith

SOS

Michael Patrick Welch is the author of the memoir *Commonplace* (2003), *Y'All's Problem* (2011), and the New Orleans novel *The Donkey Show* (2003). He freelanced for *Gambit Weekly* for many years, served as a staff writer and editorial assistant for the *St. Petersburg Times*, and penned a column in New Orleans' oldest music magazine, *OffBeat*. Welch currently writes a column about New Orleans for *Vice* magazine. His writing has also appeared in *Salon*, the *Columbia Journalism Review*, *Oxford American*, and several Village Voice publications. Welch also teaches a music writing class and acts as bandleader for electro-rock-R&B band the White Beach.

Brian Boyles is creative director of The People Say Project (www .thepeoplesayproject.org) and program director at the Louisiana Endowment for the Humanities. His work has been featured in *Oxford American*, *Offbeat*, the *Lens*, the *Brooklyn Rail*, *NOLA-Fugees*, *SLAM*, *Gathering of the Tribes*, and *Louisiana Cultural Vistas*. Follow him @brianwboyles.

Zack Smith is an editorial and fine art portrait photographer and has been active in the music and cultural scene in New Orleans since 2000. Since 2009 he has been a staff photographer at the New Orleans Jazz and Heritage Festival, French Quarter Festival, and Satchmo Summer Fest, and he has been a photography instructor at the New Orleans Academy of Fine Art since 2001. His artwork is widely collected and has been featured in many publications, including *Oxford American*, *Spin*, *Rolling Stone*, and *Vice*. Smith is also the drummer for the revered local rock band Rotary Downs.

Jonathan Traviesa has been photographing in New Orleans since 1997. In 2009 the Ogden Museum of Southern Art exhibited a solo show of his work in conjunction with the publication of his book *Portraits: Photographs in New Orleans, 1998–2009*. His prints are collected privately around the United States and publicly in New Orleans by the Ogden and the New Orleans Museum of Art. Traviesa is a founding member of The Front, a contemporary art gallery in New Orleans, and his editorial work has been published in news and fashion magazines around the world. He also owns the world's most memorable hair.

INDEX